Cover image – Washing the feet – Painting by Jyoti Sahi of Bangalore, India.

Editor – Maureen Edwards

Published by:
The International Bible Reading Association
1020 Bristol Road
Selly Oak
Birmingham
B29 6LB

Charity No 211542

ISBN 0-7197-0971-7
ISSN 0140-8275

Typeset by Avonset, Bath
Printed and bound in Great Britain by
Omnia Books Limited, Glasgow

WORDS
FOR TODAY 2001

Notes for daily Bible reading

INTERNATIONAL BIBLE READING ASSOCIATION

CONTENTS

3

Acknowledgements and abbreviations

*   Readings from *The Revised Common Lectionary.*

GNB   *Good News Bible* (The Bible Societies/Collins Publishers) – Old Testament © American Bible Society 1976; New Testament © American Bible Society 1966, 1971, 1976.

NIV   Scripture quotations taken from *The Holy Bible, New International Version* © 1973, 1978, 1984 by International Bible Society. Used by permission of Hodder & Stoughton Ltd. a member of the Hodder Headline Plc Group. All rights reserved. 'NIV' is a registered trademark of International Bible Society. UK trademark number 1448790.

NJB   Taken from the *New Jerusalem Bible*, published and copyright 1985 by Darton, Longman and Todd Ltd and Doubleday & Co Inc, and used by permission of the publishers.

NRSV   *New Revised Standard Version* © 1989, Division of Christian Education of the National Council of Churches of Christ in the United States of America.

REB   *Revised English Bible* © Oxford University and Cambridge University Presses 1989

RSV   *The Holy Bible, Revised Standard Version* © 1973, Division of Christian Education of the National Council of Churches of Christ in the United States of America.

This edition is my farewell to editing *Words for Today,* for the time has come at last to retire! I look forward to new challenges, but I am aware that this work has been a ministry (though I am not ordained) to tens of thousands of readers in different languages, and I shall miss that. For the last nine years, I have enjoyed a partnership with writers of different backgrounds and cultures and been enriched and challenged by them. Some are personal friends and former colleagues. Others I have contacted and got to know a little through correspondence and over the telephone. I would like to express thanks to them from the whole network of IBRA – both staff and readers – for all that they have shared and, hopefully, will continue to share with us.

This year, there is a strong challenge to change – to turn from the prevailing triumphalism of Christian and Jewish thought to recognize more of the vulnerability of God; to grow from a purely 'personal faith' to a stronger sense of solidarity with our community and the world; to cross barriers that separate people of different faiths and see God's Kingdom embracing all humanity; to share the pain of those who grieve and suffer; to dream, hope, pray and work for a better world and that the earth itself may be healed.

These challenges come from people at the grassroots – the poor, the lonely, the hungry, those in pain... They call us to a new way of living – not just detachment from possessions – but to a greater caring for one another, a deeper solidarity, a working together for justice and a more generous hospitality.

These values of the Kingdom are present in both Old and New Testaments and are presented by both Jewish and Christian writers for all who have 'ears to hear'. As I have said before, don't dismiss the new challenges and difficult questions. Keep an open mind and allow the Spirit to lead you, as Jesus promised, to discover new truth. Truth is infinite and we'll never know all there is to know. For God 'whose love is broader than the measure of (our) minds' calls us to journey on and explore beyond the horizons we have already crossed and where we feel safe; this is what faith is all about.

Maureen Edwards

Maureen Edwards – Editor

MORNING PRAYERS

Loving God, when life seems empty
and pain and loneliness numb our awareness
of your presence,
you are with us, in and around us,
enfolding us in your love
and sustaining us with your grace.
When we cling to the disabling powers of darkness,
you knock and call us to open the door
and let in the light.
Come to us now in the freshness of this new day.
Enfold us again in the warmth and security of your love
that we may not be overcome
by the brilliance of your light,
nor daunted by the tasks
you call us to perform today.
By your Spirit, lead us gently, and encourage us
to seek healing and justice for others,
for your Kingdom's sake. Amen   *Maureen Edwards*

Father of all humankind, make the roof of my house
    wide enough for all opinions,
oil the door of my house so that it opens easily
    to friend and stranger,
and set such a table in my house that my whole family
    may speak kindly and freely around it.
                                        From Hawaii

We ordinary people must forge our own beauty. We must set fire
to the greyness of our labour with the art of our own lives. In this
kind of creation, every day becomes pure enjoyment.
                                        Kenji Miyazawa
            Dare to Dream, Ed. Geoffrey Duncan (HarperCollins)

EVENING PRAYERS

Confession
In the light of Christ's self-giving life,
    his way of the cross,
We see the darkness in our lives.
(We reflect on our personal life)

As we think of the evil and oppression in the world
    of which we are a part,
We need to repent together with our fellow-humans.
(We reflect on the world's life)

As members of a people called to follow Christ
and live in his new righteousness,
We need to repent for the evil in the Church's life.
(We reflect on the life of the Church)

The Saviour of the world, the Refuge of the repentant,
forgives and strengthens all who truly seek his grace.
He accepts us as his sons and daughters,
and sets us free from the bondage of our past.
For Christ died and rose to new life
that we might all share his wholeness
and abundant life. Amen
                                    Church of South India (adapted)

O Lord, you have said to us, 'Peace I leave with you'.
This peace that you give is not that of the world:
it is not the peace of order, when order oppresses;
it is not the peace of silence, when silence is born
    of suppression;
it is not the peace of resignation, when such resignation
    is unworthy.
Your peace is love for all people,
is justice for all people, is truth for all people,
the truth that liberates and stimulates growth.
Lord, it is this peace we believe in because of
    your promise.
Grant us peace, and we will give this peace to others.
                                    From the Waldensian Liturgy

GOD'S NEW WORLD
1. Gospel stories for today

Notes based on the New Jerusalem Bible
Joseph G Donders

Josef G Donders, born in the Netherlands, member of the Society of Missionaries of Africa (also known as the 'White Fathers'), was ordained a Catholic Priest in Galashiels, Scotland, in 1957. Formerly Professor of Philosophy and Religious Studies at the University of Nairobi, Kenya, he is now Finian Kerwin OFM Chair of Mission and Cross-cultural Studies at the Washington Theological Union, Washington DC, USA.

2000 years ago when God became like one of us in Jesus, the Christ, a new dimension was added to an Old World. In him a New Humanity was born among us. It was a newness that can animate, direct and unify our world, transforming and remaking it so as to bring about a 'new creation'.

Monday January 1   *Luke 2.8-21**
Glory galore!

Shepherds did not count in Jesus' time. Often they were the poorest of the poor, sleeping with animals (often owned by others) during the coldest and hottest of nights. They were at about the lowest level of social ranking of their society. Living 'outside' in the fields, they were regarded as outcasts, pariahs, impure, and sinners. This social disdain could not have escaped them. Their self-esteem must have been so low, overlooking their real dignity as God's handiwork.

That night 'angels appeared to them and the glory of the Lord shone around them'. In this simple story the Bible tells us not only how great those shepherds were, but how all of us, even those who know themselves to be overlooked and neglected in the world in which they live, are 'crowned with glory and beauty' (Psalm 8.5).

That night the restoration of this world began: the rehabilitation of a people estranged from God, and who are alienated from themselves and each other. It was the beginning of God's New World. No wonder the story tells that the angels remained tumbling in the sky, dancing and singing, 'Peace on earth!'

✻ *Almighty God, my Origin and Creator –*
from this New Year's day –
help me to see your glory and beauty
in all those around me, as never before. Amen

The witness

John begins his Gospel with some poetry. The prose of our daily lives is in general rather rarely interrupted by poetry. But there are moments when we are inspired and, looking through the veil of daily routines and the reality which touches us, see the Light. These moments of insight often remain but are too rare.

And yet, a famous preacher, Ragan Courtney, once wrote, 'I believe the only way a theologian can communicate sustaining and reviving thoughts to a hungry world of spiritually malnourished people is through the language of poetry... There is no other way by which we can talk of the lofty and holy things of God.'

In John's poem God's Light illuminates the dark in our world. His poem reveals the presence of God's Word among us. His introductory hymn mentions a witness to that presence. It is about Jesus' predecessor, John the Baptist. There are many other witnesses to that presence in John's Gospel: the Spirit, the prophecies in Holy Scripture, Jesus' words and works, his disciples, the Samaritan woman, the crowds, and the break-in of God's new world.

✻ *Loving God, let the Light you sent to us in your Son,*
Jesus the Christ, illuminate the apparent commonness
of our daily chores, so that we may see ourselves
bathed in your Light. Amen

Coming home

Our text reads: 'He came to his own' (verse 11). He came home; he came into 'the world that had come into being through him' (verse 10). In our time we all know stories of people who had to flee from their homes while their property was destroyed, and their houses burned. Whole regions, once prosperous and life-sustaining, are still laid to waste for years and years. Those who dare to return face utter chaos, and have to start afresh.

Comparisons are always odious – in *Much Ado about Nothing* Shakespeare called comparisons 'odorous' – and yet it is in a way like this that the Word returned to dwell with us in the chaos we had created. He came to undo anarchy, and that is why we might be allowed to use a military term when speaking about the Word's presence. That presence is like 'a pocket of resistance', a 'pocket of wholeness and transformation' in our world. The world as such did not surrender to that power of God but, within it, many did become 'children of God', dwelling where God lives and forming the beginning of a new and recreated world.

✳ *Almighty God, send us your Spirit*
so that we may co-operate in changing the face of the earth.

Thursday January 4   *Luke 3.7-22**

Expectancy

Luke describes a feeling of expectancy. People lining up in front of John to be baptized were full of anticipation. They were hoping for change: that the future of their children would be assured, that their own sins would be forgiven, justice would be done, oppression would end, and peace would be restored. When they asked John what they should do, he told them that they needed to be converted. They should change. As he baptized them, John's challenge was very radical. They should be honest and fair. If they had any extra clothing, the extras should be given to those who had none. He spoke to them about a new Spirit, the Holy Spirit. But, he added, they would have to wait for someone else to give them that fire.

We might sincerely ask ourselves whether we would have been willing to line up in front of that grubby prophet. Are we really willing to share his expectancy? Would we be willing to share his solution to the problems of our world? Are we really looking forward to the newness he foretold Jesus would start among us?

✳ *Powerful God, help me to share in your love for the whole of humanity, notwithstanding all the consequences. Amen*

Friday January 5   *Matthew 2.1-12**

Wise people

All kinds of legendary details have been added to the story of the wise people who came from the East because they had seen a star rising. They brought three different gifts, and that is why people began to think there were three men. Tradition has given them the names of Balthasar, Melchior and Caspar. They were definitely astronomers and also astrologers, and they discovered that new star.

Why did they follow that star? We do not know exactly. They must have had some expectation that something new was going to happen to this world: that the past, its sin and its guilt were going to be taken away. Looking for that newness they made another very wise decision. They were not looking for a system, a moral code, a theory, a theology, a policy, a philosophy or a new set of laws. They were looking for a child, a new beginning!

We, too, are looking for that new life. We need a person to mediate between the old and the new, between the world in which we live and God's reign to come. We all need a new beginning – the child born among us.

✳ *Loving God, help us to welcome your Son,*
not only in our own lives, but in the life of your world. Amen

Epiphany, January 6   *Matthew 2.13-18**

Take up the child

The experience of Joseph and Mary might teach us a lesson about our role in the bringing about of the renewal of the world we are so often praying for. That prayer might be deceptive. We might be tempted to leave it all to God. Joseph was sure God would protect Mary, her child and himself. God did. Every time a danger threatened, God sent an angel to warn them. That was all the angel did! When they had to flee into Egypt, Joseph had to awaken Mary. Mary had to wake up the child. Joseph had to pack their luggage. Mary had to dress the child against the cold of the night. They had to walk all the way, while the angel flew off!

Were they not left alone? Are we left alone? We might think so, but we would be mistaken. We are never left alone. Like Mary and Joseph we have all we need to do the things we are asked to do. Mary and Joseph were not lost. They had common sense, their hands, and their feet, just as we do.

✳ *Merciful God, how often are we not asking you*
to do the things you equipped us to do?
Help me to take up my task as Mary and Joseph did. Amen

FOR REFLECTION – alone or with a group

● How are you going to mark for yourself, and for those around you, the second year of the Third Millennium of the birth of Jesus Christ?

● Consider the newness and fullness of life Jesus came to introduce in this world. Do you ever take this into consideration when you make social, political and professional decisions?

1st Sunday in Epiphany, January 7   *Luke 7.36-50*

Mercy

The story is one of a new beginning. It is a story of a confession. It tells us who is playing the most important role when sinners confess their transgressions. That role is not played by the sinner, but by God. It is up to the sinner, like the woman in our story, to know where to find God. Looking for God is the beginning of a process based on love for God. Once God is found, it is God's mercy that is at the heart of the rest of the story. That story is not primarily about punishment but about forgiveness, not about judgement but about mercy, not about the past but about a new beginning, not about sin but about love. As soon as the woman has contacted him, Jesus forgives her sins. Those sins do not count any more; they are dumped in the ocean of God's mercy. When Jesus told her, 'Your sins are forgiven,' the dignitaries around her asked how that was possible. Jesus answered them when he told the woman, 'Your faith has saved you; go in peace!' That faith was the proof of her love.

✳ *Merciful God, let me never lose my faith in you.*
Spare me the thought of considering myself worthless
in your eyes. I trust in your mercy!

Monday January 8   *Luke 8.40-48*

In front of all the people

She had been bleeding for twelve years. That meant that besides the common disdain for women in her time she had been excluded from all public occasions. She was impure; anyone who touched her would be defiled, too. She was not even allowed to share in worship. Veiled and covered, she was not supposed to be seen in public except from a distance. The Old World in which she lived preferred not to see her and to forget about her.

Profiting from the excitement around Jesus – the crowd around almost stifled him – she came up behind him and touched his cloak. In a way she was faithful to the old taboos: she did not touch him. But he was touched, a power went out from him, and he said, 'Somebody touched me.' Trembling all over she confessed in front of all the people what she had done and how she had been cured.

And a new world, a new era opened not only for her who was cured, but for all those who listened to her, when Jesus did not rebuke her, but said, 'My daughter, your faith has saved you; go in peace!' The New World, the new order of things Jesus opened is as new today as it was then. Even after two millennia many of those who call themselves his disciples still have difficulties accepting it.

✳ *Almighty God, who created men and women as equals,*
we ask you to help all of us to realize that equality,
not only in word, but also in deed.

Tuesday January 9   Luke 8.49-56

From the old into the new

Does the story about that twelve-year old girl sound familiar to you? It will do to those who know of a girl or boy of the same age who has difficulties in passing from childhood to what some call real' life – the difficulty of leaving their toys behind and 'growing up'.

The girl in the story had been lying on her bed. The bystanders said that she was dead. They ridiculed Jesus when he suggested that she was not dead but asleep. He entered the room with some of his disciples and the parents of the girl. He took her by her hand and said, '"Child, get up!"'... and she got up at that very moment.' He then told her parents to give her something to eat. When you stress that point – 'Give her something to eat!' – parents with an anorexic child at home might suddenly recognize the story. Anyone who has ever been frightened by a necessary transition in life might recognize this story: a girl numbed by the fact that part of her life was over and a new, harder one was about to start. But Jesus said, 'Come on, you can make it!'

✳ *Loving God, help me to come from the old into the new!*

Wednesday January 10   Luke 14.7-14

The new courtesy

Jesus saw people filling a hall. He saw something we can still see at practically any significant event: people jostling for the first and best places, the places of honour. It is the old courtesy of domination and manipulation. He suggests a new civility, the concern of God's Kingdom. There is to be no competition but the spirit of service; no pushing with elbows but works of mercy; no haughty praying but beating one's chest; not asking who is the most important, but accepting one's place as a child in the new order of the Kingdom of God. He does not only speak of how to behave as guests, but also of how to be good hosts. He does not ask us to prepare meals for the poor, nor to lay their tables and wash their dishes. It is not bad to do that. But how often would you be able to arrange it, and what help would it really be? The new civility Jesus introduces has on its menu card the eight beatitudes (Matthew 5.3-12). If that is our bill of fare we will never lack the guests Jesus asks us to cater for.

✳ *Gentle Jesus, we ask you to open our hearts*
to the guests you would prefer to invite
without any of the differences and discriminations
which characterize the world.

Thursday January 11   *Luke 14.15-24*

The rejected invitation

We cannot deny that we hear God's invitation. It comes to us again and again. It carries a few letters in French: 'RSVP'. Sometimes we respond by telling God that we have prior appointments, just like the people in the Gospel story: a purchase, a sale, a social engagement. What we do not want to say directly is that we have another priority list. God's invitation as such can wait. In fact it *has* to wait.

We hear the music in the hall, we smell the roast on the fire, but we hesitate, we refuse. The American Quaker Thomas Kelly (in *A Testament of Devotion,* 1941) described our predicament in a striking way: 'And we are unhappy, uneasy, strained, oppressed, and fearful that we shall be shallow. For over the margins of life comes a whisper, a faint call, a premonition of richer living we know we are passing by. Strained by the very mad pace of our daily outer burdens, we are further strained by an inward uneasiness, because we have hints that there is a way of life vastly richer and deeper than all this hurried existence, a life of unhurried serenity and peace and power. If only we could slip into that Centre.'

We have seen for ourselves bits of light, rays of goodness, fragments of songs, patches of heaven, and so often we act as if we never heard or saw a thing.

✳ *Lord, have mercy!*

A new economy

Jesus did not wait until the people came to him to tell them that they were hungry. He foresaw their need, and he wanted to help. That is how God is. God foresees and provides. Just think of creation providing all the food we need. Experts keep telling us that the world produces sufficient food to feed all of us. But not all of us are fed!

When Jesus puts Philip to the test – asking, 'How are we going to feed this crowd?' – he directs the question not only to Philip but also to the whole of humankind. Philip answers by referring to the economic situation. People are hungry because they haven't the money to buy the food they need. The difficulty is the existing economic order.

And Jesus took the food that was available – given away by a child! – and made his disciples divide it just because it was there. And it proved to be more than plentiful because there were twelve baskets full of left-overs. Jesus invites us to do what he did: to break through an economy that stops us from providing for the whole of humanity. He invites us to review our list of priorities. The world is not given to some of us; it is given to all. The issue is not my profit; it is how all can profit.

✴ *Almighty God, giver of everything,*
help us to respect your intentions.
Help us to be like you in your love and concern for all.

Double vision

When Jesus tells them that they should have seen him in the faces of the starving, the thirsty, the stranger, the sick, and the prisoner, he asks us to have a kind of double vision. The daily world that surrounds us is the carrier of a reality that remains hidden to many. The temporal carries the eternal. The human carries the divine. The earthly carries the heavenly. In our neighbour's face we should not only see his or her face but the countenance of Jesus. Or – to put it in the context of these first two weeks of *Words for Today 2001* – through the old world around we should see the new one, the Jubilee World which was introduced by Jesus.

In Jesus God took sides by becoming a human being himself, hungry, thirsty, sick, a prisoner, and an executed victim. In Jesus, God's holiness penetrates our own daily life but also the lives of all those around us. It is that reality that renews the face of the earth – the face in which we have to discover the faces of our neighbours even if at first sight those faces do not show much of God's presence.

✷ *Almighty God, help me not only to discover you*
in those I will meet today,
but help me also to live that reality.

FOR REFLECTION – alone or with a group

● What would you think, in the light of Matthew's description of the Last Judgement, about joining an organization like Amnesty International?

● Try to inform yourself about the organized Peace and Justice groups in your locality.

FOR ACTION

Read for a week the 'Letters to the Editor' in your local paper. If possible do that in a group. See whether there is any topic that has to do with the establishing of God's Kingdom in this world. Write your reaction to the Editor.

GOD'S NEW WORLD
2. More gospel stories for today

Paraphrases and prayers by
John Vincent

John Vincent's latest book is 'Hope from the City' (Epworth Press, 2000), where he tells the stories of groups of people in the contemporary city – unemployed, excluded, handicapped, teenagers, kids, old people, immigrants – and then shows how some key Gospel passages 'tell their story'. Here, he uses a similar method of seeing 'snaps' in some Gospel passages.

1. Blinding lights and blind alleys
(January 14-19)

Blinding lights are sudden moments of realization, or revelation, or clarity, or judgements, or mercy. Blinding lights are moments of falling in love, or realizing truth, or encountering betrayal, or being exposed. Usually, words come hard after blinding lights. But things are never the same.

Blind alleys are the opposite. You just know, perhaps after a blinding light, that where you have been was only a blind alley, a dark passage leading nowhere.

John's Gospel, which we follow for the next six days, is all about blinding lights – moments of utter clarity, revelation and finality. But it is in the midst of many blind alleys – places and people, relationships and happenings in which there is no life, no light, no meaning, no wholeness. Essentially, the light shines in dark places and the dark places cannot overcome it (John 1.5). But it's still too blinding for us. We prefer our dark alleys. The dark is light enough for us, we say – until the blinding light.

You are now invited to look with me over the shoulder of the writer of the Fourth Gospel...

2nd Sunday in Epiphany, January 14   *John 1.29-42**
Transferring allegiance

John's Gospel probably reflects a time when there were still disciples of John the Baptist who did not recognize Jesus as Messiah. So John the Baptist, in this Gospel, continually emphasizes that he is not the light (1.20-21; 3.28), and that the one who comes after him is greater than he – that Jesus is that

One (1.15, 26-27; 3.27-30). John the Baptist is the ideal witness to Christ, the model preacher, who uses all his ministry to point to, and give way to, Jesus as the Christ. Here, John explicitly proclaims Jesus (verses 29-31) and he bears witness to the Spirit's descent on him (verse 32).

Next, two of John the Baptist's disciples, Andrew and another, are explicitly directed to the 'Lamb of God', and leave the Baptist to follow Jesus. Their conversation with Jesus ends with the invitation to them, 'Come and see.' Andrew then finds his brother Simon Peter, and he joins them as well.

So where in my story have I moved on, transferred allegiance, gone somewhere else 'to see', been compelled to be in a new place or new relationship that will totally transform me?

✷ *Blinding Light, rescue me; Blinding Light, appear*
Wherever, however, in whomever.
Light up my blind alley that I can see it for what it is,
And for what it can never be. Amen

Monday January 15   *John 2.1-11**
Drawing water
Water I live by. Every day a human being consumes gallons of it. My body is 90% water. So I don't need any other kind of water.

Jesus and his disciples are invited to a wedding with Jesus' mother. Perhaps Jesus was responsible for their contribution to the feast. But penniless preachers were not in a position to give anything, so their presence possibly contributed to the embarrassing situation. Hence Mary's request is partly to cover up for this!

This story is unique to John's Gospel. It is the first of his seven 'signs'. In the Old Testament, a sign is an event that authenticates a prophet (Exodus 3.12; 1 Samuel 10.1-9), or indicates things to come (Isaiah 7.10-16). The 'miracles' are thus seen as 'parables of the Kingdom of God'. According to John's Gospel, signs are intended to reveal Jesus' 'glory', and to produce 'belief' (verse 11). The water used for the Jewish purification rites is contrasted to the wine given by Jesus. The old is transformed into the new. The Kingdom of God is a feast (Mark 2.19). The disciples only look on. The servants are the facilitators and carriers of the 'water now become wine'.

I'm not into miracles. But I have occasionally run to water pots and filled them and run the brimming liquid to someone calling for drink, and heard them say, 'It's the nectar of the gods!'

* *I'm always carrying water for other people.*
  I'm always drawing water from the same old pots.
  Somewhere, somewhere, let it be living water.
  Sometimes, sometimes, let it be the wine of heaven.

Tuesday January 16   *John 8.1-11*

Casting the first stone

I'm not a hard person, a legalist, a puritan. But I know how people get hurt and what a person who causes hurt is all about. I've seen it and sometimes I've felt it. So when I'm confronted with someone who has betrayed another human being, broken trust, shattered simple hopes, I'm struck dumb.

The heart of this story is not that Jesus says anything about adultery except that it is sinful – 'Go and sin no more'. It is rather about whether they were going to carry out the instruction of the Law to stone her to death. So what Jesus says in verse 11 is not, 'neither do I condemn you,' but rather, 'neither will I carry out the penalty.'

Why did Jesus stoop down and write on the ground? Perhaps to give himself time to think. Perhaps because there was no answer which the scribes and Pharisees would recognize. Perhaps from embarrassment. Perhaps he was doodling, to get himself together, caught between the unspeakable deed of the woman and the terrible punishment that hung over her.

The disciples are not mentioned. Was that because the evangelist found it easier to attribute to scribes and Pharisees the natural and legal responses of condemnation? But today, don't we also look over the shoulders of the scribes and Pharisees and say, 'There but for the grace of God go I?' And over the shoulder of the woman?

Dithering endlessly between rightness and desire, halting between judgement and mercy, I look down on the ground to pick up stones, or to write in the dust. It's easy for me to forgive sins not done against me. Who can forgive those who hurt others? Only the betrayed spouse can forgive. And he is not even mentioned!

* *She will be there today. He will be there today.*
  The bruiser, the betrayer, the breaker of bonds.
  I cannot forgive what only the bruised can forgive.
  But keep me writing in the dust. Amen

Being in solidarity

The origin of Jesus' prayer that his disciples might be 'one' is a continuation of his ministry to them in his earthly lifetime (verse 11). It is a prayer that they might be kept together because only so will they be able to stick it out in the face of the world's hatred (verse 14) and the world's exclusion of them (verse 16). It is for solidarity among disciples in the face of the ignorance of the world concerning what they are really about. The solidarity they need is the same kind of solidarity that exists between Father and Son (verse 21) – one of action. 'I in the Father, and the Father in me' (John 14.10-11, 20) now becomes 'Father in me – I in the Father – they in us'. This means to love 'as I have loved you' (13.34). The common practice creates and embodies the solidarity.

The test for this oneness and solidarity of disciples with Christ is the same test as was applied to Jesus. He did 'whatsoever he saw the Father doing', because 'whatever the Father does, the Son also does' (5.19). Jesus' actions are done to please the One who sent him (5.30). So also the disciples do what they do to please the Jesus who sent them (17.18). If they remain in solidarity, in union with him, they will bear much fruit, visible in deeds (15.8), just as the Son, in union with the Father, has borne fruit visible in his deeds. These are the deeds which carry conviction to the world (17.21,23), the 'keeping his commandments' of 14.21, especially the commandment of mutual love (15.12) which was both necessitated by the world's violent hostility (16.2) and also the means of its hoped-for conversion.

My conclusion is that Christian fellowship is crafted out of crisis and brought to birth in brutal opposition and a closing of the ranks. I've experienced that, and call it grace.

✳ *Father's plan and will in Jesus,*
Jesus' plan and will in me.
A mighty movement for universal salvation,
Sailing pathetically in the paper barque of you and me.
Sail on in me! Amen

Living water

Words can mean whatever I want them to mean. I can use the same words as you use. But I do not mean what you mean. The dialogue between Jesus and the Samaritan woman is a carefully constructed series of test questions and double meanings. Everyone lives by water. It's nothing strange. I only live by what everyone lives by. Or do I?

Water is a symbol of the Law, which becomes 'a flowing spring', like God himself (Jeremiah 2.13; 17.13). So Jesus becomes a flowing spring (verses 14-15). This flowing spring is a gift from God now (verse 10), just as the well was to Jacob. In John 7.37-38, Jesus is the source of the living water. Wisdom was previously the source of living water. Whoever drinks from it 'will thirst for more' (Sirach 24.21). Now whoever drinks of Jesus' water will not thirst again (verse 14). This water is not a drug or magic potion (verse 15). Jesus does not even answer, but gets to the heart of the woman's real life by debating her sex-life! (verses 16-19).

I can't make much of this story. I'm not into word-plays. I suspect double meanings. Water is water. I drink what everyone drinks. Except that what everyone drinks, mysteriously, for me at times becomes living. It is touched, changed, flowing, alive. This I think is the revelation of the Ultimate in the mundane, the Blinding Light in the blind alley.

✴ *This day, let me drink of the water of life freely,*
   Of the dead water of taps, and of life itself,
   That it becomes alive. Amen

Friday January 19   *John 4.19-29**
A moving God
My life has been much engaged in providing little holy places, wayside chapels, street corner tabernacles, churches in pubs, shops and houses. So I know that often the only thing you can do is to build on a different piece of ground where people can stand. If it is different enough, they will have to be different in order to stand on it. I believe in a God who moves constantly to new places. But I still believe in a God of places.

The debate about whether the Jews with Jerusalem or the Samaritans with Gerizim have the correct site for God's temple (verse 21) is of no interest to Jesus, as neither site is now the point. God is not a locatable God, who receives physical worship or sacrifice. Rather, 'God is Spirit' (verse 24), and this requires not physical but spiritual worshippers.

The woman just does not 'get it', but departs to tell the story of someone who 'told me everything I did'. It brought the crowds.

The Messiah whom the Samaritans awaited was the 'other Moses' of Deuteronomy 18.15-18. They held to the first five books of the Old Testament, and to this 'other prophet' as the one they expected. Jesus' 'I am' of verse 26 recalls the Divine 'I am' of God (Exodus 3.14 – see also John 6.20; 8.28, 58).

John's Gospel has women in significant roles. Here, the woman is the bearer of the news of Jesus as Messiah (verses 28-29), just as it is Mary Magdalene (20.2,17-18) who bears the news of Jesus the Risen One. When God shifts, someone has to be the first to take the news. Perhaps women are quicker off the mark?

✳ *Moving God, neither in this place nor in that,*
  Be where I stumble on you.
  Compass me round when I flee from you,
  Tabernacle me when I run too fast,
  That you be a place for me. Amen

FOR REFLECTION – alone or with a group
Try your own 'autobiographical readings' of some of the passages. Talk or write the story as if it is about yourself.

---

2. Living it up – acting it out
(January 20-27)

Suddenly to enter the world of the first three Gospels is to enter worlds of extraordinary excitement, vivacity and activity. One action tumbles over another. It's all about 'living it up'.

What was the response of the first readers? What took place, for example, when the Gospel of Mark was first opened and read by Christian disciples huddled together in catacombs or tenement apartments in Rome, four or five years after the mad Nero had killed their fellow believers in AD64? Did they engage only in spiritual reflection? Or did they not rather say, 'If these were the battles of the One whose name we have taken, what battles face us now?' Or, when Luke's most excellent Theophilus read all that Jesus began to teach and to do, would he not have been challenged by Zacchaeus who gave up half his wealth (Luke 19.1-10), and by disciples who have to pick up crosses not once but daily, toiling up God knows what new calvaries? What behaviour, speech, lifestyle, stewardship of money were expected of them? It's all about 'acting it out' – now!

Eating and drinking with Jesus

It is a fundamental conviction of mine that the time of the Christian movement on earth – the time since the resurrection – is not a time of fasting because Jesus is taken away from us (verse 35), but a time of eating and drinking because the bridegroom is with us (verse 34), back in Galilee, just as he was before (Mark 14.28; 16.7). The whole purpose of the resurrection was that the three days had quickly gone and now it is the time of the earthly life of Jesus all over again, daily marked by the deeds of Jesus among the needy, celebrated by 'sharing food with gladness and simplicity' (Acts 2.46), daily taking up our own cross (Luke 9.23).

So much of our life in the Sheffield Inner City Ecumenical Mission has been in closing down mournful Gothic preaching places, and opening up housing complexes, shops, houses, halls and a public house – closing down the places of fasting and praying, and opening up places of eating and drinking.

And, slowly, a few astonished locals have come in to eat and drink, and even stayed for the long haul of the secret disciplines of the faithful – which of course still have some residual bits of praying and fasting. But it's better than the 'proper' churches, where it's nearly all praying and fasting, with occasional cups of tea and chat as a concession to people's humanity!

Are the new coat, the new wineskins, the wedding feast, to be newly discovered and newly manifest in every generation by a few Jesus-people who cannot abide churches as they are?

✳ *Bridegroom, get us from the Church on time!*
Emperor with real new clothes, parade before us!
New wine of heaven, spill over into our jaded lives. Amen

Taking the crumbs under the table

The holy bread is in the house of God, guarded within stone walls and stained glass windows. What strange rites go on that they do not want us to see? Special people eat holy bread, and strange ceremonies prepare them to receive it. Not just anybody can go in and eat the holy bread.

Once in Rochdale, at our weekly morning communion service, I got the feeling, half-way through the liturgy, that something moved from underneath the altar frontal. Perhaps a cat, a mouse, or just nothing? At the end, when people had gone (I did not want to look stupid), I lifted up the frontal and a little, timid girl was crouched there, looking up at me. 'Are you all right?' I asked. 'Yes. I just hid here,' she replied. 'But I'm hungry. Can I have some bread please?'

'We are not worthy so much as to gather up the crumbs under your table.' I have never since been able to say these words without being deeply moved and inwardly confused. Let only the worthy come? Those with baptisms and confirmations, and membership tickets?

The Son of Humanity is the Boss of the Sabbaths (verse 5) and the churches (verse 6), saving life (verse 9), giving food (verse 4), sticking beside his insensitive disciples (verse 1), reinterpreting all the traditions for their benefit (verse 3), making well the broken limbs (verse 10) of outsiders who happen to pop into holy places at the wrong time (verse 6).

✳ *Zeal for your house has eaten me up.*
I door-keep at your temple as one touching holy grail,
And you have always just departed.
Your bread is in your blessed cruse, under your arm,
To eat with strangers. O, let me eat with you too! Amen

Monday January 22   Luke 8.4-8

Just keep sowing the seed!

I'm often asked whether it's worth all the effort we put into running tiny street-corner chapels in deprived areas. Is the result proportionate to the work and money and the devoted people involved? I can't quickly find an answer to satisfy the average careful, money-conscious, success-oriented churchgoer. But then I think of Jesus and his parable of the seeds. It seems perfectly OK that seeds are flung all over the place, without regard to their fruitful outcome – only one out of every four seeds actually bears any ears of corn at all!

And then I meditate on the three seeds which do not come to fruition. The first one gets eaten by birds. But birds have to get fed, after all. And that's very like the people who come in to the Jumble Sale, and in the first minute, woosh! the stuff has gone! Then there's the one among the rocks, that grows and withers. But a brief life is better than nothing – like the folk who come in and find shelter with us for a short time, but then go away. And there's the seed that grows to fruition, but thorns grow with it and choke it. That's many people I know, suburbanites as well, whose

24

faith in Christ grows alongside other things, but in the end is choked by them.

But all three had a life for a time, because I sowed the seed. And the birds, and the temporary visitors, and the two-master servers – all are loved by the sower and by God, who seeks not successful planners but faithful sowing.

✴ *Sow your mystery deep in my heart,*
  Carefree, generous, unsuspecting, trusting God,
  That I, from your foolish abandon,
  May learn not to distrust or ask who is worthy. Amen

Tuesday January 23   *Mark 1.21-28**

Shut up and get out!

We're getting much better at teaching in our churches. We have *Partners in Learning,* and thousands of pieces of paper. We clarify difficult doctrines...

Mark's Gospel, as distinct from Matthew's and Luke's, has very little of the teaching of Jesus. So when Mark has someone observing, 'It is a new kind of teaching – teaching that has authority with it' (verse 27), we take notice. Now at least we are going to get some proper teaching! But no, it's only that evil spirits hear and obey! But that is teaching, says Mark. It's not a doctrine but it is about an order. 'Shut up! Get out of him!' (verse 25). And it actually works. The devil shrieks and gets out.

Just occasionally I've seen it happen, and have been involved. The truth has broken through in a single word. 'Shut up and get out!' We said it in the CND marches, in Anti-Apartheid demonstrations, in Jubilee 2000, in other demonstrations at town halls and outside embassies. And a few people might at least have said to some church people, 'It's a new kind of teaching – teaching with authority. Evil powers hear it, and (sometimes!) obey!'

✴ *I'm getting better at the teaching.*
  I say things much more guardedly,
  But I don't shout at evil, so devils don't fear and fly.
  Teach me to be a Teacher like you. Amen

Wednesday January 24   *Mark 2.13-17*

Tax-collectors and pawnbrokers

I have this thing about taxes. Every year, the simple completion of the Tax Return is a groaning agony. I'm always behind with it, put it off, hate doing it. Extracting money from others must be a lousy job. So I have no great love for Levi, son of Alphaeus. As a long-term resident in an inner city area, I do not mourn for Levi.

So what is Jesus doing, going out of his way to call Levi to be a disciple, but then, even worse, having a feast with others like him? They're not even 'sick' (verse 17). They are extortioners, unjust, victimizers of the poor. Mark does not even tell us if any of them changed. Mark has no Zacchaeus story. Maybe Levi brought his ill-gotten money with him to share with the disciple group. That would redeem it a bit.

In Sheffield, our latest project is an Ashram Community 'emporium' of shop, cafe, community room, workshops and works, plus rooms for residents. Part of the adjoining premises is a pawnbroker's shop. We were taken into it by the lady who runs it. 'All kinds of people come in here,' she said. 'They bring pieces of jewellery or gold or valuables, and we arrange some money for them for as long as we keep the article they deposit.' She stopped and looked at us. 'Often, they stay and tell us why they need the money. It's heart-breaking. And they will come back, and tell me more of their story. It's amazing what they tell you.' And she said, 'What would you do? I'm a social worker half the time. They have no-one else to ask. So I say, "Don't leave your valuables here. It's not for your good!" But they cannot do anything else.'

✳ *As a faithful disciple, I have the world sorted*
into good and bad people. But you go out of your way
To sit down and find the good in the bad.
God, I need that grace. Amen

Thursday January 25   *Luke 5.1-11*

Leaving all and following

In Luke's Gospel, Simon Peter only becomes a disciple after an apparently unexpected big catch of fish, caught at Jesus' suggestion (verse 4), perhaps as a way of compensating Peter for having taken over his boat as a platform (verse 3)! Jesus' observation of a shoal of fish hardly justifies Peter's confession (verse 8). Why Peter calls himself a 'sinful man' is not clear. Fishermen might not be the most religious group, but that did not put them in the group labelled in Luke and elsewhere as 'sinners'. Maybe Peter had an inkling of what the future might hold and blurted out, 'I'm no good.'

But I have seen this story in action in the ones and twos who have found their way to us in the Urban Theology Unit and in one of the Ashram Community houses, or the Inner City Mission street-corner churches. They come from all sorts of places, with all sorts of stories and backgrounds.

Why do they come? Why do they leave all and follow? I do not know. Like Peter, they rarely foresee what will follow. They do not usually claim at the time to have a 'call'. Often they only know clearly what they do *not* want to do, which is what they have been doing, or were trained or educated to do. They leave it all, and stumble for a while, eventually finding their vocation in a different place and with unexpected people, and often using gifts they did not know they had.

✴ *I can't do with the call, coming at me from nowhere,*
Questioning my commitments.
But keep the calls coming, even if I'm not suitable,
So that I'll get to feel I'm some good. Amen

Friday January 26   *Luke 7.1-10*

Healing from a distance

Poor people in the inner cities or the housing estates have churches built by a rich benefactor, or a richer suburban congregation. We can understand how the locals feel when the rich benefactor makes a request (verse 5). And the church leaders would also understand that such a benefactor would not really be 'into' our religion, and would not want to bother the preacher (verse 6). People with money and status just give orders and it is done (verses 7-8). And Jesus fits in with his wish, and cures the slave without personally meeting either the centurion or the slave.

In the end, the inner city has to be grateful for the 'worthies' of past and present who do good to us at a distance. But what we really need – as I said at a meeting with Government officials who asked me to talk on 'capacity building' – is 'incarnate animators'. 'What's "incarnate"?' they asked. People of all kinds, rich and poor, experts and powerful included, who will come and share our situation. 'Animators'? They are people who come to be alongside (my favourite word!) and can get people at the bottom of our society moving. As, of course, Jesus himself did.

✴ *We are not worthy to have you under our roof.*
But don't heal us from afar. Come and lift us up
By being where we are. Amen

Losing worry, gaining the Kingdom

Poor, deprived and largely unproductive people in inner cities and housing states seem to survive. They live on crisps, chip butties, sweets and sliced bread. They don't care about diet. Perhaps they think life is more than food (verse 23). They dress in unwise clothing. They look drab and dowdy. The kids wear cast-offs and hand-downs, or contemporary flash colours. Perhaps they model that life is more than clothing (verse 23). They live from day to day. When they have money, they spend it thoughtlessly. They do not save. They borrow, or pay off things on the 'never-never'. Perhaps they think you cannot add much to your life by worrying (verse 25).

Their lifestyle is rather more like the one Jesus praises than ours is. But we 'of little faith' (verse 28) don't live like that, for all our supposed belief in a Kingdom that happens, much less a provident God who feeds, clothes and provides.

But I have seen a few, mad pieces of mission, pieces of Kingdom activity, done by groups and individuals, which had this crazy, irresponsible character of self-precipitation without visible means of continuance. And I've seen food and physical provisions and money come from nowhere, once the initial leap of faith has been taken.

✳ *I'm heavily insured against personal losses,*
As, I make sure, are all around me.
But it predisposes me against Kingdom ventures.
Put me into something where I can't be so predictable.
Give me a surprise, God. Amen

FOR REFLECTION and ACTION – alone or with a group

- Try writing a mission statement for your church or yourself, based on this week's readings.
- What one thing has opened up for you *to do* from these readings?

GOD'S NEW WORLD
3. Psalms for today

Notes based on the Authorized Version by
Jonathan Gorsky

Jonathan Gorsky is the Educational Consultant of the Council of Christians and Jews. He is an orthodox Jew who has worked for many years in Jewish adult education and small community ministry.

The notes that follow are based upon Jewish responses to the Psalms. For traditional Jews, the Psalms are a primary source of prayer and spiritual expression. Jews turn to the Psalter in times of joy and times of sorrow, finding in them both comfort and reassurance. The notes refer to the original Hebrew text when this is helpful, and also fill in basic historical background when appropriate. They seek to apply the values of the psalmist to today's world and address problems for modern readers, such as vengefulness and triumphalism. Finally, they are an attempt to share the inner responses of a contemporary Jewish reader.

4th Sunday in Epiphany, January 28   *Psalm 1*

God our teacher

The first psalm is so brief, temperate and apparently straightforward that it is easy to overlook it in favour of more impassioned and dramatic poetic expressions later in the Psalter. But a glance at the original Hebrew is instructive, for it adds depth and strength to the translation.

The very first Hebrew word refers to intense feeling that is both serious and enduring. It is indeed joyous, but 'happy' is very weak by comparison with the original *Ashrei*. Also the psalmist is not merely self-satisfied: *Ashrei* signifies a longing for the happiness of one who lives according to God's teaching, rather than a declaration that the poet has already attained this exalted state, and is commending it to others. The Authorized Version's 'Blessed' is ancient, but, in its current usage, does not convey the depth of the original.

In verse 2 'meditate' is best replaced by a more passionate and vocal engagement with religious tradition, and the tree in verse 3 is not 'planted' but 'rooted'. 'Planted' recalls a fragile sapling demanding frequent care and attention; 'rooted' is already mature and knotted in the earth, withstanding the fierce assaults of stormy weather.

The original language also helps with intelligibility. The Hebrew *Torah* in verse 2 is translated as 'law'. This translation is very early indeed – it goes back to the *Septuagint*, a Greek translation of scripture prepared by Jews more than 2000 years ago and which became the Bible of the early Church. But *Torah* literally means 'teaching' and is rich and all embracing, implying a striking image of God as our teacher in all the ways of our life. The psalmist's 'delight' is now more comprehensible!

The psalm portrays the author as a man alone in a world that is scornful of his faith and teaching. A beautiful image of a fruitful tree by a stream of living water is set against the barely outlined ways of the wicked, the chaff driven in the wind in verse 4. Is this an oversimplified portrayal that does not allow for the grey areas or – apparently – the prospect of a change of heart? Or is it a portrayal of the world as seen by a man of great faith who has been deeply hurt by the scorn and indifference of his neighbours?

✻ *Help us, O Lord, to be with others,*
as You are ever present for us, even amidst our fragility
and our failings, when we are before You
as the chaff that the wind driveth away.

Monday January 29 *Psalm 2*

Triumphalism or fragility?

The beginning of the psalm reflects the self-perception of the people of Israel confronted by an untold number of enemies in a hostile world. Clearly Israel had enjoyed military success in the past, but rebellion was in the air against whatever hegemony they had imposed.

The anointed one of God is beleaguered but unafraid, for he is faithful to the Lord who sits in heaven, and whose might is incomparable. He pleads with the surrounding powers to serve God with fear and rejoice in trembling, rather than engaging in hopeless conflict.

But while the psalm appears to us as a piece of religious triumphalism, its full pathos emerges if we contrast it with the very different closing section of Psalm 89. Having taken up the theme of Psalm 2 at great length, Psalm 89.46-51 laments a national catastrophe, stung by the derision of victorious enemies. (The last verse of Psalm 89, in which the psalmist utters a blessing of the Lord, is misleading as it is an appendix that was not part of the original composition). The simple faith of Psalm 2 is shattered: pagan enemies have triumphed over the people of God, and their aloneness is infinitely compounded by a sense of being cast off and rejected. Triumphalism concealed an inner fragility, and a new faith must be constructed from the ruin of the past, with the second psalm sung as poignant remembrance rather than exultant affirmation.

✳ *Teach us, O Lord, not to lose our reverence,*
even when our hearts are rejoicing.
As we tremble before You, help us to be joyous,
even as we are scorched by the fires of Your truth.

Tuesday January 30   *Psalm 6*

An outpouring of pain

A plain reading of the psalm indicates that it was intended to be recited in times of grave sickness. The opening verse places suffering in the context of Divine retribution. God's wrath has been provoked by our sinfulness, and illness is a chastening act of rebuke. The pitfalls of this approach are readily apparent. There is so much suffering in the world that is entirely unwarranted. Even if we are less than saintly, the agony that people endure is utterly disproportionate to the normal run of their shortcomings.

But a remarkable feature of this psalm is that the remaining verses do not continue along the same lines; we might have expected penitence, contrition and a plea for forgiveness, or the gift of a pure heart, as in Psalm 51. But the psalmist expresses the depth of his pain, sometimes taking leave of poetry and speaking in prosaic simplicity, most notably in verse 3, when his language is suddenly foreshortened and gives way to a cry of desperation.

The opening verse is an expression of humility and contrition: for many people a first response to pain is indeed an assumption that it is a consequence of some personal guilt. But the psalmist helps us move beyond such feeling, and seeks to hold us in our pain. He helps us to find words that, in such times, would be beyond our capacity, so that we can pour out our heart to God who is crying with us in the depth of our affliction.

✳ *Help me, O God, to overcome the imaginings of my heart*
and to know You in Your transcendent holiness.

In my fearfulness as I stand before you,
help me to recall Your love and Your forgiveness.

Divine power

The original language of the psalm is powerful, terse and rough-hewn; it is inevitably toned down by earlier translations. For example, the Authorized Version's opening word 'Give' is better than the more literary 'ascribe', but 'maketh' and 'breaketh' (verses 5-6 AV) detract from the power of the original and should be translated into a simple, contemporary usage.

In verse 2, 'the glory due to his name' is but two brief words in the original, and refers to the awesome response evoked in ancient Israel by the sounding of the Divine name. To this day, Jews treat with great reverence any document upon which one of the Divine names is written, and are careful not to destroy it.

'Worship the Lord in the beauty of holiness' also appears in Psalm 96.9, and has found setting in a much-loved Anglican hymn, but the original is not entirely clear. The first Hebrew word literally refers to a physical gesture expressing great reverence, and *hadar* is the overwhelming splendour associated with powerful natural phenomena, rather than a more convivial and domesticated form of beauty. The Jewish reading has the latter phrase of the sentence referring to the Jerusalem Temple, where the Holy of Holies was a sacred and awe-inspiring inner sanctum. (*Hadar* also appears at the end of verse 4, where it is indeed translated as 'majesty').

'The voice of the Lord is powerful' (verse 4) is a sensible translation, but it would be equally correct to find God's 'voice' in the great forces of nature.

The most moving and unexpected moment in the psalm is the final phrase. This magnificent psalm of Divine power concludes in praise of God who blesses His people with peace. Having developed an ever-increasing intensity, leading to a violent and climactic smashing of the great cedars of Lebanon, the imagery gradually quietens, the storm passes and the blessing of peace comes anew into the world.

✴ *As we find You amidst flames of fire,*
and hear Your voice in the breaking of mighty trees,
help us to know You in our daily lives.
May the blessing of Your peace be present in our hearts,
even when we are angry and afraid.

A world responsive to human feeling

The psalmist's vision of God, rooted in the Divine righteousness, justice and compassion, is joyous and all-embracing. He has touched upon ultimate reality, which stands over and against great world powers who rely on military might, and value only physical prowess. God, the creator of the hearts of all humanity, is intimately engaged with all of his creations. In relating to the Divine holiness we find a joyousness of heart that is the ultimate longing of the depths of our being.

This vision of the world rejects a purely exploitative or managerial approach to life. It emphasizes ethical conduct and sees the major moral principles as reflecting the Divine essence of all things. We must construct a world that is righteous and just and responsive to human feeling; such a world engages us at the very depths of our being, and we know the true joyousness of life. Other visions of salvation, rooted in worldly power, are dismissed as illusory, for such power leaves us alienated, alone and utterly homeless. The psalmist has faith in the all-embracing vision of life that his tradition reveals, and seems to find little hope in the counsel of the nations, which, despite its great power, appears empty by comparison.

✳ *O Lord our God, as You look upon the poor peoples*
of the earth, help our governments to see as You see.
Let Thy mercy, O Lord, be upon us
for You are our hope and our deliverance.

God's presence with the broken-hearted

According to tradition, David wrote this psalm as a fugitive, fearful of King Saul, and driven away by the man with whom he had sought refuge. In the midst of this fragile uncertainty, not knowing what was to happen to him, or what his fate would be, David transcends his circumstances, and finds refuge in his sense of God.

Sustained by the regularities of daily life, and secure in our material existence, prayer can become a communal ritual, safe and proper. When all of those securities are taken away, when we are rejected by society and no longer afforded status or respect, when we have no idea one day what will happen to us on the next, then our relationship with God is radically altered. The world of the poor man crying to his Creator is the world of truth, and all else is but a passing shadow.

The psalmist realizes that God is ever-present, and not only at the regular times set aside for communal prayer. Every moment is a time of devotion, and even the perils of the world lose their force, as he is caught up in his vision of the Divine holiness. For the great saints, turning away from the world is not an affliction, or a time of inner turmoil, when they are torn by earthly desire. The reality they know is utterly different and their appearance is transfigured and radiant, even in moments of great travail.

✳ *Help us, O Lord, to be with those who are broken-hearted,*
and not to draw back when they pour forth their sorrow.
Help us to hear as You hear, and to be near to them,
as You are near to us.

Saturday February 3   *Psalm 36.5-10*
All life is holy

Verse 9 of this wonderful psalm has been an inspiration for mystics down the ages. All life is seen in the light of its Divine source and, in contemplating God, they see the true light of creation. Life is no longer only a series of physical phenomena, but a disclosure of the energies that are manifestations of God in the totality of all things. The Divine is truly present in the most mundane reality, and even the simplest of tasks can be sanctified and made holy. Instead of analyzing creation for our own needs, and shaping some aspect of its fabric for our human purpose, we contemplate all of reality in silence and reverence; the loving kindness of God is no longer an abstract phenomenon, but it infuses every fibre of our world, and we realize that we dwell in the shadow of the Divine. In the perception of life, awe-inspired reverence is indeed before our eyes. It is no longer an acquired discipline, but a natural response to our awareness of reality. As we are silent and respectful when we enter great buildings, so it is when we contemplate the natural order of all things in the light of their Creator. Even the smallest task can be rendered sacred, for all of life is holy, and the most ordinary of people are infinitely precious and a source of great wonder.

When we lose this awareness, we are on the threshold of the world of wickedness. Transgression is indeed sin, but it is more than that; it signifies a loss of our sense of ultimate reality, for only then can transgression begin to speak to us in the depths of our hearts, and the words of our mouths be recognized as iniquity and deceit.

✷ *Help us, O God, to sanctify our daily lives, to know that the smallest of our tasks is infinitely precious before You, meriting our care and our love.*

FOR REFLECTION – alone or with a group

● Can Christians share the Jewish readings, or are there points of disagreement?
● What new insights have come to you from an approach based on the original Hebrew text?

5th Sunday in Epiphany, February 4   *Psalm 46*

God is our strength

The modern world has been characterized by an extraordinary pace of change in every aspect of our lives. The world of our grandparents can appear distant in a way unknown to previous generations, and events that seem immensely important one week are forgotten the next, when some new crisis has taken over the headlines. Understanding the signs of our times is difficult, as patterns are impossible to discern, and incessant instability means that we are often insecure and uncertain. The sense of progress and exhilaration that inspired the people at the dawn of the modern age has evaporated, and even the ordered constancy of the environment is no longer assured. We might expect that such insecurity would be inimical to the development of the religious life, which we tend to associate with calm and tranquillity, but this understanding is challenged by the psalmist who teaches us that, even in times of chaos, the essence of all things is unchanging, and the Lord of Hosts is with us.

Indeed, it is precisely in ages such as ours that we can be truly close to God, and know both His intimacy and His exaltedness, for in more stable times we are wont to confuse worldly matters with the ultimate and the eternal, losing ourselves in the apparently immutable order of our own creation and finding within it our identity and our selfhood. The spiritual life becomes marginal, and religion is assimilated to the respectability of polite society.

But in times of confusion, we rediscover the quest that is the essence of our being, and seek the streams of eternity that gladden the city of God. We find our true home in the tabernacles of the Most High and, even if the mountains are carried into the midst of the sea, we are neither fearful nor afraid.

✳ *Help us, O God, to know that it is Your will*
that we should live in our troubled and turbulent times,
for only in poverty of spirit can we truly find You.

Monday February 5   *Psalm 71 **

God and our woundedness

This is a psalm written in old age. The psalmist has grown old in a world of cruelty and unrighteousness, where he is a stranger, abused and in need of refuge. Later in the psalm, we find an expression of personal hurt, reflected in his aggressive response to his tormentors. These verses make us feel uncomfortable, and we ask how we can pray with such vengeful material.

We should understand that the language of vengeance is also the language of pain, and it is our first thought in moments when we have been brutalized or abused. It is in the dark reality of a suffering world – and in praying the psalm in its entirety – that we enter into the life of a person who, hurt and humiliated, pours out his inmost suffering before his heavenly Father. We recall that we too are capable of harbouring such emotions, and ask God to be with us and help us sustain our hope in a time when we are truly hopeless.

When our feelings are wounded, we often turn to others and say terrible things that in our heart of hearts we do not mean; when calm returns we deeply regret what we have done, and seek to make amends and obtain forgiveness. The psalmist teaches us to hear the pain that is the inmost core of our vengefulness, and know especially the particular sorrows of old people. When we hear hurtful language directed at us, we must learn to listen to the heart of our neighbour, and no longer focus on our own feelings. We respond to the pain of the world, and our lives become a place of God's peace; all who turn to us will find a refuge, and even the least of us participates on the redemption of all life.

✳ *Be with us, O God, in our times of anger,*
and help us to hear the pain
of those whose words have hurt us so deeply,
and to be with them, as You are with us.

Tuesday February 6   *Psalm 72*

A radical vision

Psalm 72 is one of the great biblical visions of the good society. In our time, which is preoccupied with market values, it represents a radical vision of the role of government.

In the market place, even if people conduct their individual transactions properly and legally, the global result can leave people in poverty and want. Wealth becomes concentrated in the hands of the few, and the suffering of the many can be very great. Those who conduct business find that competition forces them to cut costs, and move their factories to places where the labour is cheapest. Whole countries can be overwhelmed by debt to the degree that they are unable to provide for the basic needs of their people. The one form of transaction available to them is exchange, and if they have nothing to exchange then they face ruin.

The psalm emphasizes values that are communal, and gives them primacy. When righteousness is restored, peace will reign. The Hebrew for peace – *shalom* – does not only allude to the absence of conflict. It expresses the idea of wholeness, wherein we are all part of a community. Property, neither ring-fenced nor private, becomes a source of personal obligation to relieve the pain of those among us who are in want.

The righteous king will intervene, on behalf of the needy and the poor, but only a transformation in the depths of our hearts will bring *shalom* into the world. This will be the work of the Messiah, whose name will be blessed by all the peoples of the world.

✱ *Restore unto us, O Lord,*
  the ways of your holy community. Help us to share
  all that we have and not be fearful for tomorrow.
  Recall unto us that, when the needy
  and the poor of the world cry unto You,
  they cry because of our profligacy,
  and may our shame be the beginning of our redemption.

Wednesday February 7   *Psalm 96*

Transformation

The last verse of this joyous celebratory psalm is somewhat unexpected, for joyousness is suddenly associated with the presence of God as judge of all the earth, and we do not usually associate visits to courts with undue rejoicing!

The psalmist has an extra-ordinary sense of the redemptive significance of righteousness, and the role of the Divine Judge is crucial in its attainment. So many psalms and Old Testament narratives focus on social abuse, and the counterbalance is seen as justice, which will govern all our affairs and relationships in an equitable manner.

The psalmist seems to envisage that this can only be attained by Divine intervention. Justice, not instrumentalism, managerial efficiency, or the uninhibited workings of the market place will govern human conduct, and people will be drawn to righteousness, rather than self-centred individualism.

Justice is not merely an external imposition; its attainment will demand a transformation in our response to material goods, and indeed to each other. The community will form the context of the market place, and economic life will no longer result in suffering and deprivation.

✳ *May our lives, O Lord, be filled with the song*
of all the earth. Help us overcome our self-centredness,
and know in truth the splendour of Your Holiness.

Thursday February 8   *Psalm 135*

Tensions

This psalm reflects the self-perception of the people of Israel, in the age when they, alone of all the peoples of the world, worshipped God, with whom they were in intimate relationship. By comparison the faiths of the nations seemed to be devoid of any intrinsic value.

Verse 4, which refers to the notion of the Chosen People, is derived from Deuteronomy 7.6. The conception is taken by Jews to refer to a priestly vocation in the wider world; as Abraham was to be a blessing for all families of the earth, so the people of Israel were to be a light to the nations, who would find God in their way, as a consequence of Israel's example. The tension between the unique and the universal is part of the Jewish heritage. So is the related tension between the sense of intimacy with God utterly apart from the world and a converse desire that all of creation would ultimately worship the Holy One of Israel. The psalmist clearly reflects the tendency towards the pole that emphasizes the intimacy of God and Israel. This is how he reads both sacred history, and his own knowledge of idolatrous worship. Only the last verse has a slight allusion to a blessing that goes forth in the wider world.

This tension has its echoes today. How does a religious community with an intense sense of God's presence relate to the secular world? Does it withdraw into its own life of worship, or seek to be more universal in a world where, nevertheless, its people do not feel at home? The slight allusion at the end of the psalmist's celebration perhaps reflects that, for all of his sense of Divine intimacy, there is a longing for a vision that transcends the boundaries of Israel, going forth from Jerusalem and embracing the nations of the earth.

✳ *May our faith, O God, be in You alone,*
and not in the images of our own making.
Help us to be present for all creation,
even when our innermost longing is to dwell for ever
in the courts of the House of God.

Friday February 9   *Psalm 138 **

The way of compassion

The power of God differs from human assertion, for its focus is to be with those who call out in their loneliness and sorrow. The way of the great of the land is to be indifferent to the plight of those whose status precludes social intimacy. When we rise in the world we wish to be seen with the fashionable and the prominent and take great care as to who we mix with. Our lives are so arranged that we never see the poorer areas of town, driving from the suburbs to our work place and back undisturbed by the social realities around us.

The way of God is the opposite. Divine glory is incomparable, yet God is far removed from the proud and the secluded. The Hebrew original for verse 6 simply observes that He sees the lowly. God has compassion upon all of us, and is close to rich and poor alike, but once one has seen society's distress, the world of fashionable indifference is no longer acceptable. The psalmist dreams of a transformed society, when power does not betoken distance or indifference, and the fashionable realize that the world of truth is the compassion of God. All of us are infinitely precious, and have within us the Divine image, by comparison with which all of the glitter appears worn and faded.

It is not a question of making pious comments about wealth and greed. Rather is it a matter of helping each other to see the wonder that resides in all of us. We are drawn to consumerism because we have lost sight of the holiness of all life and the preciousness of every moment. When our sense of the creation is restored we realize that amassing possessions is unnecessary, and wealth does not consist of being aloof and distant from those who need us. We are moved to give thanks wholeheartedly, for we have been given a new world, and begun our journey to truth and compassion.

✳ *Help us, O Lord, to see everyone as You see them,*
  and let us not forsake the work of Your hands,
  which is present in all of us.

Saturday February 10   *Psalm 147*

The power of God's creative love

The miracle of our time is communication: we can see and be in touch with every place on earth in the space of a moment. Jerusalem is to be a revelation of God's love for all the world. The statutes and judgements that have been given to Israel are a way of creation that will provide for humanity and restore all life to holiness. The particular vision of God that moves the psalmist to joy is one of indescribable power that is simultaneously with the broken-hearted and the humble – ordinary people in the depth of suffering and pain. When Israel knows God in this way, there will be peace within her borders, for she will understand that true power lies in our capacity to be with each other in the depths of our broken-heartedness, and Jerusalem will be an inspiration for all humanity.

✳ *We pray, O Lord, for the people of Jerusalem,*
  that they may know the presence of Your love,
  and be a blessing for all the families of the earth.

FOR REFLECTION and ACTION – alone or with a group

● How do we cope with the violent language of some of the psalms?
● Is it possible to apply biblical values to modern societies when, for example, our economy is so much more complex than that of ancient Israel?

DARE TO BE DIFFERENT
1. Live simply

Notes based on the New Revised Standard Version by
Kate McIlhagga

Kate McIlhagga is a minister of the United Reformed Church in North Northumberland, a writer and grandmother. She trained as a youth and community worker before going to theological college as a mature student. She has worked in schools, housing estates, a new village and as a community minister in a Church Community Centre. Kate is a member of the Iona Community.

It's not easy to live simply, by choice, when there are children to feed and educate. It's not easy to live simply, by choice, when there are needs to be met, benefits to find, debts to pay. Many of us in this world long simply to live! So what message is there for us in this week's readings about lifestyle, about priorities, choices and opportunities?

6th Sunday in Epiphany, February 11   *Luke 6.17-21**
God's poor on Caedmon's Day

Jesus addresses a motley crowd of sightseers: the curious, those who had already committed themselves to his group and those who were on the fringes; those desperate for a clue for how to live, desperate for healing. People like us. On this plateau half-way up a mountain he delivers his bombshell, his manifesto. He turns the values of the world as they knew it (and we know it) upside down. He dares them to be different. He dares us to be different.

Like Caedmon, the 7th century lowly herdsman of Whitby, whose day it is today, we are called to see and praise God in all that is around us and deep within us.

'Blessed are you who are poor' does not mean of course that there is blessing in poverty for poverty's sake. Jesus is preaching to those who want to belong to the 'poor of God' (as the original Jesus' group may well have been called). If they confess that God's Kingdom is being brought in by Jesus they belong to that community of love and are indeed blessed. They may not have money for luxuries, they may sometimes go hungry, they won't be sheltered from life's grief, but they will live as God's community: the people of the way.

Walk more slowly today with your eyes open to seeing God around you in those you meet, and deep within. Treasure these moments. What have you seen, heard or recognized today that is of God? How can I praise God in what I do and think and feel today?

✳ *He lives his life in love and joy,*
In man and woman, girl and boy;
His purpose is in me and you,
In what we are and do;
    His love is in us when we sing
    With every God-created thing,
And praise him, and praise him, and praise him.
Arthur Scholey (1932-) Reproduced from 'The Song of Caedmon'
    by permission of Stainer & Bell Ltd, London, England

Monday February 12   *Luke 6.22-26**

Cold comfort

This combination of woes and blessings can be found throughout the Old Testament: the rich have used their wealth to buy their own comfort and ignored the needy. Woe to you who are rich, because that is all the comfort you are going to get!

This is a disturbing passage. Of course money doesn't buy love and of course there is more to life than making your first million.

Clearly, sharing what little or much we have is the gospel imperative. A modern 'woe' or cursing might be something like this:

    Cursed be garbage in an open sewer
    Cursed be the barbed wire of camps
Cursed be the gassing and maiming of children.
                 Kathy Galloway, The Pattern of Our Days
                        (Wild Goose Publications)

Now write your own woes in the context of the last week's news...

Reflect: what effect did Jubilee 2000 have on world debt?

✳ *Today, let us pray for the fat cats,*
the multi-million multinationals,
    that they may use their wealth wisely,
share their riches generously
    and allow justice a place on their agenda.

There are no pockets in a shroud – *Spanish proverb*

John Wesley's rule of life was to save all he could and give all he could. When he was at Oxford as a young man he had an income of £30 per annum. He lived on £28 and gave £2 away. When his income increased he still lived on £28 and gave the rest away.

Members of the Iona Community are accountable to each other, not only for the proportion of their money that they give away, but also for what they keep themselves.

What do we treasure? How do we value it? How can we share it? These might be relevant questions today, on the eve of St Valentine's Day, the saint associated with costly love.

Today pray for the things you treasure, whether it is being involved in action for change, or enjoying a quiet walk with a friend.

How accountable are you for the 'treasure' you keep for yourself?

✳ *Through Jesus, our greatest treasure,*
came an explosion of true love.
He shattered the splendid walls
of the proud fortresses of the world's great ones.
He put his hand in the hand of the weak
and brought peace to humble dwellings.

Gwylim R Jones: translated by Brendan O'Malley
Welsh Pilgrim's Manual (Gomer 1989)

Wednesday February 14   *Matthew 11.25-30*

Yoked to Christ

In verses 25-27 Jesus suggests that the so-called 'wise and intelligent' have much to learn from the poor. This comes across powerfully from the following experience of some aid workers. They had finished giving out small bowls of rice to each hungry family as they approached the truck. Then another group came over the hill. Carefully they swept enough rice from the floor and corners to make up half a bowl. It was gratefully received and everyone settled down to cook what they had. To everyone's dismay another little family struggled down towards them. There was silence. Then the last family to arrive – the family who had received only half a bowl of rice – stood up and welcomed the newcomers. 'Come and eat with us,' they said.

We are also invited in this passage to take on the yoke of Jesus, remembering that the demands of loving God and our neighbour are inexhaustible, as St Valentine found when he was martyred for his faith in Rome in the 4th century.

Whenever I put on my stole in preparation to conduct worship, its yoke-shape reminds me that I am not on my own, but am yoked to Christ.

Visit or send a card to someone who is alone today. Be conscious in whatever you are doing that you are 'yoked to Christ'. What can you learn from the 'poor' today?

✳ *God, Lovegiver,*
yours is the love we need and long for,
not counterfeit petty love tied with bows,
but lasting love:
Love that's there when the sweetness has gone;
love that endures beyond the barrier of pain.

Vulnerable Lovegiver,
Christ, wounded healer,
Holy Spirit, compassionate friend,
grant us love in all its fullness.

Thursday February 15   *Jeremiah 17.5-10**

Nourished for life

This passage comes from a small collection of wisdom sayings. You'll find the idea of a just person being like a green tree elsewhere in the Bible (Proverbs 11.30; Luke 6.43-45). In the midst of pressures and conflicting claims of modern life we are still called to make choices, to trust God rather than what we can achieve through our own strength or beauty or accomplishments. There is a deeper river into which we can sink our roots for sustenance and fruitfulness.

Take time today to reflect on what nourishes you. Put times in your diary when you can seek that nourishment. What time will you give today to allow God to nurture you?

✳ *Trustworthy God, may we sink our roots*
deep into the soil of your heart,
that we may blossom and flourish for you,
find in you the nourishment we need
to live justly, to love mercy,
and for a life simply lived in your presence.

A fragrant offering

This is the way those who, through baptism, have put on a new nature should behave. The suggestion is that any offence against a fellow member is an offence against the Holy Spirit. If we want to be members of God's household, we must love our neighbours. 'I do,' I hear you mutter. What happens, however, when you go shopping? Do you know if the wonderful new trainers you've bought have been made in some sweat shop? Are your coffee and tea fairly traded? Is the product you buy promoted by a firm which still pushes dried milk for babies in countries where breast is best – not least because of water contamination?

Nowadays to come away from a shopping expedition smelling of roses is increasingly difficult! Find out about fairly traded goods through your local Traidcraft outlet. Do you know how and where the money you save or invest is used? Find out about the Ethical Investments Service. Wake up to the real world. Live with integrity (verse 10).

✷ *Bless to Me, O God,*
    Each thing my eye sees;
Bless to Me, O God,
    Each sound mine eyes hear;
Bless to Me, O God,
    Each odour that goes into my nostrils;
Bless to Me, O God,
    Each taste that goes to my lips;
    Each note that goes to my song,
    Each ray that guides my way,
    Each thing that I pursue.

                    Carmina Gadelica III (Scottish Academic Press 1971)

More than enough

Living simply is not as simple as it seems. No one struggled more than the apostle Paul. Here he expresses his gratitude to the Macedonian church for their support. Living simply is even more complicated in the 21st century than it was then. Paul seems to be saying to us, 'Be content with your lot'. We would want to add, 'as long as it is just'. As long as we are prepared to live simply that others may simply live. As long as we're prepared to campaign prayerfully for a just and equal sharing of the world's resources. Always, whether we live in a suburban 'semi' or a lean-to hut, we have to remember that we can do all things through God who strengthens us.

Today let us pray for our brothers and sisters throughout the world:

out of our poverty and theirs

may we not stumble by judging each other.

✷ *Christ, brother of the poor,*
in the faces of our partners
may we see your love.
In our faces may they see your love.
Together may we abide in you,
simply celebrating the risen life of the Kingdom.

FOR REFLECTION – alone or with a group

● How far do we try to justify our present lifestyle rather than truly repent of it and allow God to change us?
● How can we live each day as God's poor?

FOR ACTION

A number of suggestions for action have been made most days this week. Look at these and try them again.

DARE TO BE DIFFERENT
2. Be peacemakers

Notes based on The Revised English Bible by
John Morrow

John Morrow is a semi-retired minister of the Presbyterian Church in Ireland. He is a former member of the Iona Community and a founder member of the Corrymeela Community in Northern Ireland. He was Leader of the Corrymeela Community from 1979-1993, and since then has been a Lecturer with the Irish School of Ecumenics.

When the Corrymeela Community began in 1965 the calling to 'be peacemakers' was at the centre of our vocation. Surprisingly, many Christians in Ireland saw little connection between peacemaking and the gospel. The priority was personal salvation. The passages for our reflection this week show that this was a serious omission. Much of Jesus' teaching deals with situations of conflict and violence, the tasks of peacemaking and the building of community. In a world where mobility and communication have brought people of different races, classes and cultures into closer proximity, the major question facing us all is 'how can we live together in peace?'

7th Sunday in Epiphany, February 18   *Luke 6.27-31**
Breaking the cycles of violence

This passage has sometimes been interpreted in a moralistic way as an almost impossible new law. It has also been understood as a purely passive response in the face of violence and oppression. Recent commentators like Walter Wink, in his book *Engaging the Powers,* have put the passage into context. He suggests that the call to turn the left cheek, after we have been struck on the right, was a non-violent challenge to the oppressor to treat the victim as an equal rather than as an inferior. A slap on the right cheek can only be given with the back of the hand – a 'put down' gesture. When the other cheek is turned the victim can only be struck with the front of the hand, as an equal, if the oppressor wishes to continue the violence (see also Matthew 5.39).

  Perhaps the most important insight is that if we simply react, in kind, in a tit-for-tat fashion, we get caught up in a cycle of violence and allow the oppressor to determine our behaviour. In other words we lose our freedom! If we can refrain from that gut reaction, and do something different or unexpected, we can sometimes break the cycle. There are of course no guarantees so we have to be prepared to suffer. When Gordon Wilson lost his daughter in a bomb blast at Enniskillen he said that he bore no ill will towards her killers. The leader of a paramilitary group said later that these words made it impossible for him to order his men to carry out a revenge killing.

Can we imagine for a moment how an opponent might be 'disarmed' by an unexpected gesture? (E.g. President Sadat, of Egypt, going to speak to The Knesset in Israel). Think of a concrete situation in your experience. Do Paul's words about heaping 'live coals on his head' (Romans 12.20c) strike a chord for you as a way of overcoming evil with good?

✳ *Lord, in the face of violence, hatred and oppression*
give us calmness, courage and clarity.
Free us from bitterness and fear
so that we may witness to your truth
in the power of your love. Amen

Monday February 19   *Luke 6.32-36**

God's model of indiscriminate and inclusive love

In verse 36 we are urged to be compassionate even as our Father in heaven is compassionate. Look at Matthew's version (Matthew 5.48) where the Greek word *teleios* is used and is often translated as 'perfect'. A much better translation is 'indiscriminate' or 'all-inclusive', meaning that our love is to be without limits. Often our love is exclusive; we love those who love us or give only when we are certain of a return. But any loving parent knows that this is not authentic love. We know that even when things have gone wrong, or when a daughter has turned her back on us, we cannot cease to care for her, in spite of everything, and to seek her welfare. When we discover that God loves us in spite of our selfishness, dishonesty, and prejudice, we are given a new dynamic power to show the same generous indiscriminate love to others, and to reach across the barriers of hate, alienation and division.

In our work with young adults in Corrymeela we sometimes find that they wish to test us out to see if our love is authentic. Their past experience may have made them feel that most expressions of love are phoney, so they may even betray a trust to see if they will be rejected!

How do we respond when our love and care are thrown back in our face? Think of situations when that has happened to you. What is the difference between sentimentality and love?

✱ *Lord, we are often afraid of the cost of love;*
when we are hurt we often close up like clams.
Help us to risk being vulnerable and generous
for your sake and so to know better
'the breadth and length, and height and depth'
of your love. Amen

Tuesday February 20   *Luke 6.37-42**

Getting beyond blame

Those of us who live in divided societies are well aware of the culture of blame and counter blame which infects the climate of our lives. In Northern Ireland it is often called 'what aboutery?'. Each time one community blames the other for a particular injustice, the other immediately responds with the words 'what about the time when...?' referring to a previous incident which gave an excuse for their actions.

It is so easy to keep score of each other's wrongs and to judge the actions of our rivals harshly, but the followers of Christ are called to look first at ourselves and to begin with a self critique of our own group, church or community. Jesus' words about the 'speck' and the 'plank' help us to laugh at our capacity for self-deception. It is too easy to look for scapegoats as the source of all our troubles. Blaming others, and asking only them to change, often means that we have to do nothing! If we take the initiative in self-examination and repentance, acknowledging our own blindness, we often get a surprising response from our enemy or protagonist.

Think of some of the scapegoats you are tempted to use in order to avoid personal responsibility for the problems of your society. For example, isn't it a bit too easy for us in Ireland to blame the paramilitaries, or the British or Dublin governments for all our troubles? Where does responsibility lie in your situation?

✱ *We confess how often we are blind,*
how rash our judgements
and how self-righteous our attitudes can be.
Shine your light on our lives and our communities
and transform us with your truth and love.
Peace will come; let it begin with me. Amen

Authentic living bears fruit

In some Evangelical circles there is a dangerous distortion of the reformation doctrine of 'justification by faith'. This stresses that good works are of no significance in salvation and that only faith in Christ matters. This passage shows that there is an intimate connection between authentic faith and fruitful lives. It is, of course, true that good works flow from faith-filled lives and that we can deceive ourselves by 'giving our body to be burned' without love. Fruitfulness in our lives is not the same as a CV made up of all the achievements we can number. It is more like the climax in the growth of a tree which has flowered and cannot help bearing fruit as the fulfilment of its very being. In human life it is the expression of a life founded on faith, love, truth and worship. Trees which are not nourished by water, fertility of the soil, sunshine and pruning are often misshapen runts. Our lives can be like that too and they can bear the bitter fruits of meanness, rancour and self-righteousness. Three of the fruits of the spirit are: love, joy and peace. We need to nourish these.

✳ *Loving God,*
   does my life reflect the fruitfulness
   of a healthy fruit tree?
   Do I give time and space to nourish it?
   Does my peacemaking grow out of a deeper peace
   which is rooted and grounded in Christ?

Are we building on firm foundations?

It is quite clear to many of us who live in Northern Ireland that the attempt to build a community here since 1920 did not have firm foundations. Those from the Unionist tradition (mainly Protestant) felt totally insecure from the start because they believed that those from the Nationalist tradition (mainly Catholic) were bent on destroying the province. On the other hand those from the Nationalist tradition felt that they were treated as second class citizens no matter how they acted. A community built on fear and distrust ultimately collapsed under stress. The work of peacemaking today is partly about digging deeper to find firmer foundations based on mutual respect, the participation of all and a more equal sharing of resources.

Our text reminds us that we can profess to be followers of Christ and yet neglect the most basic aspects of his teachings.

We can be selective in our use of the Bible, putting the stress on personal salvation but forgetting that salvation is about right relationships with God, with one another and with all creation. It is about the building of personal and community life on firm foundations. The ministry of reconciliation is the calling of us all. In a global perspective it is an urgent priority because, unless we recognize our interdependence in every aspect, we can destroy our 'common house' and bring catastrophe to all.

What are the foundations necessary for true peace in the world today? Where do you begin in your own local community? Do we pay lip-service to a form of Christianity which costs us nothing?

✳ *Lord, make us instruments of your peace:*
 Where there is hatred, let us sow love;
 Where there is injury, pardon;
 Where there is doubt, faith;
 Where there is despair, hope;
 Where there is darkness, light;
 Where there is sadness, joy;
 For your love's sake we ask it. Amen
                                    Adapted from St Francis of Assisi (1181-1226)

Friday February 23   *Luke 12.57-59*

Resolve conflicts before they escalate!

This is a very interesting passage because it describes the process by which a conflict tends to grow: the longer we put off seeking a resolution and go on trying to win or defeat our opponent, the greater the ultimate cost we may have to pay.

All forms of rivalry tend to follow this pattern and move upwards towards violence in a tit-for-tat cycle. We tend to get caught up in a spiral which 'takes us over'; we say things that we later regret as we progressively demonize one another.

The skills of mediation, which were often valued in ancient cultures, are being rediscovered today. They can make a big difference in societies where litigation and confrontation have become the norm. A mediator can help both parties in a dispute, if they are willing, to take joint responsibility for ending the conflict in the true interests of all.

But is it possible to mediate in a dispute where there is an unequal distribution of power? Other skills such as advocacy and conciliation may be necessary stages in a process before mediation is possible. The deepest levels of healing and reconciliation require above all else the recognition of each other's humanity and the need for repentance and forgiveness.

✳ *Set us free from the rivalries through which we destroy*
our relationships. Give us the wisdom and humility
to seek to resolve our conflicts before they destroy us.
Enable us to be peacemakers
and not merely peace-lovers. Amen

Saturday February 24   *Matthew 10.34-39*

The gospel often divides before it can unite!

This is probably one of the most paradoxical passages in the New Testament and seems to contradict some of our most basic assumptions about the value of family life. Yet it goes to the core of Jesus' message by emphasizing the need for our first loyalty to be to God and his Kingdom. If the values and priorities of any family contradict those of the Kingdom of God then they have to be questioned, even at the cost of division. Only when obedience to Christ comes first is there a real foundation for community and for family life.

This passage is especially relevant to the work of peace-making. Divided communities – even Christian communities – are a bit like families. Phrases like 'blood is thicker than water' abound, creating pressures to be loyal to our tribe, right or wrong. That soon becomes a basis for 'ethnic cleansing'. It takes a lot of courage to be critical of one's own tradition and to look for what is truthful and fair to all. When we try to build relationships with those from another culture we can be attacked by members of our own group with accusations of betrayal. Mixed marriage couples can be soft targets for abuse. It is only possible to build a truly peaceful society when enough people are prepared to stand up and be counted, exposing the bigotry and prejudice of those who nurture tribal loyalties. Reconciliation groups can come under fire for nurturing cross-community relations but they can also help those who are trapped by fears to discover the humanity of the other.

Are we willing, at times, to risk the wrath of our family or community to raise questions about our way of life, and our attitudes to others? Sometimes it is when we risk losing our life that it is given back to us in a new way!

✳ *Help us, Lord, never to seek peace at any price,*
but to witness to truth, justice and forgiveness
and all that makes for your peace,
whatever the cost. Amen

FOR REFLECTION and ACTION

- Is peacemaking a central focus in the worship and outreach of your congregation?
- If not, why not, and what would it mean in practice to put it at the centre?

DARE TO BE DIFFERENT
3. Let God be seen in you

Notes based on the New Revised Standard Version by
Julie M Hulme

Julie M Hulme is a Methodist minister dedicated to a life of prayer, and writing on spiritual themes. She is married to David, who is superintendent minister of the Birmingham (Elmdon) circuit, and they have two teenage daughters.

Throughout human history, those who have dared to be different have often stood alone, or become the focus of harassment or even persecution. The desire to live simply and to be a peace-maker runs contrary to currents in human society which deliberately foster the accumulation of material goods and the use of violence in the pursuit of power. It can be hard to sustain our 'difference' if we rely on our own strength. Rather, we need to allow God to be seen in us.

8th Sunday in Epiphany, February 25   *Exodus 34.29-35**
Others will see a difference

Moses spent many days alone with God on the sacred mountain. It was a time of awe and wonder. The Covenant had been renewed. The Law had been given. Moses had talked with God and known God's presence. But the people had shown themselves to be unreliable, choosing and making another god of their own. For Moses, the days on the mountain were strenuous as well as rewarding. He himself was not aware how much had changed. But others were able to see the difference.

Encounter, listening and struggle had created an inner light which, for a short time, was made visible to those around him. It marked Moses out as one who had walked with God. In the same way, as we spend time with God who is the source of the spiritual life within us, others will see the difference.

✳ *Psalm for reflection:* Psalm 36

✳ *O God of grace and glory, stay with us;*
that we may live in your presence,
and your light may shine through our dedicated lives.

Monday February 26　　　　　　　　　*2 Corinthians 3.12 to 4.2**

Grow by obeying the Word

If our intimacy with God is to develop and grow, we must make an active, positive response to what we learn from Scripture. Obedience confirms the Word in our hearts and shapes our lifestyle accordingly. It also enlarges the mysterious impact that the Spirit can have on other people through our attitudes, words and deeds, even when we are unaware of it.

Sadly, our prejudices can prevent us making a positive response to God. These prejudices may be derived from our history or culture, or they may be particular to our family or to the work that we do. Whatever their source, they must be challenged if they are preventing us from obeying God. Only through humble obedience to truth and love do we grow in grace. And we must be prepared to grow, for the beauty of God that we can see in this life is only partial. There is always more to see, more to know, more to receive.

✴ *Psalm for reflection:* Psalm 95

✴ *O God of grace and truth, live in our hearts;*
that we may glimpse your glory, and, desiring more,
become enriched in love.

Tuesday February 27　　　　　　　　　　　　*Luke 9.28-36**

Move on – encouraged by God

The disciples were astonished to see Jesus talking with Moses and Elijah, and dazzled by the light which shone from him. But it is possible that Jesus needed the reassurance of the two prophets as he considered what lay before him in Jerusalem, and that he was comforted by the voice of God speaking from the cloud. When the wonder faded, Jesus was found to be alone. And he remained spiritually lonely throughout the days which followed, as he set his face towards Jerusalem (Luke 9.51) and tried to explain to his followers what would happen there. When we respond to God, we may find that our pilgrimage takes us into a cloud of uncertainty and fear. But God will give us times of encouragement to keep us on the right road.

✴ *Psalm for reflection:* Psalm 90

✴ *O God of grace and love, stand with us;*
that we may move forward through the cloud of uncertainty,
listening to your voice, and not to our fears.

Ash Wednesday, February 28   *Isaiah 58.1-12**

Work for a communion of justice

Jesus warned his disciples that it is possible to use prayer and other acts of devotion as means of displaying our piety to others, or of claiming superiority over them. Another danger is that we become so concerned with God that we are no longer interested in human beings. The prophet speaks out against self-centred religion, even when it appears to be giving glory to God. It is not enough to seek communion with God through prayer and fasting. God looks for a positive response to the Word in our personal and social relationships. Our devotion is not welcomed by God unless it is working towards creating genuine community – a communion, not only of adoration, but also of justice.

✳ *Psalm for reflection:* Psalm 51

✳ *O God of grace and freedom,*
   increase our desire for truth;
   that we may live honestly with brother and sister.
   Increase our desire for what is right;
   that we may live justly with our neighbours.
   Increase your compassion in us;
   that we may love even our enemies for your sake.

Thursday March 1   *Joel 2.1-2, 12-17**

In disaster – turn again to God

The army of invasion is on its way! How should the people respond? The need is so urgent that the normal social customs are overthrown. Even those on their honeymoon must take notice. The peril threatens everyone, so all are called to the assembly, even those too young to understand. And the threat is of total destruction, so a total response is required. It is not enough for people to speak of repentance and tear their garments as signs of sincere mourning: they must return to God with their whole selves, and rend their hearts, not their clothes.

When disaster threatens, we can either carry on as we have done before, or we can turn again to God, acknowledging our wrongdoing, listening for God's guidance and asking for strength to face what is to come. This repentance will only be genuine if it is wholehearted and makes a difference to our attitudes or behaviour. If so, then as we turn to God in our times of difficulty, we are sifted, purified, changed.

✳ *Psalm for reflection:* Psalm 102

✳ *O God of grace and compassion, hear our prayer;*
in the time of our pain, heal us;
in the night of our sorrow, console us;
and in the hour of our need, provide for us.

World Day of Prayer, March 2   *Ephesians 3.14-21*

Be filled with God

Among the stories told about the Desert Fathers, there is the tale of how Abba Joseph went to see Abba Lot for spiritual guidance. Abba Joseph was concerned because, although he prayed, fasted, kept silence and spent much time in meditation to control his thoughts and imagination, he suspected that there was a quality lacking in his devotion. Abba Lot got to his feet and raised his hands into the sky so that his fingers, held against the sun, appeared to be on fire, and told him: 'If you will, you shall become all flame.'

Some Christians think so meanly of themselves (and also of God) that they are constantly disheartened. Others are too easily satisfied with their progress. Paul encourages us, not just to be grateful for what God has done for us, but to rejoice even more at what God can do with us in the future. While praising God, he also describes the astonishing spiritual wealth that is available to us. We can be filled with God!

Today we give thanks that we can worship with women and men all over the world, as we celebrate the Women's World Day of Prayer.

✳ *Psalm for reflection:* Psalm 138

✳ *O God of grace and hope, kindle our desire,*
that we may be satisfied with nothing less than yourself.
Inspire our living, that we may want nothing less
than to serve you with our whole heart.

Saturday March 3   *2 Corinthians 5.20b to 6.10**

Let the light shine!

A young girl, asked to define a saint, thought of the stained-glass windows that she had seen in her church and replied, 'A saint is a person who lets the light shine through.'

Paul describes how he and his fellow-apostles have struggled to be so transparent in their faithfulness to the gospel that no one could consider them an obstacle to accepting the truth of Christ's love. Though Paul's life as an evangelist has been hard, he has been determined to live up to his own preaching, both in public and in private. How can he do otherwise when he is not only a messenger, but an ambassador for Christ? Ambassadors do not only say what they are told to say. They represent their government, and dealing with the ambassador is considered to be dealing with the government itself. This is the responsibility which Paul takes so seriously that it determines his conduct – all the time.

✳ *Psalm for reflection:* Psalm 150

✳ *O God of grace and joy, release your love in us,*
that we may reveal your generosity
to all whose lives touch ours.

FOR REFLECTION – alone or with a group

● Moses' face shone because of the time that he spent with God. Do we allow sufficient time with God so that our encounter can make a real difference to our lives?

● Moses' time with God included many different elements of awe, understanding, mystery and revelation. How can we be more honest and open with God, especially when the encounter makes us uncomfortable?

● How does the story of the Transfiguration reveal the uniqueness of Jesus, and his vulnerability? How does God encourage us when we enter the cloud of uncertainty and fear?

FOR ACTION

Consider whether there are situations in which cultural prejudices prevent you from obeying God's Word, e.g. prejudices against relating to a particular social or religious group. Plan an activity which will challenge that prejudice in yourself and in others.

IBRA INTERNATIONAL APPEAL

In five continents you will find Christians using IBRA material.

Some Christians will be using books and Bible reading cards translated into their local language, whilst others use English books. Some of the books are printed in the UK, but more and more countries are printing the books and cards themselves. The IBRA International Fund works through churches, Christian groups and Christian publishing houses overseas to make these publications available.

Each year we receive more requests for help from the IBRA International Fund, with greater emphasis on helping our overseas friends to produce their own version of IBRA material.

The only money we have to send is the money you give, so please help us again by giving generously.

Place your gift in the envelope provided and give it to your IBRA representative, or send it direct to:

The IBRA International Appeal
1020 Bristol Road, Selly Oak,
Birmingham B29 6LB, Great Britain

Thank you for your help.

LENT TO EASTER – JOURNEY WITH CHRIST
1. Which way?

Notes based on the New English Bible by
Mary Cotes

Mary Cotes is minister of the United Church, Pontypridd, and part-time chaplain to the mental health unit of her local hospital. She broadcasts regularly on radio.

One of the most popular hymns we sing in Wales begins,
    'Guide me, O thou great Jehovah,
    pilgrim through this barren land...'
                                    (William Williams 1717-91)
If only being a Christian pilgrim in a world which often seems like a wilderness were simple! The season of Lent offers us a time to ask the really hard questions, examining ourselves in the light of Jesus' pilgrimage to Jerusalem. Who are we and where are we going? Is our face set in one direction as Jesus' was? Are we ready to move at all? These are some of the issues we shall be thinking about this week.

1st Sunday in Lent, March 4   *Luke 4.1-13**
Whose agenda?
If visitors from outer space were to read minutes taken of our local church meetings over the last ten years, what would they imagine Christian faith was about? I strongly suspect that were they to come to Britain they might think the essence of Christian believing is maintaining ageing buildings and raising funds!

Today's reading shames our small-mindedness. Here's Jesus grappling with the nitty-gritty of his calling. He's not worrying where he's going to live for the next three years or where he'll recruit twelve decent disciples. There's only one thing on his mind: how to be obedient to God. And that leads him to ask what should be his relationship with the earth and with those who hold power, and what should be his attitude to security and danger? If we were to allow Jesus' agenda to set ours, church meetings might be transformed. Instead of concentrating on the leaking roof, we might be focusing on issues of ecology or politics! Jesus shows us that the proof of the Spirit-filled life is the ability to ask hard questions.

✳ *Lord, forgive our preoccupation*
with all that is less than essential.
Dare us to follow you by asking true questions.

Monday March 5   *Luke 9.18-27*

Take my life...?

As chaplain to a mental health unit, I frequently come across
people who have renounced themselves so utterly through caring
for a sick spouse or elderly relative that they've ended up with a
nervous breakdown. In some cases they've become so ill they
have truly left all sense of self behind. If this is the way of self-
denial that Jesus is advocating, then I reject it outright.

I can only make sense of this passage if I understand 'self' to
mean 'the self-interest that denies the values of God's Kingdom'.
On that basis, company directors who put fat financial profit
before health and safety, or churches who count their buildings
more precious than the needs of those who might use them, are
rightly challenged to change. Those who face death rather than
collude with injustice are rightly honoured as martyrs. But by the
same token, societies which deny proper support to carers, who
often work themselves to the bone, are rightly commanded to
review their priorities. In the Kingdom of God the 'burn-out' of the
faithful can't be an option.

✳ *Lord, I long to be truly your servant.*
Teach me to recognize my limitations
that, knowing when to work and when to rest,
I might have the stamina to follow you all the way.

Tuesday March 6   *Luke 9.51-56*

Like a mighty tortoise...

Many of my favourite hymns picture the local church as an
energetic and joyous band of pilgrims, intrepidly stepping into the
unknown. If only it were true! The reality, I find, is very different.
Movement doesn't come easy to us and the bigger the church,
the harder it is to implement change. We're so frightened that
members will leave if they disagree, and so convinced of the
importance of love and unity that we bend over backwards to
accommodate all points of view, and end up progressing at the
pace of the slowest, which in some cases means remaining
completely stationary for years. Then people leave anyway
because the church lacks focus and momentum.

It seems to me that the Jesus we have here, far from being meek and accommodating, is quite ruthless. He knows the costly direction he's taking; he's on his way and nothing is going to stop him. If people don't like where he's headed, too bad. Jesus is ready, if not to punish them, certainly to leave them behind, knowing that others elsewhere will show their support for him. Dare we follow his example?

✳ *Lord, teach us to seek unity,*
but not to prize it more highly
than the other radical demands of your Kingdom.

Wednesday March 7   *Luke 9.57-62*

Excuses, excuses...

This reading is devastating. Here are three sincere and honest would-be followers of Jesus. Jesus soon wipes the smile off the face of the first: instead of saying, 'We need keen people like you,' it's 'Watch out: it'll be hard!' The second has family commitments. Her father is ageing maybe and in need of care, and quite clearly she can't leave home until he's died. But Jesus won't wait. The third is happily married and understandably doesn't want to do anything without consulting his loved ones first. And Jesus tells him he's unfit for the Kingdom! How unreasonable can he get?

Perhaps at the heart of this story lies, not an unkind and impossible Jesus, but the very nature of the Kingdom of God. It's costly; it's for NOW; and it faces single-mindedly forwards. The message is not that we just wildly abandon serious obligations, but that we realize that the needs of the Kingdom will always be more pressing and urgent than anything we can fulfil. We need to scrutinize all our motives – no matter how good and honest they seem – in the light of its demands.

✳ *Lord, I long for the patience*
which is the fruit of your Spirit.
But teach me too
the impatience of those who work for your Kingdom.

Thursday March 8   *Luke 11.29-32*

Blurring the boundaries

Whenever I hear the phrase 'wicked generation', I think of angry preachers playing God, thumping the pulpit and glowering at meek congregations trembling below! For all the humour of a caricature, it's nonetheless easy to fall into the trap of pointing the finger at our contemporaries. 'Western culture has become so secular,' we say in Britain. 'No one's interested in God any more. People are selfish and individualistic. They don't want to hear about loving your neighbour or commitment to a fellowship.' The sub-text of our message might read: 'If only *they* could be like *us.*'

Most organizations, in order to function, draw a strong line between 'us' and 'them': those who belong and those who don't. Those outside are thought of as in some way at fault, lacking knowledge or needing persuasion. But in the Church we must guard against such simplistic divisions. Called to confess that all fall short of God's glory, we can't deny that the sin we notice in others is also present in us. We share a common humanity. Condemning our wicked present-day generation implies condemning ourselves.

✴ *Lord, before I seek the speck in my neighbour's eye,*
  give me the strength to find the plank in my own.

Friday March 9   *Luke 13.22-30*

Just as I am

It often helps me to think of this narrow door as one of the many entrances into the King's castle. Jesus doesn't invite us to enter by the majestic door with the red carpet and servants bowing and scraping to the ground. Instead, we're invited to enter by the grotty side door with the paint peeling off. This is the access that domestics and humble tradespeople use. The alley leading to it is so narrow that you can't drive up in your car or carry suitcases of belongings with you. And if you're wearing too many fine clothes, or you've grown fat from persistent over-indulgence, you might just not squeeze through either. Quite simply, the narrow door leaves room only for yourself, nothing else. It won't flatter your ego to go in this way, but it's worth it. Who knows, you might just stumble upon the King himself: he's left the golden banqueting hall to wash his servants' feet in the kitchen.

✴ *Lord, I can't imagine myself*
  without my home, my comforts,
  and the roles life asks me to play.
  By your light shining from the narrow door,
  teach me who I am.

Making drudgery divine?

When I was a child, there was an annual occasion in my church called 'Women's Sunday'. It was the one time when women would lead the worship, take up the offering, preach the sermon and serve the communion. At the end of the service, the church secretary – a man – made a speech thanking the women for all their quiet, humble service to the church throughout the year. How Christlike the ladies were, he would say. The next day, things resumed as before. The men went back to their positions of leadership and all those Christlike women to making the tea!

Today's reading upholds servanthood as an ideal of discipleship. The danger of passages like this is that they can be used by those in power to keep servants in positions of servility. The words only have bite, it seems to me, when they are directed at those who can choose the role they play. So if we're talking about churches too respectable to get their hands dirty, or individual people in authority, then yes, the challenge is to walk the servant way. But let's not use these words to crush the little people, or to maintain as servants those who never had the choice to be anything different.

✳ *Lord, help me to distinguish*
the servanthood imposed upon me
from the humble service I freely choose
and in which alone your image is glorified.

FOR REFLECTION – alone or with a group
- If visitors from outer space sat in your church meetings, what would they think Christian believing was about?
- What changes would you implement in your church by the end of the year?

FOR ACTION

Find out what agencies, voluntary or statutory, exist in your area offering support to carers. Are they adequate? If not, what sort of scheme could your church set up to ease the burden that many carers carry?

JOURNEY WITH CHRIST
2. The cost

Notes based on the Revised Standard Version by
Victor Premasagar

Victor Premasagar – former Moderator of the Church of South India, writer and well-known internationally as a teacher of theology – has served as pastor in both rural and urban situations.

Lent is a time of fasting and prayer in remembrance of Jesus' forty days' fast in the wilderness. In India, it happens that in certain years, Hindus, Muslims and Christians keep fast days at about the same time. Fasting and prayer are associated with almsgiving in all religions. Fasting is also a sign of repentance and renewal (Jonah 3.6-9). The Bible emphasizes that the fast acceptable to God is setting free the oppressed, feeding the hungry, providing shelter for the homeless, clothing the naked and helping the poor and needy (Isaiah 58.3-8). These are not mere humanitarian concerns, but issues of justice and righteousness related to the Kingdom of God.

2nd Sunday in Lent, March 11   *Jeremiah 22.1-9, 13-17**
Act with justice and righteousness
Addressing the king, his servants and people, the prophet Jeremiah expresses God's concern that, instead of upholding justice and righteousness, they are oppressing the poor, the stranger, the orphan and the widow. They have even withheld wages which should have been paid to labourers who worked on the king's elaborate building projects.

Social, economic and political structures have the potential to bring well-being to all, but when misused they cause total disaster to the poor and oppressed. Both Jews and Christians should be concerned about unjust structures. The word 'justice' refers to structures which are set up to protect the poor, and 'righteousness' to ordinary people caring for them with generosity. Both activities are important. Paul calls us to put on 'the whole armour of God' to struggle against 'principalities and powers' (Ephesians 6.10-17). This is all a part of our journey to the cross.

✳ *Lord, we pray for your Spirit to guide us*
during this time of Lent, that we may dedicate ourselves,
grow in generosity and compassion,
and struggle against all unjust structures and powers.
Let your Kingdom of justice and righteousness
come upon the earth.

Monday March 12   *Luke 12.51-53*

Peace with justice

The coming of Jesus raises issues of justice in all human relations both in society and with all creation. In the English language, the word 'peace' is usually taken to mean the absence of war, unlike the Hebrew word *shalom* which means 'total well-being'. In some situations conflict doesn't take place because the oppressed do not actively protest for fear of reprisals from those in power.

In India the coming of Jesus has raised the issue of caste discrimination and the oppression of the *Dalits* (formerly known as 'outcastes'). The good news of the Kingdom of God explodes the myth that today's social and political structures are permanent and sanctioned by God. The life and ministry of our Lord raised questions about the traditional interpretation of the Law, social and religious customs and issues of economic justice. There are hints in the Gospels (Matthew 14.1-5; Luke 13.31-35) that the rulers of Palestine felt threatened by his teaching and did not want to change from exploitative policies which benefited themselves. Oppression is bound to raise conflict and unrest. Jesus came to bring peace with justice.

✳ *Lord, grant us courage to raise a prophetic voice*
against all that continues to oppress our people.
May your Church and its leaders commit themselves
to struggle for peace with justice in all spheres of life.

Tuesday March 13   *Luke 13.31-35**

Confrontation

Herod Antipas, who had imprisoned John the Baptist and beheaded him (Mark 6.17-29), heard about Jesus and wanted to see him (Luke 9.7-9). On his journey to Jerusalem Jesus was in Herod's territory and the Pharisees warned him that Herod was planning to kill him. This might have tempted Jesus to flee for safety but, set on doing the Father's will, he would not be diverted from his ministry to heal people, proclaim the good news of the Kingdom and proceed to Jerusalem, where he knew a similar and greater threat awaited him.

The Indian Church has been under severe persecution recently from those who want the Church to stop preaching the gospel and bringing people to conversion. The gospel, which says that 'the first shall be last and the last first', is a challenge and threat to unjust social, cultural and economic conditions that have prevailed for centuries. It has given courage to the *Dalits* and indigenous people to raise questions of justice and equality. The determination of Jesus to go on to the end gives courage to the Church to continue its ministry till the Kingdom comes.

✳ *Lord, strengthen your Church in all lands,*
to continue its ministry of liberation. Deliver us
from the temptation to abandon your mission
when threatened by persecution. Help us,
by our life and action, to be a sign of your Kingdom,
bringing hope to millions of people.

Wednesday March 14   *Luke 14.25-33**

The cost of discipleship

Jesus lays down three conditions for those who wish to follow him:

Detachment from family ties Following Jesus demands total allegiance and a life of renunciation and love. The word 'hate' (verse 26) is difficult to understand. The Hebrew word for 'hate' also means 'love less' and this may be the emphasis here. Jesus is calling us, not so much to hate members of our families, as to an attitude of detachment, i.e. 'to leave aside' or 'abandon'.

Willingness to carry the cross Taking up the cross is traditionally interpreted as bearing one's sufferings, pains and burdens. It should be read with the words, 'and follow me'. It would then mean following the example of Jesus upon the cross. Carrying the cross implies showing compassion and love, forgiveness and reconciliation, siding with the poor and oppressed and bearing the consequences. Because Jesus has come, died and risen, the disciple bears the cross with courage, hope and faith.

Detachment from all possessions The rich young man was asked by Jesus to sell all that he owned, give to the poor and follow him, but he could not be parted from his many possessions (Mark 10.17-22). Being a disciple of Jesus involves imitating Jesus and his way of life.

Lent is a time of self-examination to discover whether our allegiance to Jesus is total or only superficial.

✳ *Create in me a clean heart, O God,*
    and put a new and right spirit within me.
Cast me not away from thy presence,
    and take not thy Holy Spirit from me.
Restore to me the joy of thy salvation,
    and uphold me with a willing spirit.   Psalm 51.10-12

Thursday March 15   Luke 10.5-15
Mission from poverty
Jesus sent out the seventy disciples two by two, with no security or resources but with the power of the gospel and the message of the Kingdom. The instructions indicate a sense of urgency. They are sent like lambs into the midst of wolves, but they need not despair because in the Kingdom even the wolves begin to live amicably with lambs (Isaiah 11.6; 65.25).

They are to stay in the houses of those who receive them and not to go from house to house looking for better comforts. Reception by local families becomes an entry point into the community; it builds fellowship and an acceptance of the Kingdom and its values. The disciple, who is a labourer in the Lord's vineyard, is worthy of this reward of hospitality but should not seek luxury. The priority is not money, but committed men and women who want to be disciples of Christ.

Jesus asks them to pray that God, the Lord of the harvest, will send out more workers. Where will they come from? As the disciples pray, they receive the Lord's call and offer themselves to the task of mission. Where and when we as the Church have prayed for God's mission, we have been able to send out 'missionaries' from among us.

✳ *Lord, raise up from among our churches*
men and women who will offer their lives
for your unfinished mission to transform the world
into your Kingdom of justice and peace.

Friday March 16   Philippians 3.7-21*
Press on toward the goal
St Paul often describes his faith journey as a race that is run towards the goal (verse 14). In verses 7-11 he wants 'to know'

Christ and the 'power of his resurrection'. What is the power of resurrection? On Good Friday everything seemed lost. The disciples had come to a dead end; there was no future before them. On Easter Day the news of the resurrection of Jesus brought new hope and courage. Those who hid in fear came out into the open and proclaimed that Jesus is risen and that in him there is hope for all. This is the power of resurrection – creating a new future in situations where there seems to be no hope. Our future is not determined by our *karma* (a Hindu doctrine of the effect of actions from a previous life), but it is in the hands of the risen Lord (verses 20-21).

The phrase 'to know' (verse 8) is used in the Bible to mean 'to know intimately' as personal experience. Paul describes this as growing into maturity of faith (verse 15).

✳ *Lord, grant us the power of your resurrection,*
that we may run the race that is set before us
in sure faith and confidence in you.
Give us courage to trust that you will open up
new possibilities when everything seems impossible.

Saturday March 17   *2 Timothy 2.1-13*

Be strong in the grace that is in Christ Jesus

Paul encourages Timothy to grow strong in the grace of the Lord. 'Grace' is the very nature of God and of our Lord himself. Out of grace, our incarnate Lord pitched his tent among us, and we 'beheld his glory, the glory of the only Son' (John 1.14). The Evangelists do not describe anywhere the physical appearance of Jesus. They only describe his character as 'full of grace and truth' (John) and as moved with compassion and love (Matthew, Mark and Luke).

In the Old Testament, Moses asks God to show his glory (face) to him (Exodus 33.17-23). God promises to let all his goodness pass before Moses and to proclaim his name *Yahweh*. He adds that he will be gracious and merciful to those to whom he reveals himself. Here again, the features of God are not revealed to Moses but only his character of goodness, graciousness and mercy.

Today's reading reminds us that the 'fetters' and hard times we endure for the sake of the gospel bring us closer to the God of grace who sends us out.

✳ *Lord, in the coming weeks of Lent, Holy Week,*
and Easter, fill us with your grace. Transform our lives
and your world, and bring in your Kingdom among us.

FOR REFLECTION – alone or with a group

- What are the 'principalities and powers' in your context?
- What are the neglected areas in your 'mission-action'?
- Make a list of the social, economic, political and religious issues against which the Church and Christians should struggle in your country at the present time.

JOURNEY WITH CHRIST
3. Time for God

Notes based on the New Revised Standard Version by
Wanda Hayman

Wanda Hayman was born in Poland. During the Second World War she experienced both the German and the Soviet occupation and three years of compulsory labour in a German village. Her special concern as a Christian has been helping people to grow spiritually in the knowledge of God.

A friend of mine was married to the kindest man I ever met. They loved each other and worked together for the church. One thing, however, clouded the skies – her husband, busy as a minister, very seldom made any time for her and their son. For fifteen years she loyally persuaded herself that he really wasn't able to find time for them. But suddenly she thought, 'Maybe he doesn't want to. Maybe he doesn't really love us.'

Love needs time to be expressed: not lots of time, nor even regular time, but 'quality time'. That is true of all relationships, and particularly of our relationship with God. If, for most of our lives, we are so busy for God that we never find time to be with him or with our loved ones, do we really love God?

Does God want us to be slaves or lovers?

3rd Sunday in Lent, March 18   *Isaiah 55.1-9**
Time to receive
God invites anyone who is hungry or thirsty to come and receive, as his free gift, what it is they need (verse 1). He then laments the tragedy that the human race wastes so much effort by pointlessly pursuing what is worthless, and rejects his loving gifts (verse 2).

Feeling rejected
   is one of the most painful experiences:
A hand offered in friendship, not taken,
   suspended in mid-air...
Love offered, but not reciprocated...

A young German Jew, who was a refugee in Britain during the Second World War, suffered a severe mental breakdown. He was given repeated electric shock treatment. As a result of the personality changes this caused, he was never accepted to do the work with people he had longed to do. This life-long rejection was very painful. God must feel like that – and more so – when we turn away from the rich gifts he has to offer us.

God offers us real life, abundant, eternal life, but so often we prefer our trinkets.

✳ *Generous God, help us to empty our hands*
of all that they cling to,
and to come expectantly
to have them filled with your good gifts.

Monday March 19   *Genesis 28.10-19a**

Time to see God in unexpected places

How strange that so many interpreters have seen today's reading as a call to climb the ladder to heaven and to keep climbing. An 18th century hymn, by an unknown writer, says,

'Many millions have climbed it and reached Zion's hill,
And thousands by faith are climbing it still'.

If we accepted this model, we would always be trying to reach God by our own efforts. Is the Christian way all about effort? Is our faith meant to add to our burdens? If so, we would be like those idol worshippers who carried their gods wherever they went (Isaiah 46.1-4). The prophet reminded them that Israel's God always carried them.

In this dream, Jacob discovered a two-way traffic between God and ourselves. Having time for God means keeping our eyes open to see that God comes to us and is present where we are. We can be aware of this all the time.

A young gay friend of mine – one of many who stopped worshipping in the institutional church which they feel has rejected them – goes to 'his church' on Sunday. It is a gay club. There, among 'his people', feeling accepted and welcome, he prays, as he dances, to the God who is there with him.

✳ *Living God, whose face no one can look upon*
and live, so shine upon us
with the light of your Spirit that we may recognize you
in one another's faces and see
the presence of your glory among us.

Tuesday March 20   *1 Corinthians 10.1-13**

Time to accept ourselves

The Christians at Corinth had experienced the saving power of Christ but many, in an over-confident mood, had given in to the temptations around them. Having been one with Christ through baptism and Holy Communion, they felt safe and beyond any harm. Paul points to Israel's story in the desert. The Israelites too enjoyed all the privileges of the people of God. They were led and protected by the cloud of God's presence. Yet, in spite of that, when tests came they were not up to resisting them, but turned to idols, gave way to sexual immorality and were too terrified to enter the Promised Land. They grumbled and complained about their lot.

Paul tries to teach the Corinthians humility (verse 12). This is not the same as self-abasement. Humility is accepting our life as God has given it to us. It is accepting ourselves as we are, recognizing how easy it is to fail, but knowing also that, through the grace and in the strength of God, we can begin again.

✳ *Gracious God, our lives can be so hard.*
Our failures are many.
Help us to remember that all is gift and grace.

Wednesday March 21   *John 1.43-51**

Time to throw off prejudice

Was Nathaniel simply prejudiced against people from Nazareth? The prophecies concerning the Messiah did not mention it. Jesus was pleased that Nathaniel knew the Scriptures, pleased to have seen him meditating on them in the shade of a fig tree.

Jesus knew prejudice: he was from the north, a cosmopolitan area. It was not a country for a religious teacher to come from, thought the Pharisees.

When I first came to England, I was quite amused to discover that people made so much of different accents. Some people from the north, for example, tried to acquire a southern accent, hoping it would help them to get a better job!

We all have prejudices. We need to get nearer to people, and get to know them before we can see them clearly.

The following saying comes from Tibet:

'I saw a beast in the distance. I came nearer and saw that it was a man. I came nearer still and saw – my brother.'

Jesus certainly approached Nathaniel with respect. He recognized Nathaniel's deep spirituality and integrity. He was a 'true Israelite'.

If we would have fellowship with God, we must try to overcome our prejudices and see others as God sees them – as his beloved children. From the depths of their experience, they have so much to share with us if we will pause to listen and hear the voice of God who speaks through them.

✳ *Loving God, help us to see others as they are –*
sinners, and being sinned against –
see their shame and sorrow, joys and pain.
Give us compassion in place of judgement
and love in place of prejudice.

Thursday March 22   *Luke 6.12-16*

Time to learn

To be co-workers with God, we must first be learners – disciples. We must not be like those who say, 'I don't need it. I know it all.'

To grow in the knowledge of God, who is in so many ways unknowable, we need to be in a relationship with him, not just to increase our knowledge about him. 'God can be got hold of by love, never by thought,' wrote a mediaeval thinker. God is and will always remain a mystery. Only if we know God by experience can we be workers useful to God.

✳ *Give us a new integrity of heart,*
Renew in us the deeds that you love,
Justice and mercy, compassion and courage.
Then face to face shall we see you,
Knowing and known, loving and loved.   *Jim Cotter*
                                     By Stony Paths (Cairn Publications)

Friday March 23   *Matthew 6.7-15*

Time to make God's purposes our own

Prayer is a way of tuning in to God, a time to get on God's wavelength. It is a time to discover what God is doing. It is to ask ourselves what we should be doing as God's co-workers.

The prayer Jesus taught his disciples speaks of what the Kingdom for which we pray will be like. It will be an ordering of human society in which God's name will be revered, and his will will be done; everyone will have enough to eat; we shall forgive one another; we shall not put one another to the test, but will free one another from evil.

Who do you think will give food to all? If we think that in answer to our prayer God will feed his people, we discover instead that God says to us, 'You do it.'

✱ *O God, you claim me as your partner,*
respecting me,
trusting me,
tussling with me.
Support me
as I dare to be vulnerable with you,
encourage me
as I dare take risks with you,
so together we can transform our world. Amen

> Bridget Rees – Bread of Tomorrow, ed. Janet Morley
> (Christian Aid)

Saturday March 24   *John 15.1-10*

Time to bear fruit

If the purpose of our life is to glorify God, Jesus tells us how it can be achieved: we are to bear fruit. To do that we must be part of a strong, healthy plant from which we can draw nourishment. Jesus invites us to make our home in his love, as he abides in God's love. If we do, we shall be radiating the love of God, our home. As we enjoy the hospitality of that love, we shall be able to offer it to the homeless children of our age – not only those who do not have a roof over their heads, but those who have no spiritual family.

What we need in this new Millennium, it seems to me, is not so much inherited belief in God as this abiding where, as Paul says, we are hidden with Christ in God.

The fruit we can offer the world is our changed self: all our 'good deeds' will flow from the tree of which we are a part.

✱ *Christ, as you have given yourself*
to be food and drink for your disciples,
so change us that we too may become
refreshment to weary pilgrims.

FOR REFLECTION – alone or with a group

- Have you ever discovered God's presence in an unexpected place or person?
- Do you find it easy to accept yourself as you are and know that the grace of God can change you if you let it?
- Have you ever discovered a brother or sister in someone against whom you were prejudiced?

FOR ACTION

Try to make a habit of listening to strangers, especially those who do not attract you, or who are different from you. Try to understand them and their viewpoint. God does. Time for God includes time for accepting God's other children.

LIGHT for our PATH

- A 12 month, easy-to-use Bible reading plan for adults
- Daily notes, with extracts from the Bible passages for those with no Bible to hand
- Writers from a variety of Churches, backgrounds and cultures
- A helpful resource for new Christians or those new to Bible study
- Complementary to *Words for Today*

UK price £5.00

Order through your IBRA representative, or from the appropriate address on page 303.

LENT TO EASTER – JOURNEY WITH CHRIST
4. New beginnings

Notes based on the New International Version by
Peter Tongeman

Peter Tongeman, a retired Baptist minister, has worked in town and country churches, national youth leadership, and as an Area Superintendent. He was President of the Baptist Union of Great Britain for a year, and is now a freelance writer and poet.

A fresh start is essential when the past has ended in conflict, failure or disillusionment. Northern Ireland, South Africa, Bosnia, Israel – each with a history of confrontation and conflict – have found it necessary to fashion a basis for beginning again.

New beginnings are made possible by God's grace, through forgiveness, restoration, renewed vision and commitment. This week's readings explore ways in which it is possible to step out afresh with renewed hope and expectation.

4th Sunday in Lent, March 25   *Isaiah 40.27-31; 41.8-13**
New hope

The people had lost heart. Defeated by the massive Babylonian army, forced from their homes to live in exile, their capital and precious Temple in ruins, they felt as helpless as refugees do today – until someone draws alongside to give them hope.

Isaiah with words of comfort voiced what, in their misery, they had forgotten. God had not abandoned them. He knew about their plight, he cared about them and was available to help them (verses 27-29). Weak or weary, they could draw strength from him. No situation, however dark, is beyond hope.

In 1980, Mount St Helen's in Washington State, USA, blew up, devastating the countryside around for twenty miles. Everything was destroyed. It seemed nothing could live there again. Yet, within two years, young plants were pushing through the ash-covered soil. A new beginning.

There are always signs of hope for those with eyes to see. Not long ago, an ailing village church was closed; it seemed like failure. But the building was sold and the money used to build a church on a housing estate where the need was greater. Today that church is thriving.

✳ *Loving Lord, teach us afresh that there is always hope,*
even when the way is dark and we are exhausted,
for our ways are known to you; your love pursues us,
and your presence sustains. Amen

Monday March 26   *Genesis 9.1-17*

A new start

When the flood subsided, Noah and his family stepped on to dry land and set about rebuilding their lives. Life would be different from now on. The evil and corruption which characterized their community before the flood (Genesis 6.5) would be forgotten, for the privilege of survival required a changed attitude. As survivors they would prosper only by respecting creation and all living things, and dealing justly with one another. To remind them of this, the rainbow was to signify the intertwining of God's covenant love and the people's disciplined response.

Archbishop Desmond Tutu, speaking of a new start in South Africa, said, 'The rainbow is a sign of peace... a sign of prosperity. We want peace, prosperity and justice, and we can have it when all the people of God, the rainbow people of God, work together.'

✳ *Gracious Lord, we thank you for every new beginning.*
Make us responsive to what you desire.
May we live as rainbow people,
working with you and with each other to do your will.

Tuesday March 27   *Genesis 12.1-9*

New departure

A pastor, looking forward to a quiet and peaceful retirement in England, was unexpectedly invited to serve in a challenging new situation in South Africa, calling for all the skill and experience he had gained. He responded joyfully, not knowing all that would be involved, but confident of God's direction and support.

A bank official, given a year's leave of absence for community service, left the security of his office to work among deprived young people. He never returned to banking. His life took off in a new direction, and he discovered a fresh and fulfilling God-given vocation, as did Abram when he left home, the land of his ancestors, for an unknown destination, knowing that God travelled with him (Hebrews 11.8-10). At each stage of the journey, Abram built an altar (verses 7-8), signifying his continuing dependence upon God. Although he did not know it, every step he took in faith was a significant step in the story of the world's redemption.

✳ *Let my ears be alert, O Lord, to your call*
  wherever it may lead, and let me be quick to respond,
  stepping out obediently on a journey of faith.

Wednesday March 28   *Luke 15.1-3, 11b-32**
New relationships
Pharisees and religious leaders of Jesus' day felt unable to mix with 'sinners' who failed to keep prescribed regulations. How could religious propriety be tainted by such people? Jesus, who mixed with those they despised, responded with a parable.

The Kingdom of God is about reconciliation between God and us, and between ourselves and others. The son's longing to return home was made possible by his father's loving forgiveness, compared with the older brother's bitter resentment. Sin and self impair our relationship with God. When we return in humility and repentance, that relationship is restored along with a discovery that God's love, forgiving and welcoming, has been there all the time.

A pastor, commencing his ministry in a Kent village church, found the people suspicious. They trusted no one, lived amid tension, and always locked their doors. When his ministry, which demonstrated love and openness, ended years later, trust had been restored, people were visiting each other's homes and strangers were welcomed.

✳ *Lord, when I turn from sin to you,*
  you receive me with immense love and forgiveness.
  Grant me grace to deal with others
  as you deal with me. Amen

Thursday March 29   *Luke 5.27-32*
New purpose
Tax collectors in Jesus' day were notorious for extortion and dishonesty. They could charge more or less what they liked. They were classed with robbers and murderers as undesirables and banned from the synagogue. When Jesus invited a tax collector to join him as a disciple, he was offering a new purpose in living. Levi (or Matthew as he is called elsewhere) no doubt radically

changed his lifestyle, as Zacchaeus did (Luke 19.8). When journeying with Christ, our goal is no longer self-indulgence but service. Levi 'left everything and followed'.

Levi's new purpose found expression when he invited his friends and colleagues to meet Jesus. Perhaps they too would discover a Kingdom goal. Who better to share the good news with than our closest colleagues in the work-place?

✳ *Forgive us, O Lord,*
   that your purposes are so easily obscured
   by our forgetfulness. Teach us again,
   the greatest thing in all the world is serving you. Amen

Friday March 30   *2 Corinthians 5.16-21**
A new outlook
To be 'in Christ' (one of Paul's favourite expressions) sums up our thoughts for the week. Our response to Christ leads to new hope, a new start, new experience, a new relationship, new purpose in living. Paul speaks of a 'new creation'. As a snake grows it periodically sheds its old worn skin, to make way for the bright new one already growing underneath. Similarly, our journey with Christ involves progressively shedding the old nature, replacing it with what is new and Christlike. We are to get rid of bitterness, anger, slander, malice (Ephesians 4.31) and put on kindness, humility, gentleness, patience, forgiveness, and love (Colossians 3.12-14).

Saintly Edward King, one-time bishop of Lincoln, gave time and loving care to people, both inside and outside the churches. Aged 80, in his last letter to the people he loved, he wrote: 'My great wish has been to lead you to become Christlike Christians.'

What aspects of your present way of life need to be shed? What new Christlike qualities should be taking their place?

✳ *Thank you, Lord, that as I come to know you,*
   I learn to see through your eyes and to follow
   your example. Please continue to change me for the better
   and make me your ambassador of love. Amen

Saturday March 31   *Isaiah 43.16-21**
New expectations
Israel had every reason to look back with gratitude. God had delivered the nation from slavery and from the Egyptian army

(verses 16-17). He had brought them into a land of their own. Now, alas, they were temporarily in exile, longing once again for deliverance and repatriation. Would it ever happen? Isaiah raised expectations with God's promise to 'do a new thing'. They would indeed return home, not weary and thirsty as before, but with speed and well refreshed on the way (verse 19b).

To journey with Christ is to travel in expectation that what God did in the past for others, he can and will do again. In the desert of adversity, a way through is promised. Those who have no reason to rejoice will praise God afresh for his goodness.

Through daunting wastelands, he releases streams
To flood with joy each adverse, barren place,
Cool streams of courage to meet every foe,
Refreshing streams of faith and hope
And never ceasing grace.
With thanks for what is past, we gladly sing
And watch expectantly, with eagerness,
Each day for God's 'new thing'.

✳ *Lord, who has acted for our good in times past,*
give us faith to expect great things in the future,
and to attempt great things in your service. Amen

FOR REFLECTION – alone or with a group

● Think of a situation where people have lost hope. Is there a way ahead? What can you do to help bring about a new beginning?

● Is God calling you, or someone you know, to step into the unknown, like Abram? What factors are likely to hold you back? What gives you confidence for the future?

● William Carey said, 'Expect great things from God, attempt great things for God.' What, in the light of God's Word, can be expected on your journey with Christ? What can be attempted in his service?

FOR ACTION

Do you know a situation where relationships have broken down? Consider what steps you, and others, should take to help bring about reconciliation.

JOURNEY WITH CHRIST
5. Knowing what lies ahead

Notes based on the Revised English Bible by
Janet Nightingale

Janet Nightingale trained in education and has also worked for Christian Aid and Age Concern. She lives with cancer, but has been enjoying life to the full. A major interest is meeting fellow/ lymphoma survivors on the Internet where they share information and support one another.

This week's readings provide themes of reflection on how we face suffering and look forward to the hope of resurrection. World conflicts seem to be continually affecting the lives of those least able to help themselves. While meditating on these readings we may be led to understand how we might be expected to respond, through prayer and through action.

Passion Sunday, April 1   *John 12.1-8**
The burial gift
Things are hotting up. Jesus has raised Lazarus from the dead. The chief priests and Pharisees are out to arrest Jesus. Then Jesus is having supper at Lazarus' house. Martha is serving supper, true to form, while Mary is engaged on her own project. She anoints Jesus' feet with costly perfume and, immodestly, dries them with her hair.

Mary and Jesus are now the centre of attention. What does this mean? Is it a pointless waste, as Judas makes out, with his eye on the moneybags? Did she fancy him? Or was there something more, a hidden message perhaps?

Jesus says Mary has realized what is about to happen. He is to die. It is no waste to recognize that fact. Furthermore he is to die as Messiah, the anointed king. More than that: as Messiah he is the Resurrection and the Life (11.25-27). The saddest moment is also the most glorious. Amidst despair there are signs of hope.

✳ *Lord, in these days of mercy, make us quiet and prayerful;*
in these days of challenge, make us strong in you;
in these days of emptiness, take possession of us;

in these days of waiting, open our hearts to the mystery
of your cross. *Angela Ashwin*

The Book of a Thousand Prayers (Marshall Pickering 1996)

Monday April 2 *Isaiah 50.4-11**

Absolute trust

This passage is from one of the 'servant songs' to be found in the book of Isaiah. It is likely that they were written as reflections on what it meant for faithful Israelites to serve God as they approached the end of the Exile in Babylon. They have guided the thoughts of Jewish and Christian people since and, quite possibly, the thoughts of Jesus himself. The servant is roused by God and asked to speak but not provocatively. He is to listen to God and to console the weary. He does both obediently. He is not surprised to meet persecution and suffering. He allows himself to be punished as if God were on the side of his opponents. But he trusts that God will help him and therefore he can put up with anything.

Verses 8 and 9 are set in open court. God will clear the servant's name, so no one can declare him guilty.

How far do these words fit the situation of Jesus? How do they fit your own?

✴ *Dear Lord and Saviour, Jesus Christ,*
I hold up all my weakness to your strength,
My failure to your faithfulness,
My sinfulness to your perfection,
My loneliness to your compassion,
My little pains to your great agony on the cross.
I pray that you will cleanse me, strengthen me and hide me,
so that in all my ways, my life may be lived
as you would have it lived,
without cowardice
and for you alone. *Mother Janet Stuart (1857-1914)*

Tuesday April 3 *Psalm 69.13-21, 29-36*

God is near through good and ill

The psalm starts as a prayer for God's help against the powers of chaos and death. The writer wants deliverance from enemies, both on his own account and also for the glory of God's name and people. His individual voice is speaking on behalf of the whole congregation. Maybe they would say or sing the psalm, as we do hymns.

The concluding verses are a song of thanksgiving anticipating deliverance. True gratitude is said to matter more than animal sacrifice and ruined cities will be rebuilt; these suggest the psalm was written or revised for a period after the Temple had been destroyed. All nature is asked to join in a hymn of praise.

Could Jesus have used any of these verses? Could you? A writer who faced imprisonment for his faith wrote the following hymn in the 17th century, knowing well what it was like to suffer as a pilgrim following the way of Jesus.

✳ *For meditation*
Who would true valour see,
   Let him come hither;
One here will constant be,
   Come wind, come weather;
There's no discouragement
Shall make him once relent
His first avowed intent
   To be a pilgrim.
                    John Bunyan (1628-88)

Wednesday April 4   *Psalm 122*

Pray for the peace of Jerusalem

This Psalm seems to be something people would have sung together, perhaps at a King's coronation. Jerusalem is important as the capital city, where the Temple stood. The psalm is a confident prayer for peace and justice, both of which are linked to prosperity. The beneficiaries are to be the house of God and the psalmists' relations and friends.

It is a happy confident song, rather like 'What a friend we have in Jesus'. Jesus must have known it well and prayed it too. But in the short run the very opposite happened: injustice, war and adversity. Did the words of the psalm ever come true?

✳ *May it come soon*
to the hungry
to the weeping
to those who thirst for justice,
to those who have waited centuries
for a truly human life.
Grant us the patience
to smooth the way
on which your Kingdom comes to us.
Grant us hope,
that we may not weary

in proclaiming and working for it,
despite so many conflicts,
threats and shortcomings.
Grant us clear vision
that in this hour of our history
we may see the horizon,
and know the way
on which your Kingdom comes to us.   *Nicaragua*
    Windows into Worship, ed. Ron Ingamells (YMCA 1989)
       Bread for Tomorrow, ed. Janet Morley (Christian Aid)

Thursday April 5   *Luke 19.41-44*
Justice and peace join hands (Psalm 85.10)
Jesus visits Jerusalem but the people are not ready to accept
him. He weeps. He foresees disaster. If they are not willing to
have God as their saviour then they will have him as their judge.
In other words by rejecting Jesus' appeal for peace and justice
they are going down the road to militarism and ruin. This
culminated in the war against Rome in AD70 in which the Temple
was destroyed.

Luke may have added some of the passage from hindsight,
but Jesus' basic message is clear and as true now as then. Do we
seek the peace and justice Jesus wants or not? And are we
prepared to face the consequences?

✴ *Spirit of truth and judgement,*
  who alone can exorcize
  the powers that grip our world:
  at the point of crisis
  give us your discernment,
  that we may accurately name what is evil,
  and know the way that leads to peace,
  through Jesus Christ, Amen   *Janet Morley*
       All Desires Known, Janet Morley (SPCK 1992)

Friday April 6   *Luke 21.20-44*
Facing God's justice
We are not sure to what extent Jesus' words are his own or put
into his mouth by Luke after the event. They refer to the
consequences which future Jewish wars will have for the people
of Jerusalem. Two things are intended. One is an actual siege,
and something of this sort happened in AD70. Also the 'day' of the

foreigners (verse 24) refers to Daniel 12.7 where other people will run free in Jerusalem until eventually there will be a time of final judgement when God will triumph.

In every period of history there are examples of injustice. Sometimes we recognize that there are people who are confronting those involved – bringing them face to face with God's justice.

✳ *Using the news from radio, TV or newspapers, reflect on situations in the world where prayers are most needed. Pray for world leaders, for the people involved at the grassroots and for all who are working for peace and justice in those situations. Remember too Israelis and Palestinians who are seeking just solutions to their problems of living together in neighbouring countries.*

Saturday April 7   *Luke 19.28-40**

The stones will shout aloud

Jesus is setting out his stall, making his bid to attract people to his vision of God's Kingdom. His entry has religious and political significance. 'Blessed is he who comes as king in the name of the Lord!' (verse 38) is a pilgrim's blessing quoted from Psalm 118.26. It is quite different from a violent attack to take the city by force. The words, 'Peace in heaven, glory in highest heaven' (verse 38) echo the song of the angels at Bethlehem.

Some Pharisees tell Jesus to keep his followers quiet. Perhaps they are afraid his movement may get out of hand. Perhaps they disapprove of his willingness to sit lightly to the Sabbath, deal with publicans and sinners and forgive sins. Jesus replies defiantly, 'If my disciples are silent the stones will shout aloud' (verse 40). The crunch point has come and there is nothing he can do to stop it now.

We know what lies ahead in Jesus' story. But we do not know our own. Suppose there were a religious and political demonstration in your area today; if it were to be true to Jesus, what form would it take? Where would you be? What do you think would happen?

✳ *Lord:*
help us to see in the groaning of creation
*   not death throes but birth pangs;*
help us to see in suffering a promise for the future,
because it is a cry against the inhumanity of the present.
Help us to glimpse in protest the dawn of justice,

in the Cross the pathway to resurrection,
and in suffering the seeds of joy.   *Ruben Alves, Brazil*
          All Year Round (British Council of Churches 1987)

FOR REFLECTION and ACTION – alone or with a group

- What aspects of your national life would make prophets angry or cause Jesus to weep today?
- Where do you foresee disaster? What can we do to prevent it from happening?
- Where are there signs of hope?

JOURNEY WITH CHRIST
6. Who cares?

Notes based on the New Revised Standard Version by
Rajah Jacob

*Swaminathen Jacob, known by family and friends as 'Rajah',
served as Secretary of the Methodist Conference in Sri Lanka
and as Secretary for Asia and the Pacific for the Methodist
Church in Britain. In retirement in North London, he was involved
in preaching, leading Bible studies and tutoring local preachers
and, as Honarary Minister Emeritus, he served the London Tamil
Christian Congregation. He died unexpectedly just a few months
after writing these notes.*

Earthquakes, ethnic cleansing, racial riots, famine, rail and air
disasters, floods and tornadoes are all experiences of our time.
The television brings horrendous pictures of these events as they
happen. We are startled by them. Is there a God? Does he care?
Who cares? Questions come flooding into our minds. This Holy
Week, as we read and reflect on the events that took place in the
life of our Lord Jesus Christ, may we find some of the answers as
we recognize the suffering God who is with us in the midst of our
pain.

Palm Sunday, April 8   *Psalm 118.1-2, 8-29**
God's enduring love
The Psalmist celebrates the enduring love of God through pain
and suffering. He had experienced darkness of the soul which he
describes in graphic language in verse 12 (REB):
'They swarmed round me like bees;
they attacked me, as fire attacks brushwood.'
Most of us would identify ourselves with the Psalmist. My wife
and I fled from our home in Colombo, Sri Lanka, as a menacing
crowd came towards it on 25 July 1983 and, after two
hours' refuge in a kind neighbour's kitchen, we came out and saw
our house, together with all our possessions, burned to the
ground. We were 'pushed hard, so that (we were) falling'
(verse 13).

We spent a month in a refugee camp where we met hundreds
more who had even worse experiences. But the beauty of it was

that, as the sun went down and the shadows lengthened, all the Christians went into the church in the centre of the compound, to affirm the presence of God, to sing and to praise. This surprised our fellow Hindu refugees. They wanted to know how it was possible for us to say,

'The Lord is my strength and my might (verse 14)...
You are my God, and I will give thanks to you' (verse 28).

This is a psalm of confidence in God in the midst of trials and tribulation. Do we allow circumstances to overwhelm us, or are we able to say in the midst of it all,

'O give thanks to the Lord, for he is good,
for his steadfast love endures for ever'?

✴ *God, my rock and my refuge, help me to know*
the strength of your love in the midst of pain and hardship
in and through Jesus Christ our Lord and our Saviour. Amen

Monday April 9   *Luke 22.14-30**

Sharing and serving

As he shared with his disciples in this fellowship meal, Jesus knew that the time for him to leave them was near. In a way they never forgot, he dramatized his parting message. He shared with them the bread and wine – symbols of his body and blood – and he added, 'Do this in remembrance of me'. This action has reminded his disciples ever since of his sacrificial love for us and for the world. God in Christ cares. He has left us a memorial of his caring love in the Sacrament of Holy Communion.

A meal brings people together and is a bonding experience. There is a Tamil saying: 'Do not conspire to do evil to a household where you have eaten a meal.' The tragedy is that at the Last Supper betrayal was looming large. And after the meal they quarrelled among themselves as to who was the greatest. Their companionship with Jesus – hearing his teaching, seeing miracles, sharing meals with him – does not seem to have transformed them into his likeness.

How long have we been followers of Jesus? Do we say we have been transformed by him? How often do quarrels and dissension divide the fellowship in our church or congregation?

✴ *Lord Jesus Christ, give us the gift of humility*
so that we may serve others
in your spirit of sacrificial love. Amen

Tuesday April 10   *Luke 22.39-46**

Agonizing in prayer

Jesus leaves the upper room with his disciples and goes to the Garden of Gethsemane, 'as was his custom', to pray. This time it was no ordinary prayer: 'Father, if you are willing, remove this cup from me; yet, not my will but yours be done' (verse 42). We see an element of doubt. Jesus can see the dark clouds gathering: the coming betrayal, denial, and the cross awaiting him. Is this the way he must go? He is not afraid of facing the pain and suffering, but he needs to be certain that he is doing his Father's will until the end. In his anguish he prays earnestly. It is a prayer of total commitment to God.

Prayer is not an armchair exercise. Prayer is opening ourselves to God. It is being vulnerable and saying, 'I am like clay in the potter's hand; mould me and use me as you will.' This type of prayer is also dangerous. It is a total abandonment of ourselves into the hands of God. Are we prepared, as instruments of God's caring, to pray meaningfully, 'Thy will be done'? Do we show that God cares by agonizing in prayer for others?

✳ *I am no longer my own but yours.*
  Put me to what you will...
    put me to suffering;
  let me be employed for you...
  Exalted for you
    or brought low for you...
  I freely and wholeheartedly yield all things
  To your pleasure and disposal.   *Methodist Covenant Service*
                     Methodist Worship Book (Methodist Publishing House)

Wednesday April 11   *Luke 22.47-62**

Facing challenges

Jesus had reminded his disciples of the need to be alert and pray that they 'may not come into the time of trial' (verse 40). But Judas betrayed him, and Peter denied all knowledge of him. The cock crowed and 'the Lord turned and looked at Peter'. Peter understood that look. It was a look of sadness, of compassion and love. Peter was deeply moved (verse 62).

A group of Sinhala villagers in Sri Lanka heard the gospel message and asked to be baptized. The day before their baptism, a Buddhist monk stirred up opposition against them; their homes were attacked, and they were rendered homeless. The minister of their church visited them and gave as much help as he could. When asked if, after all that had happened, they still wanted baptism, they affirmed their decision.

And what about ourselves? Do we, who call ourselves Christians, stand by what we profess, or do we betray our Lord by our lifestyle? When challenged with keeping up standards and being true to the values we stand for at our workplace, in the factory or office, do we deny our Lord?

✳ *Good Lord, I have received so much love,*
goodness and mercy from you. I abound in riches
because I am yours. Yet, Lord, many times
I have betrayed you, denied any knowledge of you.
Forgive me, Lord, and strengthen me by your Spirit
that I may be true to you always. Amen

Thursday April 12   *Luke 23.1-25**

Shirking responsibility

'He suffered under Pontius Pilate.' Why is Pilate included in the Nicene Creed? He affirms that the suffering, death and burial of Jesus were historical facts: Jesus was a real human being who shared our lives. In such a One we anchor our faith.

Pilate is a man of authority, holding the scales of justice. He knows what his verdict should be. Yet he vacillates. He does not want to face the political consequences of standing by the truth, but looks for ways of escape from a just decision, and hands Jesus over to be crucified. As we say, 'he suffered under Pontius Pilate', we are challenged to recognize our failure to act responsibly when there are opportunities to do justice.

One of the first acts of the Parliament after Sri Lanka gained her independence was the disenfranchisement of a million plantation workers of Indian origin. It was a blatant act of injustice. The churches remained silent, but a Hindu professor and Member of Parliament spoke out against it and resigned his post in protest. God sometimes uses a Cyrus to show that he cares (Isaiah 45.1).

Do we have the courage of our own convictions, or do we find devious ways of escape from making responsible decisions?

✳ *With responsibility goes the courage to make right decisions*
at the right time. Lord, give me that courage at all times.

Suffering love

As Jesus is being led away carrying his own cross to the place called the Skull, they compel a passer-by, Simon of Cyrene, to carry the cross for him. He must have walked close enough to Jesus on the way to Calvary to observe Jesus' face. What effect would this have had upon his life? Might it have transformed him and inspired him to become a disciple?

Two others are also led away. They are both criminals. One joins the soldiers in mocking Jesus. He refuses the opportunity to examine his own life and dies in darkness and despair. The other man recognizes the justice of his sentence and with a contrite heart asks forgiveness. He sees light and love on the cross in the centre and prays, 'Jesus, remember me when you come into your Kingdom'. He is promised a place in 'Paradise'.

And in the centre is the cross of Jesus – a figure of majesty and compassion. 'Father, forgive them; they do not know what they are doing', and 'Father into your hands I commend my spirit', he says, and he dies with that joy that transcends pain, knowing that he will be reunited with the Father.

In verse 45 we read 'the sun's light failed' and 'the curtain of the temple was torn in two'. The veil that separated the people from God is torn away. God is in the midst of our suffering. As I write this, news comes that 3000 refugees in a church in Sri Lanka are facing artillery firing by the Army and the Tigers. Hundreds are killed and wounded. A typical week's news headlines: 'Terror among civilians' – 'LTTE mine attack' – 'Murder of Editor' – 'Bombs in the South'... News of Sri Lanka rarely gets reported by world media, but the suffering goes on. The world may forget, but Good Friday reminds us that God is there on the cross suffering with us. Do we always realize this in our lives?

✳ *Beneath the cross of Jesus*
   I fain would take my stand...

   O safe and happy shelter,
      O refuge tried and sweet,
   O trysting place where heaven's love
      And heaven's justice meet.
                                   Elizabeth Cecilia Clephane (1830-69)

Laid to rest

A week of planning and plotting, of praying and agonizing, has come to an end. Jesus, though in pain, yet in majesty, gives up his spirit in triumph with the words, 'It is finished'. Two secret disciples, Joseph and Nicodemus, lovingly and tenderly take Jesus' body down from the cross, wrap it in strips of linen and lay it in a new tomb. A silence descends on the earth!

Most of the known followers of Jesus had vanished, leaving two 'secret' disciples to do the last honours. God uses them to show his caring love even in death.

There are still 'secret disciples' in many parts of the world today, especially in Tamil Nadu in India. Social and cultural pressures prevent them from confessing their faith openly. In their own way, they honour and serve the Lord.

As we contemplate the events of Holy Saturday, let us examine our lives. Are we 'open' Christians? Do we have the courage to stand firm and be counted with Jesus?

✳ *Lord Jesus, we remember your secret disciples.*
Be with them as they try to be your witnesses
under difficult circumstances in many parts of the world.
Give courage to the rest of us
to be true and loyal witnesses until the end. Amen

FOR REFLECTION – alone or with a group

● When does our prayer lead us to think of someone or some issue and prompt us to do something about it?
● 'In the world you will have tribulation,' said Jesus. How do we face suffering and pain as individuals and together in our family and community?

FOR ACTION

Think of a particular need in your church or community. What practical way can you adopt to reveal the sacrificial love of Christ in fulfilling that need?

JOURNEY WITH CHRIST
7. Emptiness and triumph

Notes based on the New International Version by
Mark Wakelin

*Mark Wakelin is the National Secretary of the Methodist
Association of Youth Clubs. He has also served as a minister in
the Lincoln and Grimsby District and the Manchester and
Stockport District. He writes for various publications including
'Partners in Learning', and is particularly keen to develop worship
material that celebrates and includes an all-age Church.*

The core of the Christian faith is summed up in an early cry of faith:
'The crucified is risen'. The central paradox is this: the same Jesus
who was humiliated has been raised to life. It is important to
understand that the story of the passion is not like a fairy story – a
sad bit and then a happy ending. The resurrection, far from undoing
the painful mess of the cross, simply underlines it. In this drama the
triumph is Good Friday and the celebration of that triumph is Easter
Sunday. The theme explores what it means for us that our faith is
built upon this mystery, deeper than the dawn of time.

Easter Day, April 15   *Luke 24.1-12**
The empty grave
The women come in bitter grief, no King, no Kingdom, no healer,
no friend, no teacher, no guide, nothing but the ritual of death,
and the numbness of despair. Why look for the living anyway?
Here is no easy challenge to be optimistic when all is dark. Here
is no story to encourage others who believe that 'every cloud has
a silver lining'. The mystery is deeper, the hope greater, the
challenge more profound; for the tomb is empty. How hard the
men found it to hear of this explosive news from the women
whose testimony counted for nothing: unbelievable news told by
the unbelievable. Feel the challenge that begins with sadness
and ends with emptiness. Sadness itself is emptied away. Truth
is emptied of old meanings and is ready for something new. Dry
and dusty certainties, truths that hold humanity in thrall – that
might will always win, that love is fragile, that death is the certain
end and that God no longer cares. Feel the quality of the hope
that such mighty truths have met their end. Such hope is only
possible because of the emptiness that preceded it.

✳ *Take from me, O Christ, all my strength that resists you,*
   All my fullness that excludes you,
   All my ambitions that deny you,
   All my hopes that refuse you.
   Weaken me with the sadness of my dull certainties
   That I may catch the dawn of the first new day.

Action – 'I pour contempt on all my pride.'

Monday April 16   John 20.1-18*

Emptied of hope

Looking for the wrong thing in the wrong place makes finding
impossible! Mary does not recognize Jesus until Jesus
recognizes her. The one who knew Mary best reveals himself by
that knowledge. The struggle to find and recognize the risen
Christ is rendered possible by the Christ who struggles to meet
us, and to call us by our name. Jesus speaks hope into her tears
and gives a woman the first Christian sermon to preach. So
where will we find Christ? And what is the Christ like that we
seek? He is hidden away from us by preconceptions, disguised in
strange surroundings. The struggle seems too much, too
hopeless; our faith simply too fragile. Are we really allowed to
hope and believe such things? But strangely it is not our lack of
effort that is the problem. Perhaps we try too hard. Sometimes,
even when tears flow and we have no energy for the chase,
sometimes, we are quiet enough to hear the voice of One who
knows our name.

✳ *Calm my desperate search*
   That I can hear you call;
      That by your recognition of me,
      In all my muddles and confusion,
   I may recognize you,
   And know that your name is Love.

Action – Take time to rest in God's love.

Tuesday April 17   Isaiah 43.1-13*

Emptied of fear

Various stories brand people as fortunate because they have
escaped a gruesome end – freed in the nick of time, with certain
death averted. This is not my idea of good fortune! I would rather
not have had the scare. If it is fortunate to avoid an untimely end,

it is hardly good fortune to be placed in the situation where you need it!

Here in this passage from Isaiah we are given a vision of the future with neither good nor bad fortune. Instead there is God – God when it is going to be dangerous and frightening, come 'hell or high water'. It is no easy path, but a path together with God. We are called to be 'precious'; we are to be 'summoned... by name' and the path ahead will be difficult. We don't know what tomorrow will bring, but we do know that we will not be alone when it comes.

✳ *Though waves and storms go o'er my head,*
   Though strength, and health, and friends be gone,
   Though joys be withered all and dead,
   Though every comfort be withdrawn,
   On this my steadfast soul relies –
   Father, thy mercy never dies!   J A Rothe (1688-1758)
                                  Translated by John Wesley (1703-91)

Action – Hear the words 'you are precious' when life is hard.

Wednesday April 18   *1 Corinthians 15.19-26**

Emptied of death

How dreadful death is. It is too easy, I believe, to be sanguine about death and fear only the process of dying. Whatever you believe about the life to come, death itself comes as a violence that leaves mess and unfinished business. It is sometimes too easy, also, for those of us bereaved, to pretend celebration of our faith when someone we love has died. When we are filled with devastating grief, it can be a long time before we are able to rejoice. Jesus also wept and we weep with him.

We do wrong to minimize death; for by doing so we diminish the great victory. In Christ death itself has been destroyed. The last great enemy – the final river, the dread nightmare of the human race – in Christ has been defeated. This will not leave us free of either fear or grief, for both are ours in the dawn before the Kingdom comes. But they will free us from a present imprisoned by our fear, and challenge us to seek life in all our living.

✳ *The Cross –*
   Our freedom lies in your captivity,
   Our hope in your despairing cry,
   Our life in your death,
   Our future in this moment;

When evil, hell bent on death,
Was broken by the sigh of a dying God,
Whose breath poured order and life on creation.

Written by Mark Wakelin in 'Songs for the New Millennium'
© Trustees for Methodist Church Purposes.
Used by permission of the Methodist Publishing House

Thursday April 19   *John 20.19-23**

Emptied of power

Here is a passage that piles the impossible on the impossible. Christ is alive, yet appears through locked doors. His victory is recognized by his wounds. He sends those who ran away to follow the same path he had to take. He gives them power to forgive as only God can. Which part is hardest to believe? That a dead man should rise? That a risen one should walk through doors? That victory is found in the scars of the cross? That the weak should be strong? That the mighty weight of God's grace should hang upon the thin thread of human love? But all is one and there is only one question, for, 'On the evening of that first day of the week, when the disciples were together, with the doors locked... Jesus came and stood among them.' There is no resurrection without the cross. There is no victory without the wounds, and there is no Kingdom unless the weak, failed, and frightened disciples live in the light of new possibilities and breathe deeply of the Spirit that was in Christ and shaped the world.

✳ *Sometimes, frightened and alone*
We long for you to come.
But we guard our locked doors with hardened hearts.
Sometimes, when shamed at our failure,
We long for you to come,
And touch the wounds that mark our healing.
Sometimes, when weakened by our bitterness,
We long for you to come
But fear your call to follow
And forgive those who have hurt and damaged us.
Sometimes, we long for the impossible,
For life to beat death and find locked doors no barrier.
Dear God, let that sometime be now.

Action – Breathe deeply of God's grace all around us.

Emptied of meaning

I once spent a long time trying to persuade a young man of the value of the Christian Faith. He resisted, but we remained friends. I finally asked a question that should have been asked much earlier: 'What is the God you don't believe in like?' The question took him aback, and then he began to describe God in terms that made me realize how much we had in common. I said, 'The God you don't believe in, I don't believe in either.'

'God' is just a word. Our language about God is simply metaphor upon metaphor. Words can no more contain God than the Cross, creation, or the grave. The key question is: 'What is God like?' What is the content of the word 'God'? The answer is in today's reading. It is Christ who had been publicly humiliated, beaten, executed, and now appears to the disciples. Thomas, filled with ordinary doubts, is convinced only by the marks of the cross. Here he finds not just evidence that God is, but the true content of that easily misunderstood word. For God is the crucified God – vulnerable, involved, self-giving and present in our difficulties and pain.

✳ *Were the whole realm of nature mine,*
   That were an offering far too small;
 Love so amazing, so divine,
     demands my soul, my life, my all. Isaac Watts (1674-1748)

Action – Seek and serve the crucified God for this day.

Emptied of beauty

At the beginning of the rule of the Nazi party in the early thirties, the young theologian Dietrich Bonhoeffer gave a radio broadcast. He spoke out against the 'Fuhrer Principle'. This was not a particular criticism of Hitler, or of the Nazis, but of the concept of a leader to whom a nation gives unquestioning allegiance. He touched upon a core human temptation, which is for someone else to be in charge, to hide behind, to depend upon.

Jesus challenges his disciples to 'call no man father', to resist the urge to let someone else take control. But again and again the disciples seek to make Jesus such a figure of respect and honour. They want him to become a national leader and to put themselves in key positions. Peter stands in front of Jesus on the road to Caesarea Philippi and prays that the suffering Jesus had talked about might not happen (Mark 8.31-33). The response seems so angry, for Peter has shown a deep misunderstanding, as the other disciples do, perhaps as we do. Jesus teaches a new form of authority without instant appeal, one that Isaiah foretells. Here power becomes the humility of the cross, authority the power of love. The cry of dereliction from the hill of Golgotha becomes the victory cry of God's grace and creativity.

✷ *A cross at the centre of a troubling new way,*
That steers clear of glamour
And power over others.
A face racked in pain at a moment of triumph,
As love declares victory,
To liberate life.
A power that leads others to freedom
And bares in itself the cost and the grief.
This we found and rejected
But now we lay claim:
Crucified God, come into this time,
And reign.

Action – Consider the way we use our power over others.

FOR REFLECTION – alone or with a group

● What are the differences between the story of the Church and its use of power and status, and the radical challenge of Jesus?
● What difference does the knowledge that death has been defeated make to how we live now?

2nd Sunday of Easter, April 22   *Luke 24.13-35**

Empty in darkness

Two disciples walked from Jerusalem into the sunset of their hopes and dreams – walking west to Emmaus, a few miles down the road, and light years from where they longed to be. In their grief, shame and pain, another walked with them and tried to help them see that it is through darkness that dawn comes, that death is not the final word of a created world waiting for the Kingdom.

At the end of their journey they asked him to stay, and as he broke bread they realized who had walked with them in the evening of their despair and into the night of fears. As the bread was broken and shared, they knew that broken also was that despair. They turned around and headed back into the east to Jerusalem. They turned back to the location of their failures, their fears and grief. They turned back in the darkness and the night, but now they walked towards the dawn, the east, the rising sun. The breaking of that bread meant so much. It reminded them that Jesus lived life to the full. It reminded them that he had kept dubious company and welcomed outcasts to eat with him. It reminded them of the night in which he was betrayed and gave the bread and the wine new meaning. Here was food for their journey, and hope in their darkness.

✳ *Abide with me; fast falls the eventide;*
    The darkness deepens; Lord with me abide;
       When other helpers fail, and comforts flee,
       Help of the helpless, O abide with me.

                                    Henry Francis Lyte (1793-1847)

Action – Take time to remember today the Christ who was
    known when he broke bread.

Monday April 23   *Luke 24.36-43*

Emptiness and hunger

You have to be really hungry to understand the difference between appetite and hunger. The former allows one to enjoy chocolate after a fine meal. The latter makes the dullest piece of bread taste better than the most expensive food. Jesus describes himself as 'the bread of life'. He might have said something more exotic, expensive or rare. He said 'bread' – which in his culture was the staple food. It was every day, and essential.

It is for this reason that he points out that sinners and outcasts are quicker to respond to the gospel. If your life is full and you are self-satisfied, the attraction of bread, the ordinary, can pass you by. You may acquire an appetite for religion, but not so easily a hunger for Christ. If, however, you are broken and ashamed, you really are hungry for new life and hope. Jesus eats plain food with his disciples by the Lake. It is ordinary food for each one of them. By it they recognize him and understand the reality of seeing him. By it they are reminded that Christ is an everyday need of life, not an optional extra to save for Sundays and special days.

✳ *Our needy souls sustain*
       With fresh supplies of love,
    Till all thy life we gain,
       And all thy fullness prove,

And, strengthened by thy perfect grace,
Behold without a veil thy face.   *Charles Wesley (1707-88)*

Action – Live this day to the full that we may be hungry for the
love of God.

Tuesday April 24   *John 21.1-14*

The emptiness of failure

We live in success-oriented cultures. Failure is simply not acceptable and it is greatly feared. It is hard to own up to mistakes, for too much seems to be at stake. Triumphs and not disasters measure our self-worth, and that self-worth is in jeopardy if we acknowledge our failures. The disciples have not only abandoned their discipleship in the light of the disaster of the cross, but also have failed in their fishing. Surrounded by failure they meet the risen Christ.

I hate to be told to do something I think I know how to do and, when Jesus suggests a new strategy, the disciples show more grace than I would have done! Immediately the nets are full and they know Christ.

Underneath our fear of failure is a challenging reality. Moments of failure often lead to the most growth and change. It is when we find ourselves plumbed to the depths in the middle of a disaster that sometimes, strangely, we are most able to move on. It is not success despite failure; it is triumph through disaster. Out of our own depth, we discover the unfathomable depths of God. Our moment of emptiness is God's opportunity to fill us.

✳ *Creator God, we are ashamed of our failures;*
  We know we do not love enough or well enough;
  The good we would do, we do not do.
  Thank you that you accept us as we are,
  Successful and failing,
  And never give up on us.
  So may we grow in you,
  To love and live well.

Action – Let us value ourselves for who we are as well as what
we do.

Wednesday April 25   *John 21.15-19*

Emptied of shame

There are different reasons given as to why Jesus asks Peter the same question three times. Some argue that Jesus is making a play on words and this is reflected in the difference between two Greek words used for 'love'. Others suggest a simpler reason, and this makes more sense to me. Jesus is gently unpicking the shame of the past. Peter, who denied Jesus three times, is given the opportunity to respond three times. Encountering God means that the past, with all its awful mistakes, has no dominion over the future. Peter is given a task, and a lesson. The task is to be Christ for others, to nurture and nourish those who seek to be disciples.

He is also given a lesson, and reminded of the nature of the new authority Jesus has given to him. Before the cross Peter couldn't understand the purpose it played in the victory over evil. He assumed old forms of power and control, and when he recognized how wrong he was, he denied knowing Christ to a serving girl. In a way he spoke the truth: he simply didn't know who Jesus was, though up to that point he thought he knew. Now he is told that he too will walk the way of the cross, and exercise the power of love in the way Christ had done.

✴ *Thank you, generous God,*
That you know us well
And love us completely.
We have failed often,
And live in ways far less than you desire.
Unpick the tangles of our painful story,
That we may walk with you
And learn the best new way of Love.

Action – Treat others with the same grace with which God treats us.

Thursday April 26   *Philippians 1.12-26*

Emptied of self

There is something fundamentally unnatural about the claims that Paul makes in this passage. Those who hang on to the idea of the 'selfish gene', in which individuals comply with the deepest and ancient instincts to survive, would question the reality of words such as, 'For to me, to live is Christ and to die is gain' (verse 21). Like the cross itself, this talk is either utter nonsense or it touches upon a truth that must be deeper even than a genetic predisposition to live for self. Paul is picking up on some of the most challenging of Jesus' teaching. The strange topsy-turvy world of the Kingdom makes the claim that it is only by letting go of self that you find yourself. Our existence both for now, and into the future, depends on a courageous step of faith in which we resist the clamour of instinct, and clasp the greater reality of our divine origin and live for others. As Christ empties himself, so we are called to a joyful independence from our fears to reach out to the other, to our neighbour, our enemy, our God.

✳ *O God, emptied of all but love,*
Humbled, vulnerable, self-giving, selfless,
Give us such courage that we may risk ourselves;
Give us such strength that self may be weakened;
Give us such confidence that self may be given;
Give us such love that self may be found;
Give us such joy that we may be lost
In wonder, love and praise. Amen

Action – Take another step in letting go of self.

Friday April 27   *Revelation 1.4-8**

Full of hope

Part of our difficulty in understanding the constancy of God, and the hope of Christ, is that we live our lives within the prison of time: times past with all their muddles and difficulties that have shaped who we are now, for better or worse; times to come which fill us with fear of the unknown, and distract us with impossible dreams and fantasies; time now with all its pressure and demands...

Our God, though 'contracted to a span', rises above time and sees the wholeness of our being. God sees and understands what has shaped us, and broken us. Our future with all its possibilities and potential, however, equally shapes that understanding. When we look at ourselves trapped in the present, we can be filled with doubts, fear and shame. But God does not see us in this way. 'To him who loves us and has freed us from sins by his blood, and has made us to be a kingdom... to him be glory!' Think what that means: you before God, emptied of shame, perceived not just as you are, or as you have been, but in the light of your potential; your healed, cleansed, empowered, fulfilled potential. The 'now' – imprisoned in time, in the love and perception of God – is set free, and becomes the eternal moment as God's promise evokes the greatest hope.

✳ *Alpha and Omega,*
The beginning and the end,
Help us to live our lives within the context of eternity:
To judge our actions and decisions;

Never to rest or be content
Until the promise is fulfilled,
And all creation will know it together. Amen

Action – Act this day in such a way that in a thousand years'
time it will have mattered.

Saturday April 28 Psalm 16*

Full of joy

There is a challenge to the Christian who holds that God is love. It is the challenge of suffering and injustice. There are no easy answers, and most commonly the answer the Christian gives is not a philosophical one, but one that involves the costly love that Christ demonstrated. There is, however, an equal challenge to those who say, 'There is no God'. It is the challenge of joy – how can it be explained without the Creator? The heart is filled to overflowing. The Christian can sing,

'My heart is full of Christ, and longs
Its glorious matter to declare' *(Charles Wesley)*.

We are surrounded by an exuberant and joyful creation. Pleasure abounds in life and life is full of laughter, and content. To take all the risks of emptiness, of giving, sacrifice, trust – expressed as they all are with a courageous and practical love – is to be happy. It is a happiness that is deep down in your heart, and not just there. It is a happiness that may lie unbroken when all around is full of pain and suffering, but not just then. It is happiness that can also surface from your depths and spread from you to others as water in a dry and dusty place.

'You will fill me with joy in your presence,
with eternal pleasures at your right hand' (verse 11).

✳ *Joyful, risen Lord,*
From the empty tomb you came and declared the end of death.
Thank you for this day of life;
For creation in its wild variety;
For relationships with their complex beauty and satisfaction;
For suffering that can never touch the deepest well of joy;
For now, this moment in our day,
When you keep us safe
And become our refuge.

Action – to take time this day to relish the pleasure of life and
to rest in God who is our refuge.

FOR REFLECTION – alone or with a group

- What effect does the hope of the coming Kingdom have upon the way we feel and act now?
- Think how you feel when a guest arrives in your house but takes no pleasure in anything you offer. Think about the God of life when we overlook the joy of creation.
- What is the best thing about being alive?

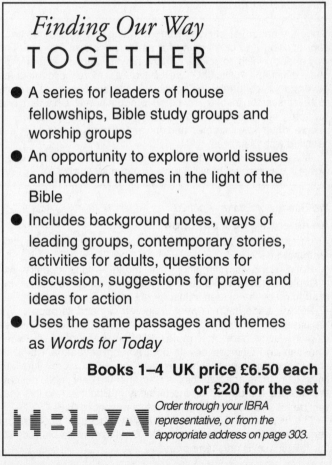

NEW ROADS AHEAD
1. Change of direction

Notes based on the Revised English Bible by
Ralph Lee

Ralph Lee is superintendent minister of the Kowloon circuit of the Methodist Church in Hong Kong. He has also served for five years in Britain through the World Church in Britain Partnership of the Methodist Church.

Since the handover of Hong Kong to China in 1997 life has been very exciting and challenging for all the people of this city. The way ahead, which coincides with the new millennium, is uncertain and difficult. Politically, we have a more executive-led government; culturally and religiously, we are becoming a more pluralist society instead of being predominantly Christian and western; economically and socially, life is getting harder for people on a low income, and inwardly more people are less satisfied with their lives.

Is there a voice from the Church? Will the Church remain where it was before, or will it have to move forward?

3rd Sunday of Easter, April 29   *Acts 9.1-9**
An emerging new direction

As directed by the voice, Saul went into the city and 'he was blind for three days'.

Hong Kong is changing. The motto – 'one country two systems' – mostly works but the direction in which we are moving is affected by the hidden influence of Central Government.

Politics aside, faith is what shapes a city and its people. We are caught up increasingly by the influence of traditional Chinese religion, and there are more head-on encounters between Christian and Chinese beliefs both among government officials and in the community which is evolving along more pluralistic lines. Christmas, for example, is no longer the only public holiday. We now have a day off on the birthday of Buddha, and this may well be followed by Taoist and Confucian special days.

The year 2001 is with us. The way ahead is unclear, but certainly challenging. Our sight, like Saul's, may be blurred, but this 'blindness' is only temporary.

✻ *Out of chaos you created order; your Spirit hovered*
over the darkness, and you created light.
We trust you to give us sight to see our future;
on you we depend, Lord. Amen

Monday April 30   *Acts 9.10-20**
Life turned to God
The Spirit is always at work changing our direction in ways that at first don't seem possible, even to the extent of a complete turn-around. At a Christian social service board meeting recently, I listened to the activities of outreach social workers among marginalized children and young people in three deprived areas. The director told us that social workers are no longer just middle-class university graduates and 'do-gooders'. Instead, they include many who suffered abuse at an early age at home or school and others who have survived a period of being 'on the streets'. They have been touched, moved, educated and now want to practise the love they have received by caring for others.

Where some drug rehabilitation programmes have failed in Hong Kong, Christian drug rehabilitation centres have done a great job. I know one young person who is now a minister and he is not the only one whose life has been changed by God.

Ananias was reluctant to go to 'Straight Street' but Saul was waiting to have his sight restored. We too believe God enables us to turn and follow him with gladness. Reluctant, unwilling we may be, but we are to reach out to those on the edge of our society.

✻ *Lord, give us hope that our lives and communities*
will not go down the slippery road of despair.
Help us, while waiting, to see the vision
and be healed with strength and courage
so that we can encourage others to turn to you. Amen

Tuesday May 1   *Acts 9.21-31*
A go-between needed
'On reaching Jerusalem he tried to join the disciples, but they were all afraid of him, because they did not believe that he really was a disciple. Barnabas, however, took him and introduced him to the apostles' (verses 26-27b). God acts and travels at high speed but we move in the slow lane, trying to catch up. It takes a while for us to grasp the implications!

Macau, in December 1999, reverted to China after being a Portuguese enclave for over 400 years. Both this and the handover of Hong Kong happened at midnight; flags were lowered and new ones hoisted in a packed hall attended by dignitaries. Then the new head, the Chief Executive, was sworn in. Yet, on the next morning, the general public saw only the new emblem on the government buildings.

It was a drastic change from past history, a totally new direction. Could the people trust the new head of government and the way that he will lead? Their knowledge of him is only sketchy because he is elected (directly and indirectly) by China. He is trusted by China but can people here also trust him?

✳ *Lord God, you have your plan for us,*
but we know very little about the future.
Give wisdom to those by whom we are governed
and inspire them to lead us with justice and compassion.

Wednesday May 2   Acts 10.1-16

Vision – challenge and opportunity for change

Since 1 July 1997, when Hong Kong became a special Autonomous Region, the Right of Abode issue for children of Hong Kong residents has been a focus of controversy. The Court of Final Appeal ruled in their favour, but the Government claimed that an estimated 1.67 million people would then come to live in Hong Kong – in a time of economic recession – taking up jobs and welfare benefits. People worried that their standards would be lowered; new immigrants – unskilled and uneducated – would make a mess of their clean city. What they failed to see at a deeper level were opportunities for change. The new arrivals would bring in younger labourers (some even more educated and skilled than the locals); and the Chinese would resist social welfare. Self-reliance has always been their motto!

Short-sightedly, the Government (surrendering its own jurisdiction) asked Central Government to re-interpret the Basic Law in order to curb the influx of a 'large exodus' of its citizens' children. The aim was achieved, but the opportunity lost.

The vision Peter had was an alarming one for a traditional Jewish Christian. To cross the safety line and absorb the 'profane and unclean' was uncomfortable and frightening, but if Peter had not acted, and if others had not supported his decision, Christianity would have remained an exclusive religion.

God gives us visions and opportunities, and we have to take up the challenges when they are there.

✷ *Lord, help us not be too scared to welcome strangers into our midst. Create in us an open mind to expand our circle and be willing to share your love with others. Amen*

Thursday May 3   Acts 10.17-33

Faith builds and fosters community

One Sunday evening, in a nearby side-street, my wife and I spotted an old Chinese antique furniture shop. We went in to have a look and a conversation with the owner opened up. He was the third generation to run the shop and showed me some old photos. Among them I recognized the Abbot of a Taoist temple whom I had met some years ago. I told him I was a Christian minister. Immediately, there was a bonding between us, the beginning of trust, and he invited us to visit the floor above which stores his precious collections.

Hong Kong is rapidly becoming a multi-faith society: it is no longer predominantly Christian in its thinking but also Confucian and Buddhist. There is a loosely-knit federation of six major religious bodies which gathers occasionally to forge closer co-operation and to send out a joint, unified message to an increasingly empty, spiritually hungry, consumer-oriented society.

God led Peter with this vision and inspired a secular, alien centurion Cornelius to invite him to his home. Both moved forward and began a dialogue. Peter found a large gathering. There is always a listening ear if one is ready to cross the traditional boundary, to a different race and culture. They are eager to 'listen to everything that the Lord has... to say.'

✷ *Holy Spirit, speak to our inner heart and change us so that we are not afraid to venture out to people of other faiths. Give us courage to share our faith in a society that seeks a spirituality which goes beyond brand names for religion. Amen*

Friday May 4   Acts 10.34-43

God is bigger than you think!

It's reassuring to hear that 'God has no favourites'. Jesus is for the whole people in all nations; be they Jews or Gentiles,

Christians or non-Christians. This we all know and can recite easily yet, in practice, often forget. We say that only 'members' can receive the 'services' of the Church; and this is nothing less than religious apartheid.

A group of ministers recently asked for a meeting of the local union of churches to explore how they might use some of their long-standing investments. The church people were reluctant. They had been put off on a previous occasion when they applied for permission to build another 'home for the aged' and the Government would not agree to 80% of beds being assigned to Christians. And so the idea remains an idea. This exclusive mentality is outdated in a multi-cultural society. God will eventually be marginalized by Christians. Our understanding of God is limited if we continue to think like this and do so little in a hungry, empty world.

We need a new attitude and then our actions will be different. Only when we begin to pay more attention to non-believers, will our God be accepted by people beyond the Church!

✷ *God, we often look inside rather than outside,*
and move inwards rather than outwards.
Change us that we may see others first
so that your name can be spread across the earth,
to all people, in all nations. Amen

Saturday May 5   *Acts 10.44-48*

God prepares the ground work

How often it is true that God waits for us, ahead of everything! If we have the faith and love to take the first step, the Spirit moves with us as we take up challenges for God's mission.

The church where I serve decided to plant a new congregation in Tin Siu Wai, in the furthest corner of the New Territories near the border with China. The area is completely new to us. It is full of immigrants from China, grassroots people and, being a new town, it's not without family problems. When we first convened a special meeting of the church council in August 1998, we boldly said 'YES' to God, knowing we had neither human resources nor money. All we had was a strong desire for mission, and 21 church members who joined the pioneering group. After many visits, studies, plans and preparations, the new church – meeting in a primary school – was dedicated a year later. Within a few months, the congregation had grown to 80-100 people.

In spite of economic recession in Hong Kong, people are looking for spiritual nurture to fill their empty lives; they seek community and want to participate in church life. Many, who don't know much about Christianity, are eager to get to know Jesus. A woman, who recently came to live here from China, asked to be baptized and invited her husband to come. A family, who had long wished to become Christians, but without a church to relate to, came and were also baptized at Christmas.

The Christian community in China itself is expanding, fast! A minister told me recently that they had to call in the police to disperse the crowd waiting outside his church to get into the Christmas service! They were mainly non-believers, so he promised to hold another carol service at New Year.

Mission is God's work. God's Spirit works in those whose hearts and minds are open and gives us courage and faith to move ahead.

✳ *Lord, quite often we hesitate, undecided,*
afraid to venture out for your mission.
Change us, we pray, so that with gladness and
without hesitation we go where you lead us,
knowing you will never be satisfied
until your name is accepted by all. Amen

FOR REFLECTION and ACTION – alone or with a group

● What are the principles on which we can begin to build a more harmonious, multi-faith society?
● 'God has no favourites'. What challenges does this truth make to your relationships with others in your neighbourhood? What challenges does it make to your church?

NEW ROADS AHEAD
2. Crossing new boundaries

Notes based on the Revised Standard Version by
Jane Ella Montenegro

Jane Montenegro is a lay pastor and Christian Education worker in empowerment programmes with and among women, young people, children and rural churches. She also writes educational materials for the National Council of Churches in the Philippines and is a member of the Asian Women's Resource Centre for Culture and Theology.

Paul's journeys are inspiring lessons of faithfulness and risk-taking. The stories of his experiences of the work of the Spirit have truly nurtured women and men of many generations to face threatening situations.

Today, Christians everywhere struggle to cross new boundaries, making Christ matter to individuals, families, communities and whole nations. They live alongside 'the unclean', mingling with all kinds of people in the cities, extending hospitality, guiding and inspiring new generations, risking lives, bringing light to homes and crossing barriers. All these are expressions of faithfulness to God's call to Kingdom building.

4th Sunday of Easter, May 6   *Acts 11.1-18*
Purity and exclusivism
A Christian friend invited me to attend meditation at a holy place. Excitedly I said 'yes' and asked if I could bring some friends. No, she answered, they might be 'meat-eating'! Immediately, these very same texts, especially of Peter's vision, came to mind. After a heated debate, I felt a deep sense of rejection on behalf of my friends who could not conform to the practices of this group. And so I replied, 'I may come another time, but not now.' I may have lost the chance to know the portents of these end-times and the heavenly wisdom given only to a 'select few' but what affected me most were thoughts like: What would Jesus have said?

It is about 2,000 years now since Peter encountered these issues of purity and exclusivism among and between Jews and Gentiles, and the problem still exists today. In what form does it appear in your context?

* *Grant me a penitent heart, O God,*
  that I may live more closely to Jesus' ways of loving
  and embracing all, instead of separating myself
  from the 'uncleanness' of this world.

Monday May 7   Acts 11.19-30

The city of God

Antioch of ancient times was the seat of power, commerce and a cosmopolitan lifestyle. So is Manila today. One pastor from the village remarked, 'I hate Manila; it's so polluted, congested, and all kinds of human depravity are in it.' A Manila-born pastor replied, 'That is true, but God also loves Manila.' The village pastor changed. She began to watch and pray for the heavily made-up young prostitutes, and grimy street-children sniffing drugs. She gave gifts with blessings to old beggars even when she knew they were maintained by underworld goons.

Just as in Antioch, the gospel of Jesus Christ is intensively preached everywhere in this city today: in buses, market places, malls and by all kinds of media. Kind-hearted folk respond to human-made disasters and natural calamities: free treatment is given to the poor; scarce, precious resources are shared with joy; many advocates seek justice amid employer-employee disputes; hundreds of domestic helpers and professionals provide regular support to needy home churches and families...

* *O God of the cities and villages,*
  give us the heart of Christ who treated others
  as sister, brother and friend,
  that we may bring about love and justice,
  making every place a New Earth today. Amen

Tuesday May 8   Acts 13.1-12

Respecting God's messengers

In the Philippines, it is common for itinerant preachers to meet with people from all walks of life, as Barnabas, Saul and John Mark did. One such preacher, hearing about a couple's infidelity, prayed with them and counselled them to remain faithful to each other, but the woman vehemently denied the affair. She began to devise ways to destroy the preacher, accusing him of being a trouble-maker and a money-lover. Gradually, her children began to defy her commands. Her teenage girl had a relationship with a married man and bore him a son. Her younger brother engaged in the pornography business and the eldest brother moved into an illegal logging trade.

It is the custom of villagers to offer hospitality to any preacher of the gospel of Christ and never consciously to despise him or her or the work of God. Yet there are unrecorded incidents where individuals, families or churches encounter problems when they intentionally malign or belittle a servant of God.

✳ *Forgive me, O God, when I am critical of church workers,*
  forgetting that I too, have motes in my eyes,
  and need your saving grace every moment of my life.

Wednesday May 9   Acts 13.13-16, 26-33, 38-39

Freedom and joy

Paul must have struggled when he preached to deeply conservative Jews and Gentiles in the context of Roman society. And so do we in this age of high technology and modernity. Even in countries where Christianity is a state religion, church members make compromises rather than truly find their security in Christ. They would rather invest heavily in armaments to protect themselves. They spend millions on amusements and comforts in pursuit of happiness. In the Philippines, supposedly the only Christian country in Asia, with a population of 60 million, only ten million copies of the Bible have been released in the last ten years, while the film and gambling industries thrive by billions.

The gifts of freedom from slavery and forgiveness of sin in Jesus Christ remind us again and again to put our trust in God. Will our young people know Jesus Christ better than today's sports idols? When will we break away from a violent culture which makes them carry arms as toys or for real?

✳ *O God, help us to discern how to nurture our children*
  to experience Jesus and his gifts of freedom and joy.

Thursday May 10   Acts 13.42-52

Loving and forgiving

One hundred years ago, foreign and local Filipino evangelists encountered excruciating difficulties when they brought the message of Jesus Christ and the Bible into a Spanish colonial form of Christianity, strong animism and Islam. They were pelted with stones and human faeces, or hounded by machetes and flaming torches. Yet, only in rare cases did they shake the dust off their feet since, most of the time, they were sheltered by protective families. Today, the Bible-reading migrant workers who go to Saudi Arabia have to hide or risk imprisonment.

Also today, many Christian parents struggle to know how to bring up their children in the midst of peer-culture, the attractions of shopping malls, modern gadgetry and the media's penchant for lust and violence. Gone are the days of acquiescence and obedience. But these parents do not simply give up.

✻ *O God, to be a light at home is no easy calling.*
  Nor could we shake the dust off our feet from our own people.
  Give us the patience and discernment we so badly need,
  that we may learn the meaning of love and forgiveness,
  again and again, until we become your New Creation.

Friday May 11   Acts 14.1-18
Healing and wholeness
The proliferation of Christian groups today is often a cause of conflict. In many cities and towns there are internationally linked groups or locally initiated sects. Many groups are known by the names of well-known healers. They draw hundreds of listeners who join them at prayer by radio or television. They attract crowds with their attractive streamers, choirs and bands of musical instruments.

Yet simple, indigenous faith communities are always quiet. Their healers live very simply: they pray and fast and depend on God's sustenance. They do not have contribution boxes, nor do they exact payments. Their healing ministry is centred on God's graciousness and power. They speak the same words Paul and Barnabas spoke to Gentiles and Jews in Iconium some 2000 years ago (verses 15b-17).

It is God who heals. The human healer is simply a vessel of God's power, lest patients worship the healers themselves.

✻ *Forgive us, O God, when we forget*
  that healing comes from you
  and that we are but stewards of your creation. Amen

Saturday May 12   Acts 14.19-28
Crossing male territory
The persecution Paul experienced was followed, centuries later, by the persecution of women who dared preach on the mutuality

of women and men as a sign of God's Kingdom. In 1654 Elizabeth Fletcher and Elizabeth Leavens in Oxford, England, were dragged through a muddy pool, and suffered pain and the indignity of water being siphoned from a pump into their mouths. In Boston, Elizabeth Hooton was tied to a cart and dragged through the streets for claiming her God-given right to preach in public (Karen Armstrong, *The End of Silence,* Fourth Estate Limited, London 1993).

In the 16th and 17th centuries, thousands more were burnt at the stake and tortured to death because they dared to cross male territory by preaching, teaching and baptizing in the name of the Saviour Jesus Christ. They stood firm in their conviction that Jesus empowered the women on that first Easter morning 'to go and tell' the good news. They firmly held to the belief that in Christ 'there is neither male nor female' (Galatians 3.28).

✳ *O God of history, your vision of love and peace*
is a continuing call to us
especially in the face of dreadful realities.
Grant us courage to endure,
to do and say what is just and right, in Christ's name. Amen

FOR REFLECTION – alone or with a group

● In what ways do you think today's affluence has softened and, perhaps, weakened, the hard grit of pioneering evangelization?
● How can Christians today cross the boundaries of other very different families to share their faith with them?

NEW ROADS AHEAD
3. Cross over and help us

Notes based on the Revised English Bible by
Salvador T Martinez

Salvador T Martinez teaches theology and ethics at the McGilvary Faculty of Theology, Payap University in Chiang Mai, Thailand. He is a minister of the United Church of Christ in the Philippines, an international associate of the Common Global Ministries Board to Thailand, director of the Programme for Theology and Cultures in Asia (PTCA) and editor of the PTCA Bulletin.

'Cross over and help us' was the plea of a Macedonian Paul saw in a vision. Convinced that it was God's call for him to bring the good news there, he set out to go immediately. Paul was one who, in spite of difficulties, would say, 'But I do not count my life of any value to myself, if only I may finish my course and the ministry that I received from the Lord Jesus, to testify to the good news of God's grace' (Acts 20.24 NRSV). Today there are similar pleas from people whose lives are constantly threatened, people who live in poverty, who are daily faced with oppression, injustice and violence. They are waiting to hear the reality of the gospel:

'...good news to the poor,
... release for prisoners,
and recovery of sight for the blind;
to let the broken victims go free,
to proclaim the year of the Lord's favour' (Luke 4.18-19).
'Cross over and help us!' Is anyone listening?

5th Sunday of Easter, May 13   *Acts 15.1-21*
To settle a controversy
Throughout its 2000 years of history, the Church has had its share of controversies – usually doctrinal. They often develop into political controversies. Some have resulted in major splits: the great schism in 1054 between the Western and Eastern Churches, the division between Roman Catholics and Protestants in 1529, the separation of the Church of England from the Roman Catholic Church in 1534, and so on. The present

is no different: theological and political controversies go on to undermine the unity and harmony of the Church.

One of the firsts of such controversies occurred in Jerusalem on the issue of whether Gentiles should be circumcised or not. What transpired in the Jerusalem Council changed the direction of the Church (thanks to cool heads). With the compromise that was reached, Christianity freed itself from becoming just a Jewish sect. It obtained an identity of its own and became the missionary church that brought the good news to all the ends of the earth. More than ever, the world needs men and women who have vision, spirit and courage to bring resolutions to the many conflicts that divide religions, nations and people today.

✴ *O God, your Church has been rocked*
with so much dissension; forgive us
for being poor witnesses to your resurrection.

Monday May 14   *Acts 16.1-10*

To proclaim the good news

A subtle but devastating hindrance to the reign of God on earth is apathy. There are injustices and inequalities out there, but like the priest and the Levite in the famous story of the good Samaritan, many Christians do not bother to find out, let alone lay their lives on the line, take a stand or remedy situations of need. The early Christians learned that discipleship means to deny oneself, to take up the cross and follow Jesus. Paul and the other disciples were persecuted and put in prison because they dared to follow in the steps of Jesus. They spoke the truth and challenged the status quo. Do we have the same vision that inspired and guided the early Christians? Does the Spirit continue to speak to us? Are we so focused on the agenda we have set for ourselves that we can't see God's surprises along the way? Or do we see situations that need our help but choose to turn away? 'Cross over to Macedonia and help us!' Are we listening? Are we willing to take up the challenge?

Father Michael Rodrigo of Sri Lanka said, 'We should not be afraid to die for the people if and when the time comes.' And die he did as he was shot saying the Mass.

✴ *O God eternal, reveal to us your will;*
help us to understand your mission
and make it our vision.

118

To drive the evil spirit away

In most Asian countries, people still believe in evil spirits literally inhabiting the earth. Rituals are performed when building a house, moving to a new home, giving birth, or when someone is sick. Illnesses are still attributed to evil spirits. Some claim to be possessed by a 'spirit of divination' like the slave girl in our reading today. In Thailand, some people maintain a spirit house to appease the spirit-owner of the land. Offerings of flowers and food are daily offered to the spirit that dwells in the land.

We may not believe in the spirit world as some people do, but evil lurks in our midst just the same. The men who employed the slave girl made money out of her. This is the real evil. Our world needs to be purged of the evils of greed brought about by consumerism, selfish ambitions that trample on human rights, religious and ethnic racism and other prejudices that foster injustice and violence. We must guard and fight against these evils – 'drive them away' – for they destroy both humanity and the human community. Paul and Silas were jailed because they opposed vested interest and evil.

✳ *O holy and gracious God, there are evils in our midst.*
  Give us the will, the courage and the power
  to 'drive them away'.

To bring deliverance

In contrast to Lydia (verses 14-15), the jailer's conversion came in a dramatic fashion, and there was another difference. Lydia was a Gentile and a business woman. She was already a worshipper of God when the Lord opened her heart and she responded. She was baptized with her household and her home became a centre of hospitality for the early missionaries. In contrast the jailer must have been hardened by his life and work. It took an earthquake to shake him into fear and ask the question, 'Sirs, what must I do to be saved?' Paul's answer was clear and precise, 'Put your trust in the Lord Jesus and you will be saved.' The jailer's genuine repentance was expressed as he washed the wounds of his prisoners, brought them to his home and fed them; he was baptized and shared the joy of his new faith with his entire family, and he faced the authorities without fear the next day. God is no respecter of persons. God moves in mysterious ways to bring men and women to repentance.

*✴ O Lord of love and compassion,
deliver us from our pride, our selfishness,
our prejudices and our fears.*

Thursday May 17   *Acts 17.1-15*

To witness to the resurrection

Each year in November we commemorate the life of Dr Daniel McGilvary and other missionaries who came to Northern Thailand in the late 19th century amid great opposition from religious and secular authorities. At one time, Dr McGilvary and his colleagues were advised to leave the kingdom because of increasing persecution, but he refused and said, 'I could not see that it is the will of Providence that mission should be abandoned.' The early missionaries in Thailand faced great difficulties, but they had faith and hope that God in his own time would bless the seeds they were sowing and bring a great harvest.

Paul met great opposition in Thessalonica and other places where he preached the gospel: 'in city after city the Holy Spirit assures me that imprisonment and hardships await me' (20.23). Only his faith in the Christ who suffered and rose again kept him going. Mission partners who have laboured through the ages in many parts of the world have been similarly inspired and emboldened by their faith in the resurrected Christ, and by the encouragement and support they received from the people with whom they worked.

*✴ O God of the cross and resurrection,
pave the way
for your Kingdom to be realized on earth.*

Friday May 18   *Acts 17.16-23*

To discover the unknown God

At the time of writing there is a report by Associated Press, being published in newspapers around the world, of a prayer booklet released by a certain fundamentalist faction claiming that Hindus have 'darkness in their hearts that no lamp can dispel'. The statement has ignited protest from Hindus all over the world. The arrogance of this statement is the kind of attitude that antagonized many people of other faiths during the 19th century missionary movement. As Christians we cannot make absolute claim that we have the only answer. Paul's understanding of the 'Unknown God' helps us to realize that God is at work in all places and at all times. Some missionaries spoke of 'bringing God to the heathen' as if God can be carried in a basket! MAC Warren writes, 'Our first task in approaching another people, another culture, another religion, is to take off our shoes, for the place we are approaching is holy. Else... we may forget that God was here before our arrival' (*A Handbook of Theological English,* Peter Sewell (SPCK).

✳ *O Creator and Lord of heaven and earth,*
  help us to be tolerant and humble
  as we share our faith with other people.

Saturday May 19   *Acts 17.24-34*

To live in the being of God

One of my favourite childhood stories was the story of Pinocchio, the wooden doll who became a boy. At first he did not have a developed conscience and little Jimminy Cricket functioned in that role, telling Pinocchio what to do and what not to do. The problem was that he would run away and get into trouble. 'If I could only get inside of him,' Jimminy Cricket would say, 'then I could be with him all the time and help him.' This is the goal of our journey to maturity – when concepts of right or wrong, which are given to us by our parents and society, become internalized so that we want to do what is right on our own. Isn't this part of what it means to say, 'in him we live and move, in him we exist' (verse 28)? Isn't it the goal of every Christian, to internalize God's purposes so that they become our desire and joy? This is something we have in common with other faiths. Buddhists, for example, have a tradition that the path to happiness is to bring the body and mind into harmony with the heart, with the environment and with society. We can agree with this because we believe that God who created the world and all that is in it is 'the universal giver of life and breath', indeed of everything.

✳ *O God in whom we live and move*
  and have our being,
  help us to live in harmony with all that lives.

FOR REFLECTION – alone or with a group

● What is a 'missionary'? Today we talk of 'mission partners'. Reflect on the reasons for the development of this new title. What challenge does it make to the way we carry out God's mission in our own community?

121

● How can Christians work together with people of other faiths in order to realize a truly human community?

FOR ACTION

Check your denominational prayer calendar for the names of mission partners your church supports. Pray for one of them and write a letter of encouragement to him/her today.

NEW ROADS AHEAD
4. Do not be afraid

Notes based on the New International Version by
Ebere O Nze

Eberechukwu Nze, a Nigerian theologian and former principal of Methodist Theological Institute, Umuahia, Abia State, has travelled widely and represented the Methodist Church Nigeria in many international conferences, workshops and seminars. His graduate and postgraduate studies were done in the USA and Ireland. He is now Bishop of Abakaliki in Ebonyi State.

Fear is an enemy of progress. It creates doubts about the unknown and blindfolds the eyes of vision. Fear builds anxiety which distorts logical reasoning and breaks down bridges of faith. Fear can kill. When it diffuses courage, we stumble because we are not standing on the secure foundation of belief and trust in God. No wonder, then, that the words 'Fear not' appear so many times in the Bible.

As we read the passages for this week, let us draw strength from the fact that God, who spoke words of courage to people like us in the past, speaks to us today with the same power. God does not change because our God is an eternal Being. With God, each new day brings a uniqueness which paves new roads for us to tread.

6th Sunday of Easter, May 20   Acts 18.1-17
The gospel defies attack

It is a common experience for mission partners and preachers to face stiff opposition when their message threatens a people's cultural and moral practices. This was Paul's experience when he arrived in Corinth, and when he met Aquila and Priscilla.

When every avenue of work seems closed to us, God opens up another way: the expulsion of Aquila and Priscilla from Rome brought them to Corinth where their support meant so much to Paul, and later on their house became a meeting place for the church (1 Corinthians 16.19).

After Paul's initial success in the synagogue and outside, it was not surprising that he was attacked for his preaching. But he had a vision (verses 9-10), in which the Lord encouraged him to continue to speak in Corinth, for there were many people there who needed to hear the gospel. His mission there led to the conversion of influential men like Titus Justus and Crispus the ruler of the synagogue whom Paul baptized. Even Gallio, the proconsul of Achaia, decreed that Paul had every right to preach the gospel.

As we meet other people, do we have courage and sufficient confidence in the love of God in Christ, to share our faith with them? It could be for them the beginning of the work of salvation.

✳ *May the faith of those who have gone before us*
inspire us with boldness to proclaim the message
of the Kingdom. In Jesus' name we pray. Amen

Monday May 21 *Acts 18.18-28*

Mission strengthens believers

Paul drew much inspiration from his success at Corinth, and this encouraged him to continue to spread the gospel, moving on to new places. 'Iron sharpens iron', they say and, likewise, faith sharpens faith. Our Lord's victory is a continuous one unless we stop co-operating with him. Aquila and Priscilla saw how much strength Paul was given by God to face opposition in Corinth, and this inspired them to be faithful in their witness. In turn, they helped to sharpen and deepen the faith of Apollos. God used them to raise up an outstanding witness to the truth, one who was to be a special blessing to the church in Corinth.

There are many Christians whose faith and sense of mission are shallow, and others who have encountered the Lord in a more personal and deeper sense. But for all, both ordinary and great, we become more effective witnesses when we are aware that we share an experience of the living Christ. It was this ordinary couple Priscilla and Aquila, who were tent-makers and who had been expelled from Rome, who instructed the well-educated Apollos to become the instrument of God's message of salvation. And it was through listening to the simple message of the gospel that rulers of the synagogue in Corinth became influential Christians.

If you want to measure your greatness, do so through the mirror of the gospel.

✳ *Dear Lord, you lived a life of simplicity,*
but today your name is so great and widely known.
May your Holy Spirit teach me
to understand you more clearly, that I may
serve you better, in the precious name of Jesus. Amen

The rewards of perseverance

There is much that we can learn from Paul's ministry in Ephesus about the great things God can do for us when we overcome fear. Paul's faith had been jolted by the fierce persecution in Corinth but the vision and encouraging words of God – 'Do not be afraid; keep on speaking... For I am with you' – sustained him and enabled him to move forward and be used by God again.

Just as Aquila and Priscilla had found that Apollos needed their help, so also Paul found a group of disciples in Ephesus who knew only the 'baptism of John', and he led them to receive the Holy Spirit.

The Holy Spirit leads us from mere religious knowledge and from the frustrations of our inadequacies to recognize the grace of God at work in our lives, and to know the peace which only the Spirit can give. When we really open our lives to the activity of the Spirit and allow the Spirit to work through us, then God can use us in ways beyond our imagining. God is looking for hands, like ours, to use.

Today's reading also demonstrates how, in conquering fear, Paul dealt a death-blow to superstition and the power of magic in Ephesus. This act opened new opportunities for the evangelization of Asia Minor.

What superstitions, charlatans and materialistic values exist in your community? How will your living by the name of Christ be used by God to demonstrate God's truth and to redeem the lost?

✷ *Lord Jesus, your presence casts out fear*
and your words are so reassuring. Open our eyes
and minds to perceive the truth of your Word
that we may grow in faith and live every day
with courage. In Jesus' name we pray.

Challenging today's gods

In today's reading, Paul challenged the gods of the Ephesian world. Even Demetrius the silversmith testified that Paul's witness in Ephesus had brought the people of Asia to consider the way of Christ as an alternative to the worship of Artemis. And the city clerk acknowledged that Paul had done nothing disrespectful or sacrilegious towards their goddess. The rabble-rousers were the Ephesians themselves.

The real issue behind this incident was the vested interest of silversmiths and goldsmiths who were losing business; the god they were protecting was their own materialism. Isn't the same true today? It is also true that this god will ultimately be rendered impotent. Those who spend their lives defending such a god will be put to shame. Our Lord Jesus Christ cares for and protects those who live by his power.

The truth of the gospel destabilizes the magical powers and gods of every age and breaks solidarity with evil powers.

✳ *Dear Lord, you are the source*
of every power that overcomes. Give us the faith
that can destroy the idols we have made
that we may live by the victory of the gospel.
In Jesus' name we pray.

Ascension Day, May 24　　　　　　　　　　　　*Acts 20.17-24*

Faithful to the call

Today as we celebrate the ascension of our Lord (Luke 24.50-53), and recall the awesome responsibilities which he left upon the shoulders of the first apostles, we also reflect on Paul's farewell speech to the elders at Ephesus. He outlines his calling and the principles by which he had carried out God's mission. He had faced danger and opposition, and now faced the future with confidence.

From personal experience he admonished the elders to be faithful to their responsibilities as shepherds of the flock God had committed to their charge. I know from my own experience, as a bishop of the Methodist Church Nigeria, what it is like to preach the gospel in today's world. We face opposition, trials and threats, both within and outside the Church. The infection of the 'world' is never far away and wherever there is truth, falsehood attacks it. Paul's message is real today.

God has chosen people who serve him humbly and faithfully, and God who calls us to this service does not abandon us on the way. Like Paul, we are to testify to God's grace. Are we going to be faithful to the end?

✳ *Our gracious God, you call people in every age*
to witness to the greatness of your gospel
and the sufficiency of your grace.
May all whom you have called to total commitment
experience the fullness of your power.
In Jesus' name we pray.

Recognizing the essentials of the call

The call to serve Christ is the most delicate and sensitive one we can ever experience. It leads us to speak 'soul to soul', as Paul did to the Ephesian elders. Sometimes, in the African context, it seems that the ministry of the Church is looked at as an easy career. This is far from the truth. The call to ministry is the most demanding and challenging.

Paul knew this, and he was anxious that the Ephesians should realize it too. They were overseers of the flock of God, called and chosen by God. As Ezekiel had emphasized, they must shepherd the sheep and not lead them astray (Ezekiel 34). It is rare to see, in both Church and State, leaders who will lay down their lives for the people they are called to nurture and lead.

Paul also reminded them of the danger ahead. But for those who trust the Lord, this will be a means of keeping their faith intact and the Church pure. Jesus' victory was won through suffering, and he beckons us to follow in his way. 'Be of good courage, I have overcome the world,' says Jesus. The Lord who calls us to serve gives strength to accomplish every task.

Whatever your calling, can people under your care discover the love which God revealed to us in Jesus Christ?

✳ *Victorious Lord, you do not make vain promises*
to those you call to serve. Give us grace to depend
upon your conquering power, that leaders at every level
may work through the difficulties of leadership
with hope and joy, through Jesus Christ our Lord.

Obeying to the end

Wherever Paul went, there was a Christian community waiting to welcome him and wishing that he might stay longer when the time came for his departure. This still happens. One of the great privileges of belonging to the Church is the discovery that you have friends all over the world: wherever you go, you are sure to find a Christian community who will welcome and care for you.

The reference to the daughters of Philip the evangelist throws interesting light on the ministry of gifted women, and supports the conviction that God has called both men and women to serve as ministers of his Church.

Paul was now set to make his final journey to Jerusalem. Paul is an outstanding example of Christian leadership. Nothing could have been more definite than the warning of the disciples at Tyre and the symbolic and vocal prophecy of Agabus at Caesarea, but nothing could deter him from the course he had chosen. He persisted in his readiness to suffer all things for the name of the Lord Jesus. The narrative here is reminiscent of Jesus setting his face to go to Jerusalem (Luke 9.51), and preparing his followers for what was to happen there (Luke 9.22).

✳ *In your faithfulness, O Lord, we have believed*
that you will ever be our Lord. We pray
that you will guide us until the end of the journey,
that we may ever dwell with you.
Through our Saviour Jesus Christ we pray. Amen

FOR REFLECTION – alone or with a group

● Find other places in the Bible where God says, 'Do not fear' or 'Do not be afraid'. Make a note of the times during the period of this exercise when you have feared situations. Share your findings with others in your church or fellowship group.

● Try to assess any progress you have made in developing confidence.

NEW ROADS AHEAD
5. The Spirit leads us on

Notes based on the Revised English Bible by
Christopher Hughes Smith

Chris Hughes Smith, a Supernumerary Methodist minister living in Nottingham, was on the staff of the Student Christian Movement, and served in circuits in Leicester, Birmingham and Lancaster (UK). Whilst Chairman of the Birmingham District, he was Joint President of the Birmingham Council of Christian Churches. He was General Secretary of the Methodist Division of Education and Youth and latterly has been President of the National Christian Education Council. He was President of the Methodist Conference in 1985.

Your church today is primary evidence for the resurrection of Jesus Christ. The epistles, which describe the character and quality of life in Christ, are as directly for us as they were for first century congregations who knew Christ alive among them. The same is true for St John's Gospel which emerged in Gentile Ephesus. If the writer heard Christ, among the congregation in Ephesus, say, I am the bread of life, the light of the world, the good shepherd...' then, with the living Christ among us in our congregations, there is the eternal possibility of our hearing Christ too. This gives St John's Gospel a new kind of historical significance!

7th Sunday of Easter, May 27   *John 14.15-24*
Preparing for Pentecost
The Christian calendar is being formed. John wants to prepare the congregation in Ephesus for Pentecost. How does the Spirit come? Can the Spirit actually be experienced as Pentecost is celebrated?

Preparation for Pentecost starts with love, obedience and expectancy (as in Acts 1.4 and 8). The coming of the Spirit is the response of the Father to the request of the Son and replaces traumatic emptiness with a sense of fulfilment. Fellowship is the experience of the Spirit – 'We the life of God shall know...' The life of God is expressed in Christ's phrases – 'I am in my Father' and 'you in me and I in you' (verse 20). Love, obedience and expectancy are not qualifications which the coming of the Spirit

129

rewards. They open up life and being for the indwelling of God, on God's initiative. This is how the mind of Christ understands the Spirit, on the basis of his own experience. Jesus' knowledge that he is sent by God is the origin of his sense that the Father will send the Spirit again and again.

✳ *Send us the Spirit of thy Son,*
  To make the depths of Godhead known,
    To make us share the life divine.

Charles Wesley (1707-88)

Monday May 28   *John 14.25-31* *

Expecting...from God

Leaders with insight prepare their followers for the future. Jesus' preparations for his death ('departure' or 'exodus' in Luke 9.31) were sometimes obvious and sometimes subtle. The instruction to those healed to say nothing, 'the Messianic secret', may have been such a subtle preparation, Jesus storing knowledge of his ministry in the experience of individuals, a memory to be stirred to life when the first Easter preachers came. 'Yes, we remember him,' the hearers might say, and the work of the Spirit begins in a new group. What is to be expected is not the disintegration resulting from the appalling horror of Jesus' death, but a coming together of friends who centre on him. This integration, in Jerusalem, Judaea, Samaria, and now, John hopes – in the Gentile world of Ephesus – is the wholeness that is the purpose of creation. Nevertheless, the brutal inertia of evil wants to prevent the coming of the Spirit. Love and obedience to the Provider, the *Abba,* which are the core of Jesus' being, are the only language on offer as testimony to the world. Love and obedience provide enough energy for moving forward to where the Spirit is given.

✳ *Come, thou witness of his dying;*
    Come, remembrancer divine,
  Let us feel thy power, applying
    Christ to every soul, and mine.   *Charles Wesley*

Tuesday May 29   *John 15.18-27*

Facing evil

Christ's will sustains faith (not 'belonging to the world') in face of impossible odds. A Methodist minister, tortured by being kept standing for five days, asked his interrogator, 'Are you afraid to die? I'm not.' And the interrogation ended.

Hostile forces subject the friends of Jesus to hatred. Christ's choice of his friends is ridiculed. But the suffering of Christ is both the clue to the meaning of ridicule and hate, and the source of strength and grace to face them. Hostile attitudes to the friends of Jesus are signs of attitudes to Jesus and show lack of knowledge of God. They make the cross of Jesus contemporary. Indeed Jesus' ministry continues to be provocative of evil. Hating God summarizes the hostility provoked by goodness.

Pentecost is the surge of love and life, originating in the same energy that sent Jesus. The Spirit's energy points to Jesus, and Jesus' followers are assured in their own testimony. They have been Christ's from the beginning – even in Ephesus at the end of the first century, or wherever you are in 2001!

✳ *Though the sons of night blaspheme,*
More there are with us than them;
God with us, we cannot fear;
Fear, ye fiends, for Christ is here!   Charles Wesley

Wednesday May 30   *John 16.1-15*

Finding reality

In a dominant culture steeped in Christianity, Christian minds become preoccupied by maintaining links with cultural power. Consciences become blunted to issues that put power at risk through confrontation with the culture. With notable exceptions – the Confessing Church in Nazi Germany or Moravians under the Holy Roman Empire – Eastern and Western Churches have suffered this dilemma for centuries. Dissenters bear the consequences of holding the faith: exclusion from society, even death. The killers – themselves enmeshed by culture and faith – believe themselves to be servants of God. Forewarning is strength. Thus, 'setting forth Christ as evidently crucified before people's eyes' (John Wesley's definition of preaching) and the Eucharist bring strength for the ravages of human life. Jesus does not invite us to 'unyielding despair' (Bertrand Russell); he promises his 'other self', the Spirit, who will give growing understanding of the profoundest issues – sin, justice and judgement. Truth will be revealed 'in the toils, the conflicts, the sufferings we shall go through in Christ's fellowship' (Schweitzer). Discipleship is being engaged by and in the dynamic life of God, Father, Son and Holy Spirit – for the world.

✳ *My talents, gifts and graces, Lord,*
   Into thy blessed hands receive;
And let me live to preach thy word,
   And let me to thy glory live.

Charles Wesley

Thursday May 31   *Luke 24.44-53**

Sovereignty, suffering and sending

The end of the Easter appearances is the beginning of Easter for the rest of us. The parting from Jesus did not create despair, but led to fulfilment and joy. The glory of transfiguration (Luke 9.28-36) is the fulfilment in Jesus of Moses and Elijah. Here is added fulfilment of divine worship from the Psalms. The Old Testament is the taproot for Christian spirituality, and the experience of fulfilment resolves the tension between continuity with Hebrew Scripture and the discontinuity of the Christian tradition. We should all like to know the references made in verses 46 and 47! The Servant Songs (Isaiah 42.1-4; 49.1-6; 50.4-9; and 52.13 to 53.12) provide ideas for interpreting Jesus. Luke, with the other Gospel writers, expresses the power of Christ's sovereignty by linking the Messianic King of Psalm 2 with the Servant who suffers but whose suffering brings light to nations outside Israel. The 'sending' will happen again and again. On their return to Jerusalem, did these disciples sing Palm 110.1 to celebrate the sovereignty of Jesus?

✳ *Sent by my Lord, on you I call,*
   The invitation is to all;
      Come, all the world; come, sinner, thou!
      All things in Christ are ready now.   *Charles Wesley*

Friday June 1   *Isaiah 44.1-8**

Led to life

The context of the Pentecostal gift of the Spirit is creation. There is no apartheid between the spiritual and the material, the personal and the natural world, the individual and the group. All human awareness is available for the attempt to describe the indescribable: birth, rain on bone-dry earth, flourishing trees at the water-side, new and renewed identity.

The Servant Songs come from this section of Isaiah. It took the exile – being away from their own land, from the hard-won settings of painfully formed institutions – to bring insight into the work of God as Creator. Without the signs of God in the communal life of settled Israel, the people of God discovered signs of God in the natural world (Isaiah 40). It is the Servant of the Lord who understands the signs. The inward sense of God and God's inclusive activity belong to one another. Time is God's. The eternal challenge is that the individual-in-community be outwardly true to inward awareness, and find courage to testify to others in the same way that God's testimony has come to the community.

✳ *Come then, O Lord, thy light impart,*
  The faith that bids our terrors cease;
Into thy love direct my heart,
  Into thy way of perfect peace.   Charles Wesley

Saturday June 2   *Ephesians 4.7-16**
Sovereignty and service
John Wesley explained Methodism by these verses. They occur in the Ordination Service. Through Christ's sovereignty, God uses individuality to shower blessings on the human race (verse 8). His purpose is to fill the universe, and this is against a world view where earth was flat and heaven a dome. Though the years since the time of Jesus are short compared with the history of life or the age of the planet, the quality of life perceived in Jesus is the breakthrough into new possibilities for all. Epistles and Gospels consistently testify that Jesus in the midst of humanity fulfils creation itself. This implies that humans are interdependent and that creation is capable of communicating God. The gifts are specific, with the persistent purpose of maturing humanity in the measure of Christ. The Church is first the fulfilment, and then an agent, of love. Growth towards maturity happens in two ways – speaking the truth, not in destructive anger, but in love that enables positive response, and the functioning of each part, using the gift God has given. The body of Christ, thus built up, is no self-serving empire, but a self-spending servant.

✳ *Move, and actuate, and guide:*
Divers gifts to each divide;
Placed according to thy will,
Let us all our work fulfil.   Charles Wesley

FOR REFLECTION – alone or with a group
● Consider the communal life of your congregation. Is it out-going? Do members have open opportunity to talk to one

another about Christ? Do members value one another? Does your congregation face or dodge the tragedies (the 'Judas factors') of human experience? Are they 'all together in one place'?

- At what points do you recognize in your congregation 'the harvest of the Spirit' (love, joy, peace, patience, kindness, goodness, fidelity, gentleness and self-control – Galatians 5.22-23)?

FOR ACTION

If it is impossible to focus answers to these points, why not aim at preparing your mind to respond to them at Pentecost next year? The Church and your congregation remain the material with which God is working!

Pentecost, June 3   *Acts 2.1-21**

Fusion, then mission

Not a journalist's record, this testimony to Pentecost is contemporary. By it, every group of Christians may understand their own experience. Today's remembrance of Pentecost holds the possibility that the gift will happen again – and again. The previous chapter explains Christ's command and promise and the disciples' deepening awareness of their worth to one another. The searing memory of Judas remains. The Spirit comes and the individuals are made a community. The new bond of life – God's self-sharing – depends not on common genes, nationality or geographical origin. Jesus is the centre of the group's allegiance; the selection of Matthias shows that (Acts 1.15-26). The community is accessible because its life is persistently out-going. Pentecost reverses Babel, and the gospel of Jesus breaks out of its geographical/cultural enclave and is heard in ways that each group can own.

And the interpretation by Peter? Joel 2.28-31 (quoted by Peter in verses 17-21) is one of the few places where the Spirit of God is described as coming to a group of people. The God-inspired community exists for all humankind in its differing social status, gender and age. Pentecost points forward. Will the Spirit come to your congregation today?

✴ *Assembled here with one accord,*
   Calmly we wait the promised grace,
 The purchase of our dying Lord:
   Come, Holy Ghost, and fill the place.   *Charles Wesley*

Community speaks to community

An introductory letter from a prospective visitor to your congregation spells out what Jesus has done for the human race. Paul is 'in the Spirit'. Though a great individual, he is expressing, coherently for the Roman world, the intellectual ferment of the Spirit-created fellowship. The work of Christ is interpreted in each generation and culture. In the West, 'democracy' is often seen as the sum-total of individuals. This omits the multitude of interrelating groups. In countries with political freedom, the sense that Christians are bonded together in the life of God has been dissolved by rampant individualism and competitiveness – in business, commerce, politics, education, and sport. Competitiveness brings the danger of fragmentation and total disintegration – shown by oppression and exploitation. Into this maelstrom, God sends the Son. Ordered life is not denied but fulfilled, uncovering the truth of the human condition. The Spirit's life, Christ's parting gift, is wholeness, wherein none feels threatened or diminished. The wholeness fulfils the purpose of God in all things. Right relationships with God and creation are restored.

✳ *Thou only art able to bless,*
   And make the glad nations obey,
 And bid the dire enmity cease,
   And bow the whole world to thy sway.   *Charles Wesley*

Life together

From a coach between Capernaum and Cana in Galilee, I saw a dozen men walking through a field. This is the scale of the beginning of God's work in Jesus. Christian congregations can think of themselves as insignificant for God's purpose. That leaves out the Spirit, through whom Christian congregations have the power of life working within them. Again, Western individualism and cultural imprisonment (by boundaries and buildings) ignore this. The health-giving power of a healthy community is glimpsed from time to time. The life of the Christian community is health-giving and life-giving because of its relationship with God, and is the result of 'justification' – a right relationship with God. The power of God, bringing Jesus through death to life, engages with illness, ageing and mortality. When the Church fails as a community, the merciful God, not limited by that failure, acts through other communities – families, sports clubs, campaigns, work groups, unions and associations – but these are less than, and different from, the possibility available through Christ. And the difference can be as sharp as that between life and death.

✶ *King of Glory! Soul of bliss!*
Everlasting life is this,
Thee to know, thy power to prove,
Thus to sing, and thus to love: Alleluia!   *Charles Wesley*

Wednesday June 6   *Romans 8.14-17**

Coming into our own

John Wesley used these verses frequently. Clothe the word 'Spirit' in the text with your experience, however limited, of Christian community. Understanding is hindered by forgetting the earthliness of those in whom the Spirit dwells. The Spirit releases people from fear. Communal fear destroys the acceptance of diversity. In Northern Ireland, prior to the outbreak of violence, fear polarized those Protestants and Catholics who had lived in one another's communities. Violence feeds on fear.

The Spirit-community is delivered from both, and lives in dependence on the loving care of God as Father. During a holiday in Israel, we heard a child call to his father, 'Abba, Abba!' Rituals of intimacy and confidence, in face of contrary appearances, are rooted in Christian assurance. Many oppressed, disregarded or scorned people – like the first disciples – become truly human in the Spirit-community of real people. This community depends not at all on social status, worldly achievement, or even moral purity. It is alive with the life of God and in the process of coming into its own – suffering with Christ, and with him entering more deeply into God.

✶ *Away with our fears,*
Our troubles and tears:
The Spirit is come,
The witness of Jesus returned to his home.   *Charles Wesley*

Thursday June 7   *Romans 8.18-25*

In passionate anticipation

Connections are now made which set the vision of the Spirit-community ablaze. The company at Rome, tiny in power compared with the might of the Empire, is addressed by one who knows similar little groups around the Mediterranean. They do not know that the Empire will carry the Christian gospel to its furthermost frontiers. But the ultimate connection of these congregations, and yours, is with the universe itself. The universe is on tip-toe anticipating the glorious liberty which is the expectation of these groups, contrary to superficial appearance. Contemporary suffering is all too real. 'The cross is not some theological invention. It is what the world does again and again to those who disclose what God is doing' (Michael Wilson). Paul is aware of a 'dolorsphere', a layer of suffering throughout the universe, which is endured, like birth-pangs, because it will lead to undreamed-of life. The Spirit-community (your local one, and/or the thousands of people in many countries who read this passage today) is likewise looking forward to liberation. As Seamus Heaney said on the first day of the 1999 Northern Irish government, 'Hope and history will rhyme'.

✳ *Hasten the joyful day*
    Which shall my sins consume,
  When old things shall be passed away,
    And all things new become.

                                                     Charles Wesley

Friday June 8   *Romans 8.26-30*

From weakness to glory

The work of the Spirit is not limited by the way we might measure people's faith. The inward life of the 'weakest' group, as a whole and through individual members, is made strong in the eternal power of the Spirit. God, persistent in will and purpose, knows his own ways. These verses cause endless discussion about free will and predestination, though the latter word is avoided in modern translations. Some of the difficulty is avoided if the verses are not exclusive. So little is known or understood about the ways of God, but we know God through Jesus! In a culture 'opaque to the gospel' (Basil Hume), Western Christians become dimly aware that 'something is going on'. The awesome speed of technological change creates further bewilderment, and uncontrollable multinationals seem to threaten humanity. In the midst of our puzzlement, with the text and with life, Christ emerges, establishing a relationship with us. The purpose of God's will is here described as the creation of a large family of siblings who will be led ultimately to know the presence of God's glory, fully human at last.

❋ Knees and hearts to him we bow;
    Of our flesh and of our bone,
Jesus is our brother now,
    And God is all our own.   *Charles Wesley*

Saturday June 9   *Revelation 1.9-20*

The Spirit and the glory of Christ

Institutions of the Church often hide the reality and simplicity of life in the Spirit. The imprisoned preacher wants to be with his flock on the Lord's Day. The Word, usually spoken, can be written for them. 'In the Spirit', distance is overcome. Fifty years ago, a Singapore Methodist said to me, 'You're going nine thousand miles home. One day you may be a minister. Never forget, however far apart we are, we are together in him.'

'In the Spirit', the Word spoken and written lives on after its 'first time', and becomes the Word for different situations. The Spirit is the go-between in space and time. Above all, Christ, here described by many references, is indescribably radiant with the glory of God. At first sight remote from us, 'in the Spirit', these verses show that whatever our agenda or activity, Christ is Lord of the Church and of congregations. The Church is caught up in the life of God, Father, Son and Holy Spirit.

❋ Father, Son, and Holy Ghost,
    One in Three, and Three in One,
As by the celestial host,
    Let thy will on earth be done;
Praise by all to thee be given,
    Glorious Lord of earth and heaven.   *Charles Wesley*

FOR REFLECTION – alone or with a group

● Traditionally we have seen guidance as an awareness in individuals – of a call, or a way forward through a difficulty. How can we develop in a congregation the sense that the Spirit leads its whole life? Is it true that the mechanisms are in place, but that we do not use them in this way?

● In 1 Corinthians 12, Paul uses the limbs of a body as an illustration of Christian fellowship. What steps can we take in our congregations to see that both the wholeness of the congregation and the support of the whole for each limb (member) are effective ?

● A 'water-table' is the way we have of talking about the nearness of water to the surface. Is the 'Spirit-table' a long way below, or near to, the surface in your congregation, or Synod, or Assembly, or Conference? How is the life of the Spirit amongst you shown?

FOR ACTION

Find a way of making a link with a group of Christians who are on the other side of a barrier (ethnic, political, cultural, geographical or denominational). Then find out about Christ from them. Expect new power (energy, maturity, drive, and love) to be given. Celebrate the outcome!

NEW ROADS AHEAD
6. Letting go of the past (Galatians)

Notes based on the New Revised Standard Version by
Brian Haymes

Brian Haymes, minister of Bloomsbury Central Baptist Church, London, is author of the Looking At' series (IBRA). He has served as President of the Baptist Union of Great Britain.

Paul's letter to the Galatians is full of energy and passion. Right from the start we are aware that something crucial is at stake. For Paul, it is nothing less than the gospel. The work God has done in Jesus is one of liberation. This is the epistle, above all, of Christian liberty.

The fact is that Christians can lose the liberty which God gives in the Spirit through Christ. Christians can return to old habits and ways which enslave rather than express that life which is God's gift. Attitudes and practices of the past can become more important to us than the creative experience of the life in Christ. How did we come to be free people before God? Was it what we did and do? Or is it what God has done and keeps on doing? We shall find this ancient letter from Paul not only taking us back to foundations but also challenging us about new roads ahead.

Trinity Sunday June 10   *Galatians 1.1-10**
A blunt beginning

Paul's letters usually begin with notes of thankfulness, often followed by a word of greeting highlighting some aspect of God's salvation. But the letter to the Galatians has only the briefest of greetings and affirmations. Paul, it seems, cannot wait to get to the point.

In this briefest of beginnings the main issues are being marked out. Paul states clearly that his calling is from God and not of human authorization. He tells the Galatians that he is astonished that they have already turned to another 'gospel'. He pronounces an absolute condemnation on those who preach anything other than the gospel he proclaimed. What is going on?

Clearly some in the churches are suggesting that Paul is not a proper apostle. This calls into question his whole life and work, amounting to saying that the Damascus Road incident was a sham.

More than that, they are suggesting that Paul has trimmed his preaching to gain human approval. He has distorted the gospel to his own ends. There can hardly be a more serious set of charges. Paul is blunt because nothing less than the truth of the gospel is at stake. Whenever that happens urgency and passion are required.

✳ *This is the day that God has made,*
We will rejoice and be glad in it.
We will not offer to God
Offerings that cost us nothing...
We will seek peace and pursue it.
In the name of the Trinity of Love,
One God in perfect community. Amen
The Iona Community Worship Book (Wild Goose Publications)

Monday June 11   *Galatians 1.11-24**

The gospel is the gift of God

There always have been arguments about authority in the Church. Who can speak for God? The Church has suffered from more than enough false prophets.

Paul, unusually, gives us some autobiographical details, but only for a special reason. He reminds his readers of his early life and his attempts to stamp out the message of Jesus Christ. But God met him on the Damascus Road and called him to proclaim Christ, even among the nations. So, for Paul, the message and the call to preach it are not of human origin. God has made known the gospel of Jesus Christ.

It is not Paul's personal status or reputation that he sees as being at stake. That is only of consequence in the context of the work of God and the revelation of Jesus Christ. Perhaps here we have a test for true servants of God. Do we care more for the gospel and its proclamation than our own reputation? Do we serve God, regardless of how others see us, or are we more concerned for ourselves? And are we willing to account for our calling to others?

✳ *Thank you, gracious God,*
for what you have done for us all in Jesus Christ.

Tuesday June 12   *Galatians 2.1-10*

Accountability

In the end every disciple and every Christian leader is accountable to God for their words and deeds. The responsibility to seek and do the will of God is laid on us all. There are tasks that God is asking us alone to do. So we pray that God will guide us and help us do his holy will.

Paul believes God has called him to preach the gospel among the nations. But he shows spiritual wisdom in consulting other Christians about this. He makes it clear that he is not trying to gain their approval but he is recognizing the importance of Christian fellowship.

One of the weaknesses of the Church, especially in the western world, is the way Christians can become very individualistic. We are not always so good at recognizing that God may well confirm his guiding through others. He may also tell us through them that we are on the wrong track! Paul went and talked with others, testing out this sense of calling from God to whom, in the last analysis, he is accountable. That is faith in the form of courage.

✶ *Father, thank you for the fellowship of the Church,*
and for all the ways you guide us.

Wednesday June 13   *Galatians 2.11-21**

The gospel at stake!

Peter's decision not to eat with Gentile Christians was too much for Paul. Peter might be an acknowledged leader in the Church but his actions contradicted the gospel. So Paul spoke out boldly.

It was Paul's conviction that what God had done in Jesus was for everybody, Jews and Gentiles. What was more, people were put right with God not on the basis of how correctly they kept the law given to Israel, but on whether they trusted God's gracious work in Jesus.

Paul had tried to live righteously by 'the Law' and found it impossible. No one could ever justify themselves before God if that was the requirement. But in Jesus, in his death and resurrection, God had shown his love for us, saving love that we can trust in faith. It is God's grace that saves us. If we could ever justify ourselves then there is no point in Jesus' death. Peter's actions seem to imply that keeping 'the Law' was still the way. He had to be opposed for the sake of the gospel of grace.

✶ *Thank you, living God, that you come and live*
in all who trust your saving grace.

Some very blunt speaking

Paul's passion is obvious. The urgency of the letter is no better
expressed than at the moment when he called the Galatian
Christians 'fools'. What has provoked this outburst?

It is not easy to say but many teachers think that some of
Paul's opponents are saying that simply putting your faith in what
God has done in Jesus is not enough. Perhaps they were
teaching people that they must also keep the old law of Israel to
be saved. Whatever it was, it amounted to saying that Jesus
Christ was not enough.

Paul appeals to experience. The Galatians know that the Holy
Spirit has been at work among them. Now, how did that happen?
Was it because they kept the law, or because of Jesus? Was God
so evidently at work among them because of their performance or
because they had trusted God?

We ought not to think this is an old argument of long ago. All
Christians face the temptation of trying to add something of our
achieving to Christ. It often takes the form of cultural customs or
moral achievement. To imagine that we need to add anything to
what Christ has done is to deserve the title 'Fools'.

✱ *Gracious God, may our desire to serve you*
never replace our gratitude for what you have done for us.

An appeal to history

After appealing to the Galatians' experience, Paul now presents
an argument from history. It concerns Abraham whose obedient
trust in God was what brought Israel historically into being. No
one doubts that here was a truly great and righteous man. At the
back of this argument is the question: who are the true heirs of
God's promises to Abraham?

What made Abraham so special? It could not be that he kept
the law because the law had not yet been given. Abraham is
important as one who trusted God and that was 'reckoned to him
as righteousness'. On the basis of trusting the gracious promises
he went out into the future and God kept his promise that in
Abraham all nations will be blessed. So the true heirs of the
promises of God are those who, like Abraham, trust in the
faithfulness of God.

So who or what are we trusting in? Our own achievements?
The correctness of our theology? The moral quality of our life?

Our education, position, wealth, family, nationality? All these, because they are so good and valuable, can tempt us away from trusting the promises of God in Christ. Thank God for the example of Abraham.

✳ *Forgive us, living God, whenever we forget*
our roots in the history which tells of your grace.

Saturday June 16   *Galatians 3.19-29*

A truly revolutionary claim!

God's law and the gospel of grace are not in opposition to each other. Grace came first and then the law as a gift of grace to teach us how to live as God's people – but only until Christ came. Now that Christ has come the law is not our basic need, for now we are called to live by faith in the Christlike God. In Christ we are sisters and brothers, by faith.

Paul believes a new people of God is being brought into being. He speaks of baptism 'into Christ', putting on Christ. And all who are so baptized are called to a new way of life where the old distinctions drawn in the world are no longer significant.

National distinctions (Jew and Greek), social economic values (slave and free), gender differences (male or female), these are not decisive in Christ. Sadly we must admit that the Church has not always lived by this faith. We have participated in forms of educational, economic, nationalistic and sexist oppression of others. What a challenge for 'NEW ROADS AHEAD' to live out this vision where all are one in Christ!

✳ *Gracious Father, give us a vision of our one family*
united in Christ and help us to treat all who own your name
as sisters and brothers in him.

FOR REFLECTION – alone or with a group

● Reflect on Paul's affirmation of being justified by faith alone. Are there ways in which the churches you know make this difficult to believe?
● Discuss the response of Paul to Peter as described in chapter 2. What practices in today's Church might be a denial of the gospel?
● Arrange to meet with some Jewish people to talk about Abraham and the meaning of faith.

Abba, Son and Spirit

All around the world today Christians are gathering to worship God. We speak of God as Trinity. That word is not in the Bible but it is deep in the heart of our faith. God is One but is Creator, Saviour and Sanctifier; Father, Son and Holy Spirit.

In today's passage Paul brings together *Abba* (Aramaic, meaning 'Father'), the Son, and the Spirit. The Galatian churches may not know the word 'Trinity' but they have come to call out to God as *Abba* (as Jesus did). They do this because God sent his Son so that they might realize they are God's children. And this is no theory since God the Holy Spirit prompts them and us to cry out to the God who has sought us in his love. We are God's children and heirs: what a thought to ponder on the Lord's Day!

The Galatians are still fussing about special days and seasons. Is this another way by which the Galatians think they will be saved by being extra religious? It is important to keep the Lord's Day but that does not save us. Salvation is the gift of God, the triune God whose life we are called to share.

✷ *May the grace our Lord Jesus Christ,*
the love of God our Father,
and the fellowship of the Holy Spirit be with us all today.

Pastoral pain

This is a deeply touching and tender part of the letter. Paul has been furious about the Galatians, even to the extent of calling them 'fools'. But that was only an expression of the pastoral heart he has for the church members. He recalls how they first welcomed him and would have given anything of themselves to help the one who brought them the good news. But now the much beloved friends have been led astray and turned against their first pastor.

Paul uses the image of a mother, caring for children, and bearing birth pains until the child comes to life and health, until the Church 'has Christ formed in you'. Mothers care. They risk their lives that children should be born. Until the end they always seek the well-being of their offspring.

What a powerful image this is. It reminds us that passionate care sometimes shows itself in fierce and penetrating ways. That is what love does. The opposite of love is not hate, for we only hate what we feel strongly about. The opposite of love is indifference, which is not caring. Paul cares, passionately. But then so does the Christ Paul so eagerly serves.

✴ *Passionate God,*
thank you for those who care so much for us.
Thank you for our pastors.

Tuesday June 19   *Galatians 4.21-31*

Law and promise

Paul uses a kind of argument that would have been well understood in his day. The ancient teachers often used allegorical interpretations of Scripture. An allegory is a story understood symbolically. The characters in the story are interpreted in other terms and a deeper meaning is seen in them.

Paul likens Hagar's son to those who are slaves to a way of life based on keeping the covenant of law. No one in that condition would ever be free. Their religion is a load they must carry to show how righteous they are. But Isaac was the child of the covenant of grace and promise, as are all the true children of Abraham and Sarah. What characterizes these people is their trust in the promises of the faithful, gracious God. They are not slaves to law but free people.

This is Paul's great theme re-emerging. Those who put their trust in Christ are set free from the burdens of legalism. They are not required to justify themselves but to trust in Christ their Saviour. The difference is between a religion of duty and a life of joy. The paradox is that it is in Christ's service that we find our freedom.

✴ *Free us, O God,*
from all unnecessary desires to justify ourselves to you.
May we trust your promises
and enjoy your free, life-giving grace.

Wednesday June 20   *Galatians 5.1-12*

Freedom in Christ

Christ freed us in order that we might be free. That is Paul's great theme. Those who think they can impress God enough by keeping all their religious scruples have set themselves on a treadmill from which there is no escape. Trying to fulfil all the law perfectly to justify themselves is like being in prison.

We notice the vehemence of Paul's language. So much is at stake, even today. We try to impress by what we do for God. Take the issue of baptism. There are differences of opinion about baptism. Should children be baptized, or only those who are able to declare their faith in Christ for themselves? These are important questions but it is not the outward act of baptism in any form that saves us. What matters is 'faith active in love'. If we decide to walk the road of religious achievements then there will be no end to it. We shall be as good as saying that, whatever God has done, more is needed and we shall supply it. But now we are trapped because there will always be more to do. But why are we doing all this if Christ has done what is necessary and liberated us to be free?

✳ *Help us, loving God, to have such faith in you*
  that we are free to live in love.

Thursday June 21   *Galatians 5.13-26**
Freedom, not licence

All this talk of freedom can be heady stuff. Does this mean we are free to do anything? Does the law of God no longer have any significance for us? Some of Paul's opponents were probably suggesting that he was advocating a very lax attitude to life where anything goes because Christ has set us free.

This is a travesty of Paul's position. Paul understands the Christian life to consist in love for God and therefore love for our neighbour. He can identify ways of living which are a denial of the life in Christ. He calls them 'desires of the flesh' and we notice that they are all selfish. By contrast those who live by the Spirit, whom they have received through Christ, live in ways which please God and are going to benefit others. Paul calls Christians not to a life of self-indulgence, but to live in the Spirit and, as Friedrich Schleiermacher the theologian put it, the fruits of the Spirit are nothing but the virtues of Christ. The point is that we find freedom in the service of Christ, not the demand of law.

✳ *Come, Holy Spirit, so fill my life*
  that it shines with the glorious liberty of a child of God.

Friday June 22   *Galatians 6.1-10*
The law of Christ

Those who think too much about themselves, especially their status before God, are not going to be available to live the law of

147

Christ. This is because Christ lived for God and others, not for himself. So Paul urges pastoral care, one for another. Jesus spoke against those who placed heavy burdens on others and did not lift a finger to help them (Luke 11.46). Paul is clear that helping one another to carry the loads we must is Christ's way of life.

We reap what we sow. The person who goes around criticizing others will soon have no friends. Those who spread around doom and gloom will eventually become gloomy people. Those who spread dissension in the Church of Christ will find themselves isolated. Hence Paul's direct appeal to do good to all, not so that good may be done to us, but because that is the way of Christ and so is a characteristic of the Church of Christ, the family of faith. There is a sense of urgency about this. The opportunity for living this way is now!

✳ *Loving God, help me to take every opportunity*
to live your way for the sake of others, and for your glory.

Saturday June 23   *Galatians 6.11-18**

New creation!

Paul signs off in his own handwriting. It has not been the easiest letter to write. We have noted his deep pastoral concern for the churches, so deep that he can be very direct when they have put themselves at risk by wandering from Christ and his gospel. How he longs for them to have all that Christ gives.

The summary of the whole letter is in the phrase 'new creation'. That is what God has done and is doing in Christ. The old world order, marked by sin and inevitably leading to death, has been redeemed by Christ. The cross and resurrection of Jesus are the turning point in the whole history of creation, whether people realize it or not. Paul lives to tell out this story. He will boast of nothing else. Really what matters is not the old law, or lack of it, but 'new creation is everything'.

This has been a costly ministry for Paul. He bears on his own body the marks of belonging to Christ. But he would not have had it any other way. Christ Jesus has set him free from the law of sin and death. And Christ has done that for all who put their trust in him. So we leave the past and go into the future with Paul's prayer:

✳ *May the grace of our Lord Jesus Christ*
be with your spirit, brothers and sisters. Amen

FOR REFLECTION – alone or with a group

- Reflect on your own life in the light of Paul's contrast between the works of the flesh and those who walk by the Spirit.
- Bear one another's burdens. Can you think of ways of doing this more effectively in your church?

FOR ACTION

Write out a summary of Paul's argument in less than 100 words. Share your summary with a friend and discuss it together. How would you tell out Paul's message today?

SUFFERING AND A GOD OF LOVE
1. Why have you abandoned me?

Notes based on the New International Version by
Elizabeth and Mark Lakin

Elizabeth Lakin has been a teacher for twelve years, and has spent the last nine years teaching children with moderate learning difficulties. Mark qualified as a barrister in 1986 and works for the Crown Prosecution Service of England and Wales.

When in November 1992 Katie was born, only five months into Liz's pregnancy and too premature to survive for more than a few hours, we were devastated. When, in May 1995, Daniel was born and died in identical circumstances it was worse. Why had God allowed or even caused this bitter, double tragedy? What had we done to deserve it? Our reflections upon the biblical texts are written in the light of this experience. They are, in the main, jointly compiled, and some are our individual thoughts.

Sunday June 24   *1 Kings 19.1-15**
Where are you, God?
We haven't been regular worshippers since October 1996 and our church attendance within that time has been, frankly, occasional. Some may consider this, alone, evidence that our reflections will be bereft of insight or, at least, reason why we ought to be writing, 'Why have we abandoned you?'.

We just stopped feeling the presence of God in our life of worship. Sundays became an exercise in empty ritual, and orthodox teaching required us to accept a view of God and his involvement in the world that did not seem true to our situation or, if true, only increased our suffering. After all, the more power and control you ascribe to God the more responsibility follows.

Orthodoxy has presented us with a triumphalist God who destroyed cities, brought down plagues and raised up great kings, who is in the rock-shattering wind, the fire or the earthquake. Gentle whispers are, well, not very Godlike, but then nor is sharing in our humanity and vulnerability even to the cross. And when you haven't been to church for three years it is comforting to know that God can be gentle.

❋ Even when we don't come to you, God, come to us.

Monday June 25   *Luke 8.26-39**

I beg you, don't torture me!

The depression that followed the death of Daniel was, without doubt, made deeper and darker by the fact that I was a Christian. In that sense I can identify with Legion's plea.

When my ability to function at work was severely challenged; when relationships began to fracture; when, in a classic spiral into depression, I despised myself for being so weak and worthless, my faith – if a rock – was a burden to carry, not a firm foundation.

What if the Old Testament stories were true and my refusal to accept their absolute veracity an affront to God? What if my God was as jealous, condemning and judgemental as those stories would sometimes show? What if, as I certainly felt, my failings of thought and deed – which I would gladly list for your entertainment were they not so exceptionally ordinary – were now being weighed against me and our loss was a richly deserved punishment?

If we refuse to discard images of God based more upon our desire to control others through fear than upon a pursuit of the truth, we can expect to find that when we enter the dark places of mental anguish God will shine out like a branding iron.

❋ When we feel the need to speak of power,
let it always be the power of your love.

Tuesday June 26   *1 Samuel 1.1-18*

The long wait

I empathize with Hannah and her 'bitterness of soul'. There are times when I feel God has let me down and has forgotten me. Then I feel guilty for these thoughts. The Church promotes motherhood as an ideal, and to be unable to have children is an immense burden on me.

Hannah's rival 'kept provoking her'. I have felt provoked by the ease with which those around me have had children compared with my difficulties, initially in carrying children to full-term and latterly in conceiving. Friends with children, perhaps feeling uncomfortable for me, have at times excluded me from their activities, and I have felt abandoned.

Are Christian people meant to promote the family so much, so fuel the expectations that all women should become wives and mothers, that those unable to – or choosing not to – feel 'great anguish and grief'?

I do feel anguish and grief and a sense of loss both for my children and my childlessness.

When Hannah poured out her soul to the Lord she was answered with a child, Samuel. I still await my answer.

✳ **God, grant me the strength to accept today**
and the patience to await tomorrow.

Wednesday June 27 Job 23.1-7

Helpful advice

The bitterness and disturbing honesty of Job's complaint flow as much from the 'support' bestowed by his friends as from his ills. It works like this.

If you say that God has a plan, worked out in such minute detail that every flower in every field, every petal on every flower, every dewdrop on every petal is there by God's express ordinance, then is not also every famine, flood, earthquake, disease and war? Is not all poverty God's wish?

If you credit God with bestowing the good but blame all ills on our wickedness, our tendency to break our covenant with God, then who is at fault when freak weather takes homes and lives? At whose door do we lay the pandemic and who made our babies die? Us?

Is it better to accept tragedy as an inevitable risk, the unpalatable partner of the dangerous vitality that life requires and which frees us to see upon the cross a supremely vulnerable God, not causing but sharing our pain?

✳ **Loving God, help us to see you,**
not in the cause of our anguish,
but on our road to recovery.

Thursday June 28 Genesis 3.1-24

In defence of original sin

Adam and Eve were, in their innocence, that which English lawyers would term *doli incapax*, incapable of sufficient ability to distinguish between right and wrong to be punishable at law. That, after all, is what consumption of the apple bestowed. So where is the justice in God's reaction? What place has love in their eviction from paradise and our resultant troubles? It is not enough to say that they disobeyed the express will of God, because they could not have known that to do so was wrong.

This passage might be taken to present a view of God that we simply cannot accept: God who set Adam and Eve up to fail – God who created all of the circumstances, from their inquisitive nature to the presence of the serpent and, let's be frank, the tree itself, from which their disobedience was inevitable.

In the supreme sacrifice of the cross God showed himself to be bigger than that.

✳ *Forgive us,*
when we make you small enough to fit on a page.

Friday June 29 *Psalm 22.1-11**

So why have you abandoned us?

It was easy to feel the presence of God in the immediate aftermath of the loss of our children. The intensity of our grief was a bridge, a hot-line, if you will, to God's love. Perversely, we even felt special, privileged to be given a unique insight into the nature of God.

The feeling of being forsaken came later: when friends felt guilty at the health of their children; when our barely suppressed anger forced upon them impossible standards of sensitivity; when that anger overflowed, and people saw only the unpleasantness and not the pain; when we turned our anger on each other; when, despite people's expectations, our faith was not enough to assuage the pain and, ultimately, became an additional burden; in the guilt; in the wretched self-loathing of depression – that was when it was hard to feel God at work in our lives. That was when we felt abandoned. That was when all the glories of God and stories of his great benevolence counted for nothing. Maybe those were also the feelings of Christ when he uttered the words of verse 1 on the cross. Like the pain of crucifixion, the pain of grief is real and even faith is vulnerable.

There is no advice as to how to come through such a time, except, perhaps this. It is so very unlikely that you are to blame.

✳ *May we always feel your loving presence.*

Saturday June 30 *Isaiah 9.2-7*

Hope

There are, it seems, stages in the grieving process. In time, if we are fortunate, and, thankfully most of us are, the pain loses its sharp edges and the loss, though never erased, becomes bearable. In the darkness, light begins to shine once more.

If we had been writing this two years ago we would have found verse 6 difficult indeed. Katie and Daniel had been so tiny that their frail frames could not carry the simple exertions of life, let alone the weight of the kingdoms of the world. Today, however, it brings hope.

Our experiences have often made us reflect upon that which we can no longer believe. We have had to jettison images of God so as to make sense of our loss and to revitalize our faith. You have the right to ask what we do believe. Well this.

In a baby born in Bethlehem, in a man who lived in first century Palestine amid the anxiety of occupation – who taught us to love each other even when we are enemies – God is revealed.

If we could love Katie and Daniel, knowing that they could give nothing in return, then how much more unconditionally can God love us? We know of no greater source of hope.

✳ *Wherever we are, be there also and make your love known.*

FOR REFLECTION – alone or with a group

- What are the qualities of the people to whom you turn when you need support?
- Which facets of God's nature make it easy to bring your problems to God, and which are a barrier?

FOR ACTION

Resolve never to speak of God in ways that will make faith an extra burden to those in anguish.

SUFFERING AND A GOD OF LOVE
2. Weep with those who weep

Notes based on the New Revised Standard Version by
Glyn Simmonds

Glyn Simmonds, a Methodist minister who has served in circuits in the Midlands and South Wales, is now retired and lives in Rogerstone, Newport, Gwent.

Reflecting on the given verses of Scripture, I have found myself reliving my responses to my wife's illness and death in 1997 from ovarian cancer. The years since have been full of the hurt and pain of not having her with me. The loneliness is untamed. This experience is shared too by the separated, the divorced, those who have been in other kinds of partnerships, and the single. Death and broken relationships are a taboo subject. Those who want to talk find few who will listen! The Church itself does not handle it well! It is long past the time when we should be reviewing our stance. Let us remind ourselves of the words of John Donne: 'No man is an island, entire of itself.'

Sunday July 1   2 Kings 2.1-14*
Partnership

When Elisha was reminded that Elijah was going to be taken away, he responded, 'I know; be silent.' The thought was too painful. This can be so when we know that a child, wife, husband, or close friend is dying. We have become so absorbed in each other that the death of one creates havoc in the life of the other. Coping alone is unthinkable. Often we close our eyes to what we know is going to happen, because we cannot imagine how we will possibly deal with it. When my wife was dying of cancer I avoided facing the facts. It was too painful. The thought of being without her was unbearable. I wanted to cling to the present as long as I could. 'I know; be silent.'

But if, when life is good, we are able to talk about and understand that this happens to us, we are more able to help ourselves and others. That is why Jesus, well ahead of his approaching death, tried to prepare his disciples for what was to happen (Mark 10.32-34). They felt despair. I understand that!

Elisha would have understood it! I also understand, as Elisha would have, their joy when Jesus said later, 'I am with you always, to the end of the age' (Matthew 28.20).

✴ *God, you have trusted us with our own humanity.*
We trust you to help us handle it.

Monday July 2   *Mark 10.32-34*
A reversal of roles
I remember during my wife's illness, that we knew to be terminal, realizing there were times when she needed to be alone. She needed 'space'. She understood what was happening better than anyone else, and needed to understand it, to be able to face the future for her and me with confidence.

Jesus, knowing this to be his last journey to Jerusalem, told his followers of his approaching death. In the circumstances we might think he was the one most likely to give way to fear, and that his followers would have supported him. But Jesus was the rock and they were sand. In his adversity, he gave them the strength and support they should have given him.

How often in my experience, and probably in yours, has this proved to be true. There were occasions when I know I should have been giving encouragement and support but knew all the time that I was the one receiving it. On one occasion, someone said to me, 'I felt that I needed help and support but I was the one who gave it.' Can you identify with these experiences?

Identifying with the feelings of others is the first step to being able to encourage and support them in their need. The followers of Jesus took a long time to reach that point. Do we?

✴ *Lord, help us to have inner strength*
and enough to spare
that we may share the pain of others.

Tuesday July 3   *Matthew 26.31-46, 56b*
Failure and disappointment
If you have ever experienced disappointment – and I am sure you have – you will know how Jesus felt in the garden. He must have had great expectations of his disciples, but they withdrew their support when he needed it most. Self-centredness took over, and they failed him. We may have had similar experiences in the church or among friends: when we need them most, they are

incapable of helping us. They keep their distance. That hurts, and we are disappointed.

Look at yourself: are you as supportive as you might be? There may be someone, in crisis, looking to you for encouragement and support and you are doing little to help. S/he will be disappointed in you, and you will be disappointed in yourself. Take hope! Jesus turns failure into victory. He encourages those who falter. He does not sit back and complain about his followers' failures, but tries to redirect them in the way they should go. What he has done for others he can do for you.

✶ *Lord, when you are wearied by our hesitation,*
give us a clear mind and a dedicated heart
to do what is good and right
without disappointing anyone.

Wednesday July 4   John 19.25-27

Loneliness

At the height of his torture on the cross, Jesus continued to think of the needs of others. Looking down on his mother and 'the disciple whom he loved', he introduced them afresh to each other: to his mother, 'Woman, here is your son', and to the disciple, 'Here is your mother'. He united the two people most likely to be affected by the pain of loneliness and bereavement. It would have made it easier for them to share their deepest feelings, and for the bond between them to deepen.

There is nothing worse than this loneliness. Others have told me so, and I have experienced it. It is traumatic! Since my wife died I have concluded that if I were sentenced for some crime I could not receive a heavier sentence. Jesus knew this feeling at the centre of his agony on the cross: 'My God, my God, why have you forsaken me?' (Matthew 27.46).

I read two entries in the 'Lonely Hearts' column of a newspaper. One called herself 'a pub enjoyer' and the other 'a church goer'. I would have thought that both pub and church were places where friendship could be found. It would appear not, for them. Even on the cross, Jesus was deeply aware of the possibility of months and maybe years of loneliness for his mother and closest friend. He acted to prevent it! Are we so busy that we do not notice the lonely?

✶ *Lord, give us eyes to see and the spirit to act.*

Human limitations

Notice Martha pointing an accusing finger at Jesus: 'Lord, if you had been here, my brother would not have died.' At that moment, Jesus must have been acutely aware of the limitations he had accepted for himself in becoming man.

The two words, 'Jesus wept' show his natural reaction, like Martha's and Mary's response. But the love of God also moved the incarnate Jesus. The accusing finger carried some truth because he chose not to be in Bethany when he was needed (verses 5-6). While in the flesh he would always be unable to be everywhere. This must also have moved him to tears.

As soon as Jesus had ascended (Matthew 28.20), he was free to be with his followers in every age and every place. Now in his name we are called to be where the need is, letting him work for good in and through us. Paul called it being 'one body in Christ' (Romans 12.5). May we, his followers, not cause him to weep because we fail to let this happen.

✳ *Lord, remembering that we are all part of your body,*
   the Church, help us to live out a caring ministry,
   that we might share your tears.

Being alongside

After reading the verses from Ezekiel, read Psalm 137.1-4. Allow what you read to touch the depths of your spirit. It is the song of Jews in captivity in the 6th century BC. 'By the rivers of Babylon we sat down and wept.' What agony of spirit! What depths of depression! Ezekiel had possibly been taken into exile in Babylon with the first wave of Jews ten years earlier. He watched as the second wave of exiles arrived, and then came and sat with them for seven days identifying with their grief, stunned (NRSV), dumbfounded (NEB), lost for words. Perhaps he relived his own feelings of ten years before.

It is easy to observe at a distance, but it is hard to understand or feel what others are experiencing. The judgements we often make reveal our ignorance of the pain and help neither them nor ourselves. We need to listen closely to grasp how they feel. The pastoral place is not to stand apart, but to 'sit where they sit'. Until we can do that we cannot offer real support.

✳ *Lord, grant that we may find you in times of despair.*
  And, through love for others,
  enable us to come close to them and support them.

Saturday July 7   *Romans 12.9-16*

Compassionate love

Whatever else is our aim, our first should be to attain a spirit of
Christ-like compassionate love. If we have that spirit, we will be
able to reach out as caring people touching those who need our
touch. How bewildering life is to those who look through a veil of
tears. They need support and true friendship.

In these verses Paul is setting out the nature of love that a
Christian should display towards others. It is affectionate,
respectful, liberating, sympathizing, uniting, gracious and
engaging. Having these Christ-like qualities allows us to be all
things to all people in making their grieving journey easier. We
weep with those who weep. When we open our hearts and minds
to being hospitable it will be possible to turn some of the weeping
into joy and share that also.

✳ *Dear God, let the true nature of love dominate who we are.*
  Let us not be so full of self
  as to be blind to the needs of others.
  Let all we do be done with Christ in mind,
  seeking no praise, no reward, no glory,
  except to know that we are doing your holy and perfect will.
  The grace of our Lord Jesus Christ be with us all.

FOR REFLECTION – alone or with a group

● How do we find emotional strength to cope with the
  unthinkable in our lives?
● How can we put ourselves in the place of others and
  understand how they feel?
● How do we identify the loneliness of other people?

FOR ACTION

Look below the surface of other people's lives. Try and see if
there is any kind of confusion, loneliness, hurt or pain there. Then
act as a friend and not as an acquaintance.

SUFFERING AND A GOD OF LOVE
3. God of healing

Notes based on the New Revised Standard Version by
Alison Beever

Alison Beever is an Anglican priest working in a parish in Reading (UK). She is chaplain to a local women's centre, and has a particular concern for the way the churches treat people perceived as 'different', especially those who have disabilities and those who have survived sexual abuse.

It is ironic that, as we explore the theme 'God of healing', we approach a topic which often divides Christians and causes pain and judgement. Division comes when we try to limit the work of God and our understanding of this ministry: when we impose our own healing agenda which is so often limited to God curing the ills of those for whom we pray.

This week we will focus on a wider understanding of the healing work and intention of God who draws us towards a right relationship with him and a fullness of life which transcends the limitations of medical 'models of cure'.

This week there is one prayer to be used after each day's study:

✳ *God of healing,*
show us our need to be healed,
show us your world's need of healing,
and show us how we can share
in your mission to make us whole.
Help us bring your healing and fullness of life
to all the places we visit,
to all people we meet,
and deepen our understanding of your will for us
as we seek your ways,
in the name of Christ. Amen

Sunday July 8   *Genesis 8.1-22*
Wholeness not painlessness
A friend coming through severe depression once told me that he would not change where he was and what was happening to him.

160

Despite the pain, he had a sense of becoming more himself than he had been before. I share his reflection from my own experience of intractable pain – the feeling towards a 'becoming' I would not otherwise know. For each of us our journey is towards healing. This is a very different experience from the 'if only's': 'if only I could start over again, make a clean break – it would all be different'. In the story of Noah, despite the devastation of the flood, God does not make a completely new beginning. The world remains, and the work of re-creation builds on this world, saved by Noah's obedience. From chaos and destruction come healing and new possibilities.

God promises healing to the world and to each of us, but the promise is not for a painless existence. Psychologists tell us that some 'conflict and pain' are necessary for human development. They belong to being the humanity God intended us to be, and to creation itself (cf. Romans 8.22).

✳ *God of healing, show us our need to be healed...*

(Continue with the prayer on page 160)

Monday July 9   *2 Kings 5.1-14**

Know yourself

Many traditions have stories about people who die and come to judgement. Faced with the question, 'Who are you?' their responses rely on their status or profession – I'm a mother, teacher, wife of... husband of... They are almost always sent back to discover who they are, and their own identity or name.

Naaman perhaps has to learn not only to be obedient to God in his search for healing, but that he is Naaman. He cannot rely on his wealth, authority, or standing with the king; nor even on being a tool of Yahweh in his people's victory.

Part of our coming to wholeness, and living the healing of God, is to know ourselves as we are – not a false humility, nor a puffed-up pride – but a knowing who we are and what our name is. How else will we know ourselves called by God (cf. Isaiah 43.1)?

✳ *God of healing, show us our need to be healed...*

Tuesday July 10   *Luke 5.12-16*

God's choice?

People sometimes suggest that God 'chooses' to answer some prayers and not others. For some he will 'snap his fingers' and cure; others he will leave in pain or distress. This seems especially so when prayer is 'not answered' in the way we had demanded/expected/wanted. Is our God really as whimsical, arbitrary and apparently unfair as this? Is this the God we find in Scripture?

Sometimes it seems so. But even in New Testament miracles, when Jesus cures someone it is usually a demonstration of who he is and his special relationship with God.

Today's reading points to a deeper reality. The man with leprosy asks not for a cure but to be 'made clean'; the Greek word used has a specific ceremonial and spiritual meaning. And yes, this is the will, the choosing of God, not only for this man, but for all who ask for this wholeness and cleansing in their lives.

There is, of course, a double meaning within the story. For the man with leprosy, it is this cleansing in the ceremonial context which makes him acceptable to his community; a social healing for the outcast, and for the community which rejected him in his need.

✳ *God of healing, show us our need to be healed...*

Wednesday July 11   *Luke 5.27-32*

Does God believe in you?

A friend, the vicar of a medieval town centre church, is used to petty acts of vandalism. He tells how one morning he looked up at the church tower and immediately thought, 'Oh no! Someone has pinched one of the hands off the clock!' It took him some moments to realize his mistake. It was actually twenty to eight!

It's easy to be paranoid about security, and judgemental of people. But whilst we need to be realistic about human nature and take precautions for our property and personal security, it is quite another issue to get locked into an attitude of permanent suspicion. How easily we go around expecting the worst in people, in our world, and all too often in ourselves – just as in Jesus' day people ostracized tax gatherers. We imprison people in our suspicion, and forget what extraordinary, surprising creatures human beings are. We imprison ourselves in doubt, and lose sight of who and what we are able to be, but we can turn our lives around, repent of what we have need to, and live in a right relationship with God and others.

One of the most life-changing, healing and shocking things about Jesus was the way he treated people. He had no illusions about what they were like, but he insisted that there was more to them than their failure. The real challenge, and our real hope for healing, isn't so much to do with whether we believe in God. It's to live up to the fact that God believes in us.

✳ *God of healing, show us our need to be healed...*

Thursday July 12   *Luke 8.40-56**
With God, it is good to be woman'
While people are 'outcasts'; while we judge some to be less than others and create second class citizens politically, economically, socially, and religiously; while we deprive some of the basic rights of belonging and citizenship... our world cannot know peace, nor fullness of life in God. Yet this peace is not dependent solely on governments. Each of us needs to look at our hearts and lives, discover who we diminish and deprive of personhood, then speak words of acceptance and healing. It is only as we speak such words that we move into the wholeness of a right relationship with God and his people.

It is no accident that these two stories are interwoven: the older woman, troubled for years of bleeding, being treated as an outcast, and issued with a death sentence if she approached others; the younger, perhaps in today's understanding a classic anorexic, afraid of growing up and the separation from her father which menstruation would bring. Jesus' gift to each of them is not primarily their physical cure, but his acceptance of them as the women they are. He speaks to the bleeding woman and the dead child, making himself unclean; he accepts them as human beings. They are not unclean because of their gender. I believe that for each this is the heart of their healing – the acceptance and implicit blessing of their womanhood.

✳ *God of healing, show us our need to be healed...*

Friday July 13   *Isaiah 57.14-21*
Peace be with you'
'Peace, peace to the far and the near, says the LORD;
    and I will heal them' (verse 19 NRSV).
When changes were made to the Communion Service of the Church of England, 'sharing the peace' was met with mixed reactions. Some welcomed it as an expression of love and community; some hated it because it disrupted quiet times and forced unwanted contact with others.

Yet to wish someone *shalom,* 'the peace of the Lord', is one of the most powerful prayers and blessings possible. It is a life-changing greeting. You cannot wish 'peace' for somebody whilst holding on to resentment or refusing forgiveness. *Shalom* (the Hebrew word for 'peace') is not just an absence of conflict; it has excitement and depth in its meaning. It hopes for wholeness and completeness, an unbroken relationship with God, a deep well-being for the individual, for society and for creation, worked out in justice, trust, openness, wholeness, and interdependence.

Shalom is the ultimate prayer of healing for the world and all in it, and it is the expression of God's will for his people. If we have *shalom* we live in right relationship with other people, with God, with the world, with ourselves. It is a blessing that encompasses all reality. It is not a human achievement but a gift of God in spite of human achievement.

This is the peace proclaimed by angels at Jesus' birth, and the peace proclaimed in today's reading, despite people's failure and determination to go their own way: peace, *shalom,* wholeness and healing.

✴ *God of healing, show us our need to be healed...*

Saturday July 14   Acts 3.1-10

Not in our own strength

One scene in Monty Python's 'The Life of Brian' shows a beggar who has been cured of his disease. Far from being grateful for this he is next seen shouting and complaining that his livelihood has been removed – and how dare someone do this to him! A comedy film reveals an uncomfortable truth. Today, amongst the poorest people of our world, and often where the tourist industry most impinges on the life of poor communities, people deliberately injure and mutilate themselves to eke out a living by begging.

Whilst this is a condemnation of many of us in the richer parts of the world, and of systems which keep two-thirds of the world's people poor, it reminds us of the risk and immense changes that we will have to make if we follow God's healing agenda. If we pray for God's healing for the world, we have to be prepared to change systems and work for the justice which gives life to all, if we pray for healing for ourselves we have to be prepared for changes that affect all of life.

We cannot change the world in our own strength but, with Peter and John, we can give what we have – our prayer in the power of Jesus' name – and the risk of praying.

FOR REFLECTION – alone or with a group

- In the apparent devastation of our world, can you hear God's promise of wholeness? How are you called to work within and towards this purpose of God?
- Consider the labels or titles you hide behind. Who, with God, are you?
- To whom do you need to speak *'shalom'* this week?

FOR ACTION

Identify individuals or groups in your society who are labelled or implicitly understood to be outcasts. Try to find a way to approach one of those you find hard to accept, and initiate a conversation. Can you speak and hear words of healing and acceptance? Perhaps turn this action into a prayer that can be shared.

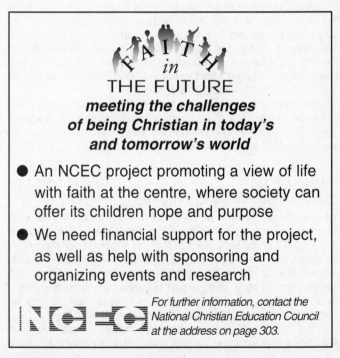

FAITH
in
THE FUTURE
meeting the challenges of being Christian in today's and tomorrow's world

- An NCEC project promoting a view of life with faith at the centre, where society can offer its children hope and purpose

- We need financial support for the project, as well as help with sponsoring and organizing events and research

For further information, contact the National Christian Education Council at the address on page 303.

SUFFERING AND A GOD OF LOVE
4. The healing Church

Notes based on the Revised English Bible by
David Dale

David Dale, a minister of the United Reformed Church, served as Moderator of the General Assembly in 1995/6. He was convenor of the URC Health and Healing Committee and chairman of the Churches' Council for Health and Healing. He is the author of 'In His Hands' (Darton Longman and Todd) and 'The Love that Heals' (United Reformed Church).

Lesslie Newbigin told of a time when he was working for the World Council of Churches and was almost overwhelmed by requests for help from mission hospitals throughout the world. He could not see how the massive help they required might be provided. He shared this problem with Dr Ademola who was at that time in charge of health services for the Government of Nigeria. Dr Ademola was silent for some time and then he said, 'You must not forget that the primary unit of healing is not the hospital but the Christian congregation.'

This was a new thought in the 1960s when technology was supposed to provide the answer to all our problems. I wonder how many local congregations see themselves as 'the primary unit of healing' in their community? Does yours?

Sunday July 15   *Luke 10.1-11,16-20**
Jesus sends out the seventy-two

Here Luke records the sending out of 72 disciples (some early manuscripts say 70). They went in pairs, a practice continued in the Early Church. They were to look for support from the people to whom they were sent; they were to travel lightly and not seek luxury: 'Do not move around from house to house' (verse 7b). Healing was to be an integral part of their mission and the heart of their message was: 'The Kingdom of God is near'. Some will reject this message, but that is their responsibility.

They returned with excitement, having seen signs of God's redemptive work. Satan's downfall was already apparent.

Jesus' vision of Satan's fall from heaven confirmed this (verse 18).

This may be regarded as a decisive victory in God's campaign against evil. As Christians we are called to overcome evil by good. The healing acts of a local congregation caring for people who are ill, housebound, lonely, bereaved... are all part of God's campaign against evil. The campaign continues and we are empowered to engage in it.

✳ *God of healing, help us to recognize the wonder of your victory through acts of befriending, care and kindness.*
Teach us not to exult in spiritual achievements
but to rejoice in what you have done for us in Jesus
and in his call to become a healing community.

Monday July 16   *Luke 10.25-37**

Who is my neighbour?

Most ethical systems and each of the major world faiths emphasize the need to care for our neighbour. The crucial question is: how far do we carry this responsibility?

Could it be that our neighbour today might be an asylum seeker, the mother or father in a one-parent family, a person of another faith, a child separated from parents by war, political faction or natural disaster...?

From all parts of the world today the cries of pain and loss come in and call for the response of healing love.

✳ *God of all nations, help us to discover our neighbour in the most unexpected places, and to bring your healing even to the most unlikely and unneighbourly.*

Tuesday July 17   *2 Corinthians 1.3-11*

Comforted to comfort

Saintliness did not come easily to Paul. He had to wrestle with temptation and physical weakness, privation and danger, personal attack and discomfort, and the problems of the Corinthian church had added to his troubles. Yet, when he was tempted to despair, the sufferings of Christ which flow over into our lives, released the healing power of Christ's love to bring new trust, hope and endurance.

Paul suggests that suffering can bring two wholly good results: it can bring a powerful experience of the Father of compassion and the God of all comfort. It can also make us more aware of what others are going through so that we can help them more effectively: 'to share with them the consolation we ourselves receive from God'. When JM Barrie, the Scottish dramatist and novelist, was a young boy he was greatly affected by the death of his brother. He later described the powerful effect this had on his mother: 'That is where my mother got her soft eyes and why other mothers ran to her when they had lost a child.'

✳ *God of all comfort, grant that in our suffering*
we may find your grace all-sufficient,
and our weakness the opportunity
for your power to be displayed
and your love made known.

Wednesday July 18   *James 5.13-20*
Prayer for healing
Martin Luther described the Epistle of James as 'an epistle of straw', on the grounds that it said little about the Passion and Resurrection of Christ. It does, however, provide us with a glimpse into the life of the Early Church and its concern for those who were ill. Read again verses 13-15.

The suggestion is that both prayer and praise are effectual remedies for a whole host of human disorders. The anointing with oil reminds us of the importance of appropriate ritual in a ministry of healing. In the time of Jesus, anointing with oil was used as a medical remedy and by the third century was recognized in the Church as a means of blessing.

The surprise in this passage lies partly in the suggestion, 'send for the elders of the church'. Is this a plea for collective responsibility in pastoral care? Then there is the call for mutual sharing in confession as an important element in Christian healing – helping each other to unburden ourselves and to know that we are forgiven can be a channel of health and wholeness.

We are reminded too of the healing strength that comes from knowing that someone cares for us and how this in itself is often sufficient to bring its own particular miracle of healing.

✳ *Thank you, Lord, for the renewal of the healing ministry*
in the Church today. May our hearts be healed
by the wonder of your love,
and may we be made strong in service, for Jesus' sake.

The Lord's supper

In the early days of the Church, the 'Lord's Supper' was celebrated as part of a common meal known as the *Agape* – 'Lovefeast'. Paul is concerned here about disorderly attitudes and greed which contradicted the meaning of both meals and, in verses 23-26, he reminds his readers of the way our Lord commanded us to observe this meal both as a thanksgiving – *Eucharist* – and as an act of remembrance.

This passage is the earliest written record of the institution of the sacrament. It was written at least ten years before Mark, the earliest of the Gospels.

Over the centuries, Christians have found in this sacrament something more than a memorial: they have found a reconciling and renewing presence calling them to share with others the good news of God's grace and to take part with the Church in God's continuing healing and reconciling mission.

✳ *Then grant us courage, Father God,*
   To choose again the pilgrim way,
And help us to accept with joy
The challenge of tomorrow's day.   *Fred Kaan*
                    By permission of Stainer and Bell Ltd

Spiritual gifts

Paul rebuked the Christians in Corinth for their overweening ambition to perform miracles and speak in tongues. This desire for special gifts of the Spirit made the less well-endowed feel inadequate and inferior. So Paul reminds them that all gifts of the Spirit are given, not primarily to individuals but to the Church. The Church which is the body of Christ, like the human body, consists of many parts but has an essential unity. All parts are important, and all contribute in their various ways to the value and effectiveness of the whole.

We need to learn that it is often the marginalized – those with disabilities, the elderly, the bereaved and the terminally ill – who have something special to contribute to our common life and understanding. Whilst we should not cease to value what Paul calls 'the higher gifts', we should not seek them at the expense of 'the still more excellent way', the way of love, which does not boast of achievements or miracles, nor does it exclude or ignore anyone.

✳ *Lord, send your Holy Spirit into our hearts*
that we may be cleansed and made whole in Christ.
May love be our aim and Christ our hope.

The vision and the thorn

Still somewhat on the defensive and anxious to establish his credentials as an apostle, Paul tells of a remarkable experience in which he was caught up in an ecstatic vision of God. But after the glory came the pain, and Paul speaks movingly of his 'thorn in the flesh': a physical problem which he doesn't describe for us but which served to keep him from spiritual pride and to remind him that God's grace was sufficient for all his needs.

It also brought him a new understanding of prayer. Three times he asked God that the 'thorn' might be removed. He had to learn to persevere in prayer and then at the end discover that God has different ways of answering: 'My grace is all you need; power is most fully seen in weakness.' He came to see that experiences which carry pain, weakness and distress can be used to bring new strength and fresh discoveries of the grace of God and the power of the risen Christ.

✳ *Lord God, enable us to see how,*
by the power of the risen Christ,
those experiences which trouble us may not pull us down
but lead us forward.

FOR REFLECTION – alone or with a group

● How far do you see your local congregation as a centre of health and healing?
● What does it mean to be a good neighbour in the city where people 'keep themselves to themselves'?
● How can we begin to learn from our suffering?

FOR ACTION

Discuss with your friends how together you might become better equipped to become agents of Christ's healing presence and power in your community.

SUFFERING AND A GOD OF LOVE
5. Trial and trust

Notes based on the New English Bible by
Jean Mortimer

Jean Mortimer, a minister of the United Reformed Church, is a qualified Youth and Community worker. Much of her ministry has been with young people in Urban Priority areas. In 'active early retirement' she has returned to part-time research in 'Health and Salvation' and hopes to complete her doctorate before she qualifies for a state pension! After a break of three years, during which she was helping to care for her parents in their final illness, she has recently resumed part-time teaching in New Testament Studies at the University of Leeds.

Stories of heroes and role models which tell it as it really was, without glossing over moments of darkness and doubt, are far more encouraging than those which look back through 'rose-tinted glasses'. This week's readings are about real people who encountered trials and tribulations similar to those which we experience. Their faith and trust in God did not come easily. It was nurtured alongside doubt, disillusionment, difficulty and fear. The contemporary 'catch phrases', which sprang so readily to mind as titles for these notes, underline the relevance of their stories for all of us today.

Sunday July 22   *Genesis 18.1-15**
'Get real!'
Laughter like Sarah's is brittle and cynical. It represents the hard-headed, hard-faced masks behind which many of us have learnt to hide our innermost pain. Going through the motions of getting on with life as Abraham did, when our hearts are not really in what we are doing, can blind us to the presence and power of God in our lives. This story invites us to 'get real' to our own and other people's disappointments: to 'get real' to the unexpected ways in which God hears us and helps us even in circumstances where we have almost given up hope. Pause and think of a seemingly hopeless situation known to you. What might God be calling YOU to do about it? What healing opportunities might be made

available to the people involved through your willingness to listen and share their sense of hopelessness? Are you aware of any self-help, support groups or counselling services that might be able to offer further help?

✳ *All-seeing God, help us to see and feel*
the reality of your healing presence
as we help one another
to name life's deepest disappointments and despair,
till hollow laughter and empty activity
are filled with purpose and power. Amen

Monday July 23   *Ecclesiastes 3.1-8; 7.3-4*

'Good grief!'

We usually employ the expression 'Good grief!' when we are taken aback by unexpected, shocking or perturbing events. It does not signify that we believe that grief is good. There are many aspects of the grieving process which are socially unacceptable because they cause us to feel strong emotions like anger, resentment or jealousy. If social 'taboos' or personal considerations prevent us from voicing such feelings, the loneliness and pain of grieving can be exacerbated to the point at which it becomes almost too painful to bear. Virginia Ironside has written about her own experience with moving candour and self-awareness. Her book, *You'll Get Over It – The Pain of Bereavement* (Penguin Paperback) is the most realistic treatment of the subject that I have read for a long time.

Although the Wisdom Literature is often harshly criticized for its fatalistic and deterministic view of life, the writings of Koheleth, the unknown 'preacher' of Ecclesiastes, underline the inevitability of death and mourning as inescapable realities. We may not accept that everything is predetermined, to the extent that all human endeavour is futile, but there is much that we can learn from his realism in accepting that some things cannot be avoided. Realistic acceptance of death and honesty in voicing all our emotions about it are more healthy than 'putting on a brave face'. Grief is not a good experience, but we have the assurance in Christ that all our grief is God's grief, for God does not abandon us to bear it alone.

Find out about the work of bereavement counselling agencies in your locality. Offer this prayer on behalf of someone you know who has been bereaved:

✳ *Jesus, Man of Sorrows, acquainted with all our grief,*
help us to name our sorrows,

172

to be honest and realistic about our strongest emotions
without diffidence, embarrassment or denial.
Be with..
and all who feel the pain and loneliness of grief today,
as a source of comfort and a force for good. Amen

Tuesday July 24   *John 12.20-26*
'Get a life!'

Current usage of this catch phrase implies that the person to whom it is addressed has little understanding of, or empathy with, the issues, problems or difficulties which the speaker is facing – that s/he is unable to see things from any other perspective than that of self-interest. Today's reading contains some hard sayings of Jesus about getting a very different kind of life in which suffering, sacrifice, obedience and service are placed very firmly before self or self-preservation. 'GET A LIFE INDEED!' Though this phrase would not have been used in his time, there were many who responded to his challenging reversals of accepted values in a similarly negative way. The reference to the 'Greeks' reminds us that there are people today, as there were then, who are interested in the man and his message and want to find out more. Their spirituality may be different from ours. They may not value our religious traditions but they are on a quest for meaning, purpose and values in life. What do they see when they look at us? Are our lifestyle and behaviour in keeping with the example of selfless love Jesus demonstrated in his life and his death? Do they see us defending such a lifestyle even in the face of negative criticism, harsh judgements or dismissal as foolish idealists? Or do they look elsewhere for encouragement and inspiration because they see nothing of Jesus in us?

✶ *Giver, Saver and Renewer of life,*
  give us strength to live for others, and renew in us
  the spirit of self-sacrifice and obedient service,
  that our lives may proclaim YOUR LIFE,
  given for all and risen for all. Amen

Wednesday July 25   *2 Corinthians 4.7-15*

'Down but not out'

First, try to complete the following sentences in the light of your own experience and your awareness of other people's problems (locally, nationally and internationally).

I feel/felt hard-pressed when ....

....

I am/was bewildered by ....

....

People who experience ....

....feel persecuted or hunted.

It was a devastating experience when...

was/were struck down by ....

Now read today's text and also 2 Corinthians 11.23-33 which gives a more graphic and detailed account of the hardships and trials, both physical and spiritual, which Paul had to undergo for the sake of the gospel. Compare them with the situations you have listed. Does your faith, like his, enable you to add the words of encouragement which he uses after each statement of hardship? What other forms of encouragement might you or others need in order to be able to say – but not 'hemmed in'..?

What 'amazing grace' that God places the treasure of the gospel in such ordinary, everyday pots and trusts that they will continue to be of service! Remember that grace and put your trust in it as Paul did in his weakest moments when he was very 'down' but never entirely 'out'.

＊ *For the treasure of the gospel*
the riches of God's grace;
For the brightness of God's glory
reflected in Christ's face;
contained in pots of earthenware
for use in mundane ways,
not kept safe like precious china
reserved for special days;
For all God's gracious goodness
we render thanks and praise. Amen

Thursday July 26　　　　　　　　　　*2 Corinthians 4.16 to 5.5*

'Get in shape'

While vast numbers of the world's population starve or struggle with unpayable debts that weigh them down, others vacillate between over-eating and over-anxiety about maintaining a good body image. Diets and fitness programmes may hold out superficial promises of becoming 'new women' or 'new men', but these are a far cry from Paul's concept of new life in Christ. There is some evidence to suggest that when Paul wrote this passage his earlier hopes of the imminent second coming of Christ had been modified at the prospect that his own death would come first. But he did not lose heart because he had confidence in the power of the Spirit to get his inner self in shape in preparation for the fuller life that was to come. His clever word-play on the links in the Hebrew language between the word for 'glory' and that for 'to be heavy' (see 'outweighs', verse 17) underlines the contrast between the superficial and the real issues highlighted in my introduction (page 171).

✴ *Risen Lord, help us to trust in the power*
of your resurrection; to rise above all that wearies us,
worries us or weighs us down.
Do not let our hope in that unseen eternal life with you
blind us to the harsh realities of life in this world,
or dull our sensitivity to the problems
of those who struggle daily to find enough
to keep body and soul together.
Show us how to keep fit for your service. Amen

Friday July 27   *2 Corinthians 5.6-15*

'Man alive!'

Continuing the note of confidence, Paul boldly states his personal preference for death as a means of coming closer to his Lord. This does not, however, provide grounds for complacency but expresses an overwhelming sense of responsibility to make the rest of his earthly life worthy of Christ's life given for the world. He appeals to his readers to follow this example and to base their life and conduct on spiritual values. Think of someone whose life has provided you with this kind of example.

On the international stage, Nelson Mandela or Desmond Tutu might come to mind, but all of us know other people whose names and stories have not hit the headlines. They are role models for our faith too. The supreme role model is Jesus himself – the 'man for others'. Man alive! What an example!

✴ *Man alive! Man for others.*
God with us. God for us. God standing by us.
May we follow your example
and conform to your standards. Amen

'Got it in one!'

Make a list of experiences that have caused you to question God's goodness, power or love. Though I cannot know the precise detail of the pain and anguish expressed in your list, I understand the reality and intensity of such feelings, for my own list would include the life-threatening illness of one of my sons. In a series of rhetorical questions, Paul invites us to think about personal and impersonal forces which can raise doubts like these in our minds and hearts. Compare his questions with those of Isaiah 50.8-10. Notice the appeal to Abraham and Sarah as role models in the faith in Isaiah 51.1-2. Paul does not deny that such forces exist, nor that some of them are beyond our understanding or outside our control. What he does emphatically deny, however, is that they have the power to separate us from God's love made real in the One who has suffered and died for us all.

✳ *Suffering God, be with us in our bleakest despair.*
When we are faced with impossible dilemmas,
overcome by unexpected tragedies
or overwhelmed by unbearable sadness,
help us to call to mind your Son and his cross.

FOR REFLECTION and ACTION – alone or with a group

● With which potential crisis of faith mentioned in this section do you most closely identify?

● What support and help would you look for from your local church if you had to face such a situation? Ask yourself if that support is currently on offer. If your answer is 'No', think and pray about what you can do to change this. If your answer is 'Yes', think and pray about how you might make a useful contribution to whatever service is being provided.

GOD OF LOVE AND ANGER
The book of Hosea

Notes based on the Hebrew Bible by
Jonathan Magonet

Jonathan Magonet is Professor of Bible and Principal of the Leo Baeck College, a Rabbinical Seminary in London. His books on biblical subjects include 'A Rabbi Reads the Psalms' and 'The Subversive Bible'.

Hosea is one of the most difficult books of the Hebrew Bible for readers and scholars alike. The language is very complicated and in many cases has probably become corrupted in the transmission. The image with which it begins, God's request to the prophet to marry a prostitute, is shocking on many levels and needs to be challenged. So the book invites sympathetic critique, serious questions and radical interpretations.

Sunday July 29   *Hosea 1.1-11 *****

Challenging Hosea

It is probably the most shocking opening to any biblical book. Hosea is asked by God to take a 'wife of harlotry'. It has embarrassed successive generations of readers who have had to come to terms with it in their own particular way. Earlier ones had to allegorize it or treat it as a dream. More recently some have tried to 'improve the text' by emendation and change her status or wish her away altogether. But even if you take the text at its face value it is a stumbling block for the pious, and a red flag to feminists who rightly attack what they see as an abusive view of women. We simply cannot accept the analogy of Israel as a faithless wife because it seems to justify negative stereotypes of women that have persisted down to our own time.

We will stumble over this theme again. Which means that sometimes we have to read *against* the grain of a biblical text and not simply accept it, or its presuppositions, at face value.

If it is any help, the call to take such a wife is not an imperative but a request. However it may be translated, the Hebrew insists that Hosea has a choice in undertaking this marriage.

✳ *You favour human beings with knowledge, and teach mortals understanding. Favour us with the knowledge, understanding and discernment that come from You.*

Jewish daily prayer

Monday July 30   *Hosea 2.1-15*

A suitable case for therapy

We have to assume that Hosea's first readers would have shared his cultural assumptions. A wife who would betray her husband, by taking not one but many lovers, would deserve any punishment he would bring upon her, from public exposure and humiliation to private confinement and the hint of violence. When the husband is God, how much more is He free to punish a people that had betrayed Him, worse, people who did not even recognize how far their gifts came directly from Him.

Today we would arrest such a husband for physical and mental abuse, before putting both of the partners into therapy: she for her nymphomania, he for his pathological jealousy. In time, with much work, we may even be able to effect some kind of reconciliation. Whether the children would ever be able to lead normal lives – having been given names to reflect the inner conflict in the family – is harder to tell!

Again we have to read against such a violent text. Where did the 'husband' fail to give his wife what she needed? Material things, rain and harvest, for sure, but what was missing so that she had to seek it elsewhere? And where was her loyalty, or even self-respect, that led to such destructive behaviour? We end with a flawed God and a flawed people in desperate conflict. What Hosea suggests as an answer – for us – can only be seen as a difficult and uncomfortable question.

✳ *And if I say, 'I will not make mention of You, nor speak any more in Your name', then there is in my heart, as it were, a burning fire, shut up in my bones and I weary myself to hold it in, but cannot.*   *Based on Jeremiah 20.9*

Tuesday July 31   *Hosea 2.16-23*

Master or partner?

The Hebrew here reflects a subtle change of tone – one that we have been hoping to hear. It depends on a couple of word-plays. Behind the language of Israel's 'lovers' stands the term *baal*, originally a name for the god of a particular area. The term becomes generalized by biblical writers to mean all false gods. But it also has the sense of 'master', one who has a controlling power over you.

In God's promise to change, He will no longer be Israel's *baal*, a husband who is a master; instead he will be literally her *ish*, her 'man' or 'husband'. We hear the Genesis story of the creation of woman, *ishah*, from the body of the 'man', *ish*, and the relationship changes from ownership and control to partnership, similarity and equality. It is sealed with the exquisite promise: 'I will betroth you to me for ever – with righteousness and justice... love and compassion... faithfulness.' You will come to 'know' God in all the myriad senses of the word, intimate, physical, intellectual and spiritual. We must hold onto the beauty and hope in this promise in all the emotional trials ahead in the book.

✱ *Do not send us away from our nearness to You, and do not take away from us the spirit of Your holiness. Our living God, do not leave us, be not distant from us.*

Jewish High Holyday Prayerbook

Wednesday August 1   *Hosea 3.1-5*
What shall I do with this old man?
A Rabbinic tradition gives a remarkable reading of Hosea's marital problems. When God said to Hosea, 'Your children (Israel) have sinned', he should have asked God for mercy on them, but instead he told God to exchange them for another people. God said, 'What shall I do with this old man? I will tell him to marry a harlot and have children of harlotry and then tell him to send her away. If he can do it, then I will send Israel away.'

But when God told Hosea to do so he could not bring himself to divorce her. God said: 'If that is the case when your wife is a harlot and you don't even know if the children are yours, how can I send away the children of Israel who are descended from Abraham, Isaac and Jacob?!' So Hosea saw that he had sinned and prayed to God for compassion. God said, 'Rather than pray for mercy for yourself, pray for Israel.' Hosea did so and the decrees against Israel were annulled. That is when all the negative names of his children were reversed. So that *lo-ammi* 'not My people' (1.9) is changed by the promise 'you *are* My people' (2.23) *(Babylonian Talmud, Pesachim 87ab).*

✱ *Give me, God, some help that I might serve You,*
and life that I may praise You.   *Marrano prayer*

But the earth is given into human hands (Psalm 115.16)

Verse 2 echoes the ten commandments. Three of the crimes –
murder, theft and adultery – are exact parallels. As bad as these
crimes is the fact that no one reproaches his neighbour. The
priest and prophet, who carry responsibility for Israel's abiding by
the terms of their covenant with God, have failed them – so Israel
in turn forfeits its special task to be God's 'priest' among the
nations.

The *Torah,* the revealed teaching of God, is a blueprint for
creating a just society, but that also includes obligations about the
correct treatment of the land itself and the animal world. So abuse
on any level has direct consequences throughout the creation.
The land and all creatures languish and mourn. There is a bitter
symmetry in the punishments. They have forgotten God's *Torah;*
God will in turn forget and abandon their children.

All that they do will be in vain: they will eat but still hunger;
have intercourse but not produce the children who will increase
their numbers. At this low point the prophet can only imagine God
rejecting and abandoning the people.

✳ *May it be Your will, our living God,*
  to give to every creature what it needs
  and to every body what it lacks.

                                                    Jerusalem Talmud

Across the generations

The prophet spells out in uncompromising language the sins of
Israel in worshipping fertility gods on the high places and under
leafy trees. And, if the elders perform these rites, no wonder their
daughters are led astray and follow their example.

The language of prostitution and adultery is harsh and hard to
take, for it is women who pay the price when the violence of the
language is used to justify the violence of actions.

At least for God they are not to be punished. What choice did
they have, given the values and experiences they were brought
up with? At that level we can recognize our responsibility to the
children we raise. They may sometimes listen to what we say, but
they will always observe what we actually do. Civilization is about
the history of idolatry into which each generation falls but which
the next generation sees through and combats, only to fall into
their own traps in turn. The idols may change but the
consequences they bring about are always the same whether the

idol be materialism, power, the nation, an ideology or unselfcritical religion itself.

✳ *Soon let us witness the glory of Your power when the worship of material things shall pass away from the earth, and prejudice and superstition shall at last be cut off.*

Based on Jewish Daily Prayer

Saturday August 4   *Hosea 5.1-7*

From disputation to dialogue

A Rabbinic tradition explains the references to Mizpah and Tabor. When King Jeroboam formed the Northern Kingdom of Israel, he established local shrines to discourage the people going south to visit the Temple. When this was not effective, he posted guards on these two mountains to prevent potential pilgrims reaching Jerusalem – Hosea's 'snare' and 'net' (verse 1).

Throughout history, religion and politics have been intertwined in a sometimes fruitful, often deadly embrace. The biblical references to the Northern Kingdom belong to such a polemic. Hosea, like others, sees its establishment as both a political and a religious betrayal. Whether the worship at the northern shrines is of the same God, or of local Canaanite deities, it could only be condemned in the harshest possible language.

Standing outside such conflicts they often seem absurd, petty and an abuse of the religious spirit. Standing within them it is hard not to become caught up in the feeling that others have betrayed our 'own' faith, or people, or community. Translate Hosea into the religious battles of today and the issues become familiar. Once again we have to read against the text to find ways of healing these bitter, destructive rifts.

✳ *God, give us today and every day grace, faithfulness and love in Your eyes and in the eyes of all who regard us.*

Jewish daily prayer

FOR REFLECTION – alone or with a group

● How do we deal with biblical texts whose message or content we find unacceptable?
● Husband and wife, or parent and child, are biblical metaphors for the relationship between God and human beings. What would be appropriate metaphors in today's society?

Turning back to God

The extraordinary thing with Hosea is to find amid the seemingly endless images of condemnation and his problematic, and often obscure, language, an occasional phrase of enormous clarity and religious power.

Here he offers at the beginning the hope that 'turning' to God will lead to healing. The Hebrew word, *shuv*, which means 'turn' in all kinds of senses, leads to the term 'repentance', but this hardly conveys the dynamic of the original Hebrew.

At the centre of Hosea's complaint is another of his favourite 'theological terms', for Israel has abandoned their *hesed*, another virtually untranslatable term. 'Lovingkindness' or 'mercy' are attempts, but at its centre is the idea of the 'loyalty' and 'faithful love' to be found between those bound together in a covenant, a partnership. It is a loyalty that holds them together for a thousand generations (Exodus 34.6-7), a loyalty that Hosea has already celebrated (2.19-20). This is what God wishes, not sacrifices. But even if Israel fails, God's *hesed*, faithful love, remains constant – that is the ultimate promise in the covenant.

✳ **Bring us back to You, our God, and we shall return;**
renew our days as of old.   *Lamentations 5.21*

Exile and return

It is as if in his desperation Hosea loses control of his language itself. Certainly it is hard to follow his argument at this point. Is he primarily a political critic? Israel chooses the wrong kings and leaders, she makes alliances with Assyria, the great empire that will one day destroy the Northern Kingdom itself. Or is he a religious conservative still reacting, generations later, to the scandal caused by the original breaking away of the Northern Kingdom, when King Jeroboam set up new sanctuaries to replace the Temple in Jerusalem?

The imagery is precise, hinting at the appropriate punishment for their actions: they have strayed from God, they will experience the ultimate distance from God, exile among the nations; they rejected God (verse 3), God rejects them (verse 5). All is seemingly measured and balanced.

Worse than their defection is their sudden loyalty (verse 2) when trouble arises. Yet for all their rejection, God will still bring them back from the nations (verse 10). God is now the parent who cannot let go of the children; who must watch helplessly the mess they get themselves into and nevertheless repeatedly bail them out.

✳ *For we are Your people and You are our God.*
We are Your children and You are our parent.
We are Your servants and You are our master.
We are Your community and You are our portion.

Hymn from Jewish High Holydays

Tuesday August 7   *Hosea 9.10-17*

The unforgiving prophet

The tradition of the wilderness period is a recurrent biblical theme. Jeremiah celebrates Israel's love and trust of God when they went into the desert like a bride accompanying her bridegroom (Jeremiah 2.2). Hosea has the opposite image. Now Israel, like a totally unexpected, yet highly desirable cluster of grapes, is found in the wilderness. These are the male forefathers, but their very masculinity leads them astray. At Baal Peor they allowed themselves to be seduced, despite all that God had done for them (the same harsh terminology of prostitution appears in Numbers 25 to which this passage relates).

For once Hosea steps out of his role of spokesperson for God, calling on God to punish Israel for their betrayal by their worship at Gilgal. In this continual switching of voices it is hard to tell whether God's anger actually matches that of the prophet. Rather, from other passages we detect God's torment, torn between anger at betrayal and a parental love that can hardly be articulated. The prophet himself is less forgiving. Does he exceed his task as the divine agent even as he expresses the depth and complexity of God's tortured love?

✳ *God, only if You open my lips*
may my mouth truly declare Your praise.

Based on Psalm 51.15

Wednesday August 8   *Hosea 10.1-12*

Righteousness and peace

The grapes that God encountered with such joy in the wilderness (9.10), once planted in their own land, have flourished. But their fruit is wasted, for they have forgotten God and turned to others.

Again the Hebrew text is hard to unravel. The two kingdoms, north and south, Israel/Ephraim and Judah, might have a chance, but only if they change their ways. One sentence emerges with clarity and hope, using agricultural images that point beyond themselves: 'Sow righteousness for yourselves, reap according to faithful love; plough yourself a ploughing, for it is time to seek the Eternal, until He comes and teaches you in righteousness' (10.12). God will meet you on the terms you decide: righteousness to match the righteousness you yourselves establish.

A Rabbinic comment links verse 2 with a reading of 4.17. 'Ephraim is joined, although he worships idols, let him alone.' See how great is peace! For even if Ephraim worships idols but there is peace among them ('Ephraim is joined'), the Accuser cannot touch them. But if there is no peace between them, 'their heart has parted' (10.2), then the Accuser can condemn them, 'now they will be guilty'.

✳ *May You who make peace in the highest*
   bring this peace upon us and upon all the world.
                                        Based on Jewish daily prayer

Thursday August 9   *Hosea 11.1-11**

For love is strong as death

Hosea evokes yet another image of a relationship under threat: an emotional, loving parent coping with a troubled and troubling child. The nation is a son enslaved in Egypt, and whom the father has rescued. But immediately the parent's love is abused by Israel's betrayal. The awful inner anguish of the father, torn apart by love and disappointment, is graphically shown. Almost every verse contains an inner contradiction.

'I taught them to walk... Let them go back into slavery in Egypt! Let Assyria devour them with the sword! No! How can I give you up, Ephraim? They will come again out of Egypt! I will bring them home!'

It is a nightmare of torment and an extraordinary depiction of God. It speaks to anyone troubled by unfulfilled hopes in a beloved child, who can only see disasters ahead and feels powerless to prevent them – or else too caught up emotionally to allow the young adult his or her own freedom. The phrase 'I taught Ephraim to walk' can be read as 'when I held him on my lap'. 'I have only to remember holding Ephraim as a child and my love pours out of me.'

✳ *With deep love You have loved us, and with great and overflowing tenderness You have taken pity on us... Never take away from us Your love.*   Jewish daily prayer

Friday August 10   Hosea 12.2-9

Struggling with God

At the heart of this section is yet another series of puns. Hosea plays upon the name Jacob, in Hebrew *ya'akov*. In the womb he, *akav*, 'took his brother by the heel' (verse 3). In Genesis (25.26) the twins in Rebecca's womb are in constant struggle. Esau emerges first with Jacob holding his heel as if trying to pull him back and take his place.

In the same sentence Hosea plays on Jacob's later experience when he wrestled with a 'man' (Genesis 32.25). Here the 'man' is identified as a 'messenger' or 'angel' (verse 4), and the struggle – *yasar* – which gave Jacob his other name of *yisrael*, is really with, or for, God.

Verse 5 evokes the language of yet another key moment in Israel's history, when God was revealed to Moses at the burning bush heralding the rescue from Egypt. 'The Eternal is His name/remembrance' echoes Exodus 3.15.

Hosea plays with the traditional trickiness ascribed to Jacob. But, just as Jacob, refined by bitter experience, can become Israel, God's champion, so can Hosea's people return to God. They too must give up their deceitfulness and act out of faithfulness and justice, while waiting, hoping, for God to return to them.

✳ *Help us hold fast to the good within us and to good deeds, and bend our will and our desires to serve You.*
     Jewish daily prayer

Saturday August 11   Hosea 14.1-9

Reconciliation and restoration

The raging is over and calm is restored. God and the prophet have exhausted their anger, have offered every possible argument and threat. Now the task of reconciliation begins.

It depends on confession, the acknowledgement by Israel of their mistakes, failures and rebellions against God – not vast arrays of sacrifices but well-chosen and honest words (verses 2-3). Again one phrase springs out to haunt the religious consciousness. 'No longer will we say "our gods" to the work of our hands.' This echoes the way Aaron introduced the Golden Calf and King Jeroboam the new sanctuaries at Dan and Bethel: 'These are your gods, Israel, that brought you up from the land of Egypt' (Exodus 32.4).

But everything created by human beings can become elevated to a 'god'. It needs no more than a moment's inattention. Power, possessions, ideologies, religions become idols when they lose the sense of something beyond that calls them to account. Despite the difficulties in much of his writings, therein lies Hosea's power – that he speaks critically from within his religious tradition and wishes nothing less than honesty and integrity, to match the honesty and integrity demanded by the God he serves.

✳ *Give us integrity to love You and fear You. So shall we never lose our self-respect, nor be put to shame, for You are the power which works to save us.*   Jewish daily prayer

FOR REFLECTION – alone or with a group
- What idolatry can we identify today, both personally and in society?
- How do we reconcile the fact of different religions and our shared values with the truth claims of our own particular faith?

FOR ACTION
The language of Hosea belongs to a long line of texts and traditions that use images of women in a negative way to justify social behaviour and the largely male power structures that underpin them. A possible action is to examine the way such negative stereotypes within our religious traditions, liturgies, preaching and institutions still affect our communities today.

THE POWER OF DREAMING

Notes based on the Jerusalem Bible by
Kathy Galloway

Kathy Galloway is a theologian working in the community, a poet and a liturgist. She lives in Glasgow and edits 'Coracle', the magazine of the Iona Community.

'Without a vision, the people perish.' In a sense, the history of humankind is the story of the power of dreaming. Every endeavour, every creative act, every tiny accomplishment, every idea that has affected millions, originates in a dream. Whether it is the child we bear, the garden we plant, the scientific knowledge we seek, the music we compose, the revolution we make or the prayer we offer, it is an act of faith in a different future, one that we will not necessarily see. We dream for our children, for our lands and peoples, for the whole world or for our own salvation. The power to dream is one of the distinguishing characteristics of humankind.

'God hates visionary dreamers,' cried Dietrich Bonhoeffer, executed for his opposition to Nazism. When a dream of the glory of God becomes the fantasy of the glory of a man, or a system, or an idea, nightmares soon follow and there is no peace on earth. But how are we to discern the message of our dreams, so that we do not become part of the nightmare?

1. Dreams, fantasies or nightmares?

Sunday August 12   *Hebrews 11.1-3, 8-16**
Dreaming their real homeland

'And the glory of the Lord shall be revealed, and all flesh shall see it together.' These are the words of the first chorus of Handel's great oratorio, *The Messiah*. Artists of every generation and culture have expressed the dream in enduring images, words, sounds, movements, and we return to them again and again for their power to revive our own fading vision.

'I have a dream,' cried Martin Luther King and, in his inspired leadership, he spoke for millions who endured insult, imprisonment and death. He articulated their hope – but he also shared their struggle and its cost. Like Nelson Mandela in South Africa and Aung San Suu Kyi in Burma, 'they were longing for a better homeland' (verse 16).

The book of the Hebrews reminds us of some of our mothers and fathers in the faith. They too were 'in search of their real homeland... a better homeland, their heavenly homeland.' They too endured much, lost much, risked everything for the sake of realities that remained unseen. Their faith was not theoretical; they stepped out in it, moved their bodies – and became a bridge between the dream and the reality.

'Hope is not to foretell or foresee. It is a directedness of the mind, a directedness of the heart, anchored beyond the horizon' *(Vaclav Havel).*

✴ *Be thou my vision, O Lord of my heart.*

Monday August 13   *Genesis 32.22-32*

Dreaming survival

There can be few characters in the great *dramatis personae* of the Bible for whom tormented nights could be more easily predicted than Jacob. He is a moral thug. Not only has he injured others grievously; he himself is spiritually maimed.

But what we cannot admit, even to ourselves, in the cold light of day and consciousness, returns to haunt us by night, in dream or nightmare, when we wrestle with God. Jacob, the ultimate survivor, will not just settle for being undefeated. He actually demands a blessing, and **he will not let go** until he gets one. All his life, it seems, Jacob has known what he wanted.

If we are looking for morality we will not find it in Jacob. Esau wins that contest hands down. But there is in Jacob some stubborn, unquenchable spirit of sheer daring that wins a response of respect, even affection, from God (as it does for the spirited sinner throughout the Scriptures). It is like a recognition that this spirit is a necessity of the human struggle and dream as much as Esau's goodness. It too is part of the divine image.

Now Jacob knows his own woundedness, and the knowledge will change his life. But, he has 'seen God face to face, **and survived.**'

✴ *Be thou my battleshield, sword for the fight.*

Tuesday August 14   *Genesis 37.1-11*

Dreaming our truth

Jacob was a cunning man, but not, perhaps, a wise one. Otherwise he would not have made it so obvious to his other children that he loved Joseph (firstborn child of age and love) more. Joseph, on the other hand, secure in his parents' love, was too trusting for his own good. That he had been gifted with considerable intuitive insight was to be proven again and again. That he recounted to brothers who hated him a dream in which the whole family bowed down to him suggests that his spiritual perceptiveness was only matched by his worldly naiveté. Or perhaps his motive in telling was less innocent, and he wanted to get back at siblings who made his life a misery. We don't really know, but even his father was somewhat taken aback by the exalted scale of Joseph's dream.

As Freud pointed out, and as biblical chroniclers already well knew, it is precisely the unwise nature of our dreams that has the ring of truth about them. We may fool other people, we may fool our waking selves, but our dreams can reveal our deepest desires, in all their beauty and all their shame. Yet if we can confront that truth, it will be our friend, for God is active even in the depths of our dreaming souls.

✳ *Waking or sleeping, be thy presence my light.*

Wednesday August 15   *Genesis 40.1-23*

Dreaming of freedom

Having survived kidnap and being sold into slavery by his own brothers, Joseph is falsely imprisoned in Egypt on a trumped-up charge. But even in jail, Joseph's integrity and ability cannot be hidden. He becomes effectively the chief trusty. Joseph's is an extraordinary story of a man of outstanding gifts who experienced the extremes of fortune, finding himself the object of hostility, oppression and imprisonment, yet also inspiring deep love and confidence; who acted with foresight, courage and generosity even to those who had persecuted him, and who was eventually appointed governor of a large and powerful country. Every now and then, the world is gifted with such people.

Given his somewhat precarious position in the prison, caution might well have prevented Joseph from coming forward. But Joseph always believed that his power to interpret dreams came from God, a gift which he had a responsibility to exercise – and his only request in return was for a little assistance in his own unjust situation. Such requests are too soon forgotten when fortunes change and so it proved. Still, caution never awakens the kind of trust and love that Joseph did!

✳ *Be thou my soul's shelter, thou my high tower*
  Raise thou me heavenward, O Power of my power.

189

Practical dreaming

When Pharaoh is disturbed, everyone else is disturbed too. And no wonder Pharaoh is restless – these are disturbing dreams indeed. Their images of hunger and destruction do not require much imagination to make sense of.

When I was a small child, under five years old, I lived in the country. And I remember being told this story and being quite sure that skinny, starved cows were going to come up out of the placid River Nith in Scotland and eat up the fat cows in my meadow. The fear of famine is buried deep in the psyche of all human beings, even small ones in prosperous countries.

Perhaps all the wise men of Egypt knew perfectly well what the dream meant, but none wanted to be the harbinger of bad news. That was left to Joseph, who, resourceful man that he was, spelled out not just the problem but also the solution. Joseph gives lie to our stereotype of the dreamer as vague and head-in-the-air. Scratch a real dreamer, not just a fantasist, and you find political and economic strategies. Practical measures are also a measure of faith. Real faith makes real plans!

✳ ***Be thou my Wisdom, thou my true Word***
I ever with thee, thou with me Lord.

Shattered dreams

Living in the turbulent times before the invasion and destruction of Jerusalem by the Babylonians, fearful that God had abandoned them because of their sinful ways and idolatry, the religious leaders of Israel instigated a clean-up of some of the worst local excesses. At first supportive of this move, the prophet Jeremiah became disillusioned, for 'nothing is more deadly to a nation's spiritual welfare than a reformation which is not quite radical enough' (*The Old Testament,* Robert Davidson (Hodder & Stoughton 1964). In a time of national crisis, there is always a temptation to invest hope of deliverance in some mythical 'destiny of the nation' and so it was to prove here. The 'false prophets' whom Jeremiah scourged exacerbated this tendency with their intensely nationalistic, militaristic utterances. He hated the fact that they attributed their dreams, their 'private delusions', to God.

The story of the people of Israel in the book of Jeremiah is a salutary reminder that **any** people which pins its salvation on its own history, identity, or sense of divine calling, is gravely deluded. Their hope lies only in turning to God in the practice of justice and mercy, not with reformed institutions, military solutions or instructions to the Almighty, but with transformed hearts. The broken-hearted yet faithful Jeremiah embodied his message.

✳ *Thou and thou only, first in my heart*
High King of heaven, my treasure thou art.

Saturday August 18   *Matthew 27.15-26*
When the dream dies

Men should listen to their wives more! In fact, the Gospels are full of instances in which men failed to listen to women and got it wrong. The hopes, dreams and intuitions of women are so often derided and ignored. Not by Jesus, though.

In Bosnia, I heard a man say that it is easier for the women to take the first steps in reconciliation and reconstruction because they are not carrying the guilt of having committed atrocities. It is often true that when dreams turn nightmarish – when the vision fades and hope dies – the women are still there. Because they have children to care for and life – or some approximation of it – still goes on. Because they are forced to stay as hostages, as slaves, as prostitutes. Because they are too poor to go. And because a kind of loyalty, a kind of persistence, a kind of witness, and a need to offer the rites of burial to the dream holds them.

Pilate tried to wash his hands of complicity, to claim innocence and blame others. But the blood stuck. He should have listened to his wife.

✳ *Heart of my own heart, whatever befall,*
Still be thou my vision, O Ruler of all.

> *Prayers for 12-18 August are adapted from the hymn 'Be Thou my vision', translated from the ancient Irish by Mary Byrne (1880-1931) and versified by Eleanor Hull (1860-1935)*

FOR REFLECTION – alone or with a group

● Are there times in your life when a dream has said something important to you?
● What is your vision of hope?

2. Discerning the message

A message of encouragement

The book of Daniel was written around 167BC when Antiochus, the overlord of Judah, was attempting to integrate the Jews culturally and spiritually into the Hellenistic empire of which they were a part. Of all its diverse ethnic groups, the Jews were the most resistant to assimilation, determined to maintain the uniqueness of their religion against Greek ways. With the intention of whipping this recalcitrant people into line, Antiochus marched on Jerusalem and garrisoned his soldiers in the Temple, which was given over to the worship of Zeus. He publicly burned the Scriptures and banned all distinctively Jewish practices, including the worship of Yahweh.

The offence of all this to the Jews was unimaginable. It was desecration, an assault on God. Resistance hardened and a full-scale war of independence followed. In recounting the legends of Daniel – a traditional Jewish hero of the Babylonian exile four centuries earlier – the patriotic writer sought to inspire similar courage and integrity of faith among his people, and to proclaim God's judgement on oppressive empires.

Daniel, facing the spoilt capriciousness of an all-powerful ruler who demands the impossible of the people around him, inhabits a climate of fear in which the only recourse is to one's own wits – and trust in God. How many people since then have lived like this – and still do!

✳ ***Blessed be God forever.***

A message inside history

It is characteristic of despots that they expect those around them to give them what they want without even being told what it is. They seek knowledge of what only God knows – the future – precisely because it is beyond their control. That mysterious knowledge, not just of how to interpret the dream but of the dream itself, comes to Daniel in the extremity of threat, in a night vision. It is the gift of God 'to uncover depths and mysteries, to know what lies in darkness' (verse 22). Daniel's blessing of God is heartfelt.

Power to predict the future has always been a dangerous claim. The 19th century myth of progress became the 20th century nightmare of holocaust. To claim to know the mysteries of God is the arrogant pride that goes before a fall. Many have claimed apocalyptic visions in times of terror; but truth has rather been found in the prophetic reading of the signs of the times. Located in the present, these sought to demonstrate the consequences of certain courses of action. Their call was not based on the extraordinary or exotic, on arcane signs and symbols filtered through complicated belief systems. Instead, it was an eternal, simple call to humility and repentance, to justice and mercy in the ordinary everyday reality out of which God constructs a future inside history, where we actually live.

✳ *Blessed be God for ever, who lives in time and eternity.*

Tuesday August 21   *Daniel 2.36-47*
Small messages
Nebuchadnezzar's dream of the future, interpreted by Daniel, is a ruthlessly accurate reading of the past. The greatest of worldly empires glitters, tarnishes and fades away, to be superseded by another. The Greek Empire of the 2nd century BC will suffer the same fate as Nebuchanezzar's four centuries earlier. The warning and inference are clear. God's Kingdom will shortly replace the kingdoms of the world, and it will last for ever.

We can look back, more than two millennia later, and know that this analogy holds good. Many successive empires have come and gone. Many have predicted 'the end of history'. And many have too closely identified their own particular vision of the Eternal City with what God is doing in history – and found history outlasting their vision. Truthful discernment turns out to be a bit more than trying to make the facts fit one's own agenda.

The victors who write it tend to overlook 'the history not part of history'. Hence the chagrin of the mighty, who never notice what is going on among the small, the poor, the dispossessed. They do not see the mustard seed growing and, dinosaur-like, fail to observe, in their midst, the beginnings of a quiet revolution which will turn every understanding of power and majesty on its head.

✳ *Blessed be God, who loves justice and mercy*
   and pays heed to each body and soul.

A message of change

A paranoid child-slaughtering ruler dies. A little refugee family in the middle East has a dream of return. Power passes to another member of the murderous dynasty. The protector of the family has his sleep disturbed by warning dreams and, deciding that discretion is the better part of valour, they do not go back to where they came from. Instead, they settle in a distant highland region, far from the notice of priests and princes.

From such familiar (too familiar) pieces, a pattern takes shape which will invest the ordinary, precarious existence of a family in a small occupied country in troubled times, with extraordinary meaning and significance. The earthly powers are about to be shaken to their foundations; the careless cruelty, the pride of place, and above all the fear of revelation – upon which their power is based – will be exposed in all their nakedness and shame. What is weak will master the strong; what is defenceless will confound the mighty. Time itself will be bent. The love of power in every time will be vulnerable to its own crumbling before the power of love.

It's sometimes easy to be discerning with the hindsight of history.

✴ **Blessed be God, whose Kingdom is at hand.**

What we do not know

The passage of time may clarify some things, but it obscures others. Did Jesus really mean that it was his intention to hide the truth from all but a select few? Did he speak in parables, a common rabbinical method of teaching, in order not to reveal but to conceal? Was it a way of saying that the real import of his message was for the disciples alone, those one might describe as more advanced students, rather than the casual listener? Was he in a bad mood with the thick-headedness of the crowds? Was he reflecting on the lack of equal opportunity? Are these in fact not the words of Jesus at all, but comments added by later Christians who, finding evangelization difficult, found it easier to attribute this to a divine (and mystifying) hardening of hearts?

Personally, I incline to the bad mood theory, but the truth is, we don't know. Discernment is also a matter of admitting our ignorance. Verse 12 here has often been taken wholly out of context and applied in dangerous ways for which there is no textual support. Truthful discernment is wary of projecting from its own prejudices. Its first requirement is humility – following the light we have and praying for more light.

✱ *Blessed be God, who heals and forgives those who fall.*

Friday August 24   *Luke 4.16-30*

Good news

In its original context, this message was intended to reassure and hearten. In Isaiah, these were not symbolic phrases. They spoke of real, material circumstances. They were a testimony to the good news of God's deliverance for those who were destitute. The captives in Babylon would return home; prisoners would be released; the anguish of the broken-hearted would come to an end. This is the divine manifesto Jesus chose when he announced himself as the promised One.

We are accustomed to hearing this passage spiritualized and individualized, interpreted as deliverance from our sinful selves. Clearly, there is no reason to reject this interpretation. Jesus always enlarged meaning; the good news was not just for Jews but also for Gentiles; for the sinner as well as the righteous; for the individual as well as for the whole community. But we should never forget that the manifesto which Jesus claimed as his own was as a Jew, for whom there was no salvation apart from the community, and for whom good news for the poor was exactly that.

✱ *Blessed be God, who comes to save the oppressed*
  and lifts the poor from the doors of despair.

Saturday August 25   *Proverbs 25.6-7a*; Luke 14.1, 7-14**

A different way of seeing

As with empires, so with individuals! The fall of the mighty is no more humiliating than the (inevitable) displacement of the status-seeker. The virtue of humility is rarely a prized one. Yet it is a characteristic of the new way of seeing things which is at the heart of Jesus' message. The kind of reticence and delicacy he encourages refrains from attention-seeking, and simply accepts what honour comes. In the same way, hospitality is no longer a reciprocal gesture but an open-handed generosity that is rooted in the needs of those who have less.

How well Jesus knew the way our enthroned egos delude us with illusions of grandeur, and make us calculating. As with empires, so with individuals; we are blind to the certainty of judgement and the possibility of mercy, to the truth of the other and the love of God, because **we are always looking in the wrong places**. Look around you, says Jesus, open your eyes, get yourself out of the way! The Kingdom of God is among you. It is the dream which is the reality, closer to you than breathing. The rest is the illusion.

✳ ***Blessed be God, in whom is our hope and our trust who puts songs in the hearts of people.***

Prayers for 19-25 August are adapted from the song, 'Blessed be God', by Salvador Martinez, Philippines – from 'Many and Great: Songs of the World Church', Vol. 1, ed. John L Bell (Wild Goose Publications, 1990)

FOR REFLECTION – alone or with a group

● What are some of the criteria we use for discernment?
● Where do we find discernment most difficult?

FOR ACTION

Think of a long-cherished dream you have, even if it is a little one – to make a little garden, or clear up some wasteland; to do something for young people in your church or neighbourhood, or whatever. Begin to make some detailed plans for how the dream may become a reality. Find some people with whom you can carry them through. If it's a practical dream, then the right people will show up.

THE POWER OF DREAMING
3. Dreams of hope

Notes based on the New International Version by
Burchell K Taylor

Burchell K Taylor – who has been pastor of Bethel Baptist Church, Kingston, Jamaica, for over twenty-five years – is internationally recognized as a leading Caribbean biblical scholar and theologian.

The apostle Paul refers to God as 'the God of hope' (Romans 15.13). This reminds us that our human hope for all life and the whole creation resides in God. This being the case, the promises of God, to which his word testifies, are of supreme value to us. These promises are grounded on God's deeds already seen in creation and redemption. These deeds are yet to be brought to complete fulfilment in the New Order inaugurated and guaranteed in and through the person and work of Christ Jesus and the ongoing ministry of the Holy Spirit.

Our readings share with us some of the vital promises of God and the vision and hope they represent.

Sunday August 26   *Genesis 1.1-5, 20-31*
Creation

It all began with God: 'In the beginning God...'. God's creative presence and act accounted for the ordered universe and life within it. Humankind is given unique status in relation to God and the rest of creation (verses 27-31). This is a great theological and spiritual affirmation that ought to make a complete difference.

It implies that we can make no sense of the meaning and purpose of the universe and life without due reference to God. God is the key to our understanding. Humankind is meant to live and find fulfilment in community. This involves the acceptance and affirmation of the gift of sexuality which embraces differentiation, equality and reciprocity:

'male and female
   he created them'.

The relationship of people with the rest of creation must respect the integrity of all things. We are responsible and accountable to God in the outworking of this relationship. Communion with God and commitment to his service are integral to God's dream for humanity as they were from the very beginning.

✳ *Accept sincerest thanks, O God,*
for all the blessings that flow from you in all of life.

Monday August 27   *Isaiah 5.1-7**
Frustration

This is acknowledged to be one of the most beautiful passages in the book of Isaiah. There is a poignancy about it that is most touching and a challenge that is most compelling. We are held in suspense until we get to the end where it is disclosed that the story and the experience it relates are about God and his chosen people (verse 7). Divine purpose suffered great frustration and disappointment. The people failed to fulfil God's dream for them, just as the garden failed to produce the quality fruit it was meant to produce (verses 4 and 7). And there was no justifiable excuse for this. Everything possible was done to ensure the proper fulfilment of God's purpose. God never falls short in what he does to enable his people to fulfil his hope for them.

With adequate provision and careful preparation made, we see rightful expectation come to nought. This is dramatically put in the text, more so in the original than in the NIV translation,

'And he looked for justice but saw bloodshed;
for righteousness, but heard cries of distress' (verse 7).

The reasons for this are waywardness of will and rebelliousness of spirit, and these inevitably incur judgement, which will be experienced as divine abandonment. This is indeed a dreadful outcome.

Thank God he remains a saving God.

✳ *Loving God, we confess*
our constant frustrating of your gracious purpose.
Renew your purpose within us for Christ's sake.

Tuesday August 28   *Isaiah 11.1-9*
Reaffirmation

God reaffirms his promise to secure the future and well-being of his people and the whole creation in a new order under new leadership from the old line of his promise (2 Samuel 7.10-16). The people's failure and their disappointment were not unrelated to the failures of their leaders. The people placed great hope in some of them only to find it frustrated. Leaders often displayed lack of trust in God by practising the politics of expediency and dependency which often led to compromising alliances (Isaiah 7.1-6; 31.1).

Isaiah offers a different vision, a renewed hope, based on God's promised coming of a new leader. Much emphasis is placed on his qualification and role. He would be suitably equipped by the Spirit with the right attributes. He would execute justice, defend the people, re-establish meaningful communion with God and renew the created order. What better vision could be desired for the inspiration and maintenance of hope?

Our Lord Jesus Christ has inaugurated this new order and with eager anticipation we await its consummation.

✳ *Lord, help us to take you at your word*
  that we live trusting your promises in which lie our hope.

Wednesday August 29   *Isaiah 25.6-8*

Celebration

God's people sorrow in the world but not as those without hope. Their hope gives rise to celebration in spite of prevailing realities that bring pain. Living towards God's future gives an alternative vision of reality which has a way to put the things that cause distress into proper perspective.

God's dream here is of a divine victory over the forces and powers of alienation, oppression and death. This is appropriately celebrated in royal style, recalling traditional banquets such as took place on the enthronement of a king. This celebration will be at God's invitation and it will be of universal scope (verse 7). No one else can rightly offer such an invitation because it is God alone who has power, ultimately, to defeat the victimizing forces involved, including death.

The language speaks of the restoration of human hope in terms that point in the direction of resurrection. A full-blown expression of it may not be found here but there is a strong sense that death itself does not have the final say.

✳ *We give you thanks, O God, for your victory over death*
  that you have accomplished in Jesus Christ.

Thursday August 30   *Isaiah 35.1-10*

Restoration

The prophet sets forth the vision of a day that will disperse the gloom that had settled upon the people. These words were most likely spoken at a time when the people felt hopeless and helpless in exile in Babylon. There was a future that was open to them. It was completely in the hands of God and would represent a complete reversal of the state of affairs. God will again be their Liberator and the Restorer of their welfare and well-being, just as he had been in the Exodus event. In fact, the whole experience will be like a new Exodus. This time the hostile environment of the journey will be completely transformed. It will be negotiated with ease. The fearful will be reassured, the weak reinvigorated, the disabled restored, and the unredeemed removed. It will be a community of the restored and redeemed, re-established as the place of peace and salvation that it was meant to be.

Didn't Jesus draw on this passage in answer to the query of John the Baptist about his identity? (Matthew 11.2-5). The time is indeed upon us in which the in-breaking of the new and restored order has been announced and inaugurated by none other than Jesus our Lord. Let us rejoice in hope.

✳ *Lord, may your Kingdom come on earth as in heaven.*

Friday August 31   *Isaiah 33.13-24**
Vindication
Those who pursue and benefit from oppression and injustice invariably become arrogant and seem unstoppable. On the other hand, those who pursue righteousness, and are themselves often victims because of it, are sometimes pushed to the edge of disillusionment if not despair, by such a state of affairs. There is a word of encouragement and hope for them in the words of this passage.

God dislikes oppression and has a record of taking an effective stand against it. It is promised that he will again move against all such oppressors and their oppression in decisive and victorious fashion. He will vindicate his cause and manifest his sovereignty fully and lastingly. It will be the joy of the faithful to behold his glory and to experience their own vindication in the process. This possibility must remain a source of inspiration and the basis of faithfulness in the midst of current struggles.

On the cross, our Lord Christ declared, 'It is finished', indicating that the purpose of victory and vindication of righteousness, which were confirmed by the Resurrection, were now accomplished. The faithful, who now face persecution for righteousness' sake, will find inspiration and strength in this, and in the victory and vindication yet to be fully and finally manifested.

✳ *Lord, give hope where despair encroaches upon my heart.*

Saturday September 1   *Matthew 20.1-16**

Grace

The whole story of our human hope grounded upon divine action in creation and redemption, restoration and vindication, is a matter of grace and grace alone. This finds its ultimate expression in the coming of Jesus Christ into the world as the ultimate 'Yes' to the promises of God (2 Corinthians 1.20). A good glimpse of the nature and character of this grace is given in our reading for today. Grace, that unique expression of divine liberating and life-transforming love, is entirely of the freedom and initiative of God. There is no prior claim on it from any quarter. It cannot be argued for as a right. It bears within it an element of mystery and surprise, for it always exceeds expectation and is never subject to calculation. It is revolutionary and far-reaching in the manner that it gives hope to the hopeless and remains available even to those who are offended by its generosity, if they will accept it on God's terms.

Without grace there is no hope.

✳ *Lord, give me the humility to depend upon your grace*
and the joy of sharing its benefits in Christ.

FOR REFLECTION – alone or with a group

- How do you see God's dreams for the world expressed in the story of creation in Genesis 1?
- How far do the prophets keep alive that dream, and how is it perfected in Christ?

FOR ACTION

What new steps do you need to make to strengthen hope within yourself and those around you? How will those steps help to sustain hope for the world?

THE POWER OF DREAMING
4. Transformation

Notes based on the Revised English Bible by
Clare Amos

Clare Amos, the Theological Resource Officer of USPG, has taught biblical studies in Jerusalem, Beirut, Cambridge, South London and Kent. She has also recently become honorary editor of 'The Reader', the national magazine for Church of England Lay Readers.

Several of the Bible readings this week stem from the period in Old Testament history that is referred to as 'the exile.' It was a cataclysm which shook the faith of Israel's people to its foundations. Many did not survive the time of trial, either physically, emotionally or faithfully. But some dug deep into the traditions of their past, and into their awareness that 'the steadfast love of God never changes'. And their faith helped create dreams that sustained them during the dark days of exile, and which turned into the seeds of a new future.

In our times of despair and desolation we too need our dreams and visions. For us too they become the source of a new and transformed future.

Sunday September 2   *Isaiah 43.14 to 44.5**

Dare to dream

Dreaming is dangerous. It opens us up to the possibility of change, even when it might be more comfortable to wallow in our abyss of despair or sin. Such was the attitude that confronted the prophet whose words appear in Isaiah 40-55. By the time he wrote, the people had been in exile for more than half a century. Communal memories of their homeland had faded: being slave labourers to the Babylonians had at least a tolerable familiarity to it. And they could even defend their outlook as a kind of pious acceptance of the punishment that had been meted out to their sinful forbears.

Not so, said the prophet. It is to the future and not the past that you should be looking! God is going to do something new, and far greater than anything you have experienced before. Grasp courage in your hands and dare to be led out into freedom. God can recreate the wilderness you think is waiting for you. God has the future in his hands – and you too!

✳ *The past is comfortable. I feel so secure there.*
No, I don't want to move. I don't want to change.

But God is doing for you a new thing,
do you not see the way he has made for you?

Let me stay behind, freedom is too frightening.
I want to say No.

I'm not a bad person, just afraid to be forgiven now.
I don't want God's risky challenge.
It is too costly to stand up and be restored.

But Jesus offers you acceptance,
pledges to you the Yes of his own life.

If only my friends would carry me,
resting me gently in your presence
I might begin to say – Perhaps.

The future is being formed; I am invited into it.
Am I brave enough to trust God's faithfulness,
to offer my assent to his love?
In the community of the faithful I find a welcome;
those around me testify, giving their Amen.
I will allow Christ to set his seal upon me,
I am free to declare God's praise,
I will say Yes for evermore.
                                                    Clare Amos
                        Based on Isaiah 43.14 to 44.5 and Mark 2.1-12

Monday September 3   *Isaiah 51.1-16*

Colours of creation

Sometimes our dreams for the future need to be fed by the memories of our past. So the prophet draws on the story of Abraham and Sarah – how God's faithfulness to them had overcome all the odds (verse 2), and God's incredible rescue of his people from the roar of the sea and the hordes of Pharaoh (verses 10 and 15).

The future will be just as sure as this past. But gradually, as the writer continues, his vision draws him out of historical time, to the moment of creation when time itself began. The prophet speaks of God's victory over the forces of chaos, symbolized by the figure of the dragon Rahab, which allowed creation itself to take place (verse 9). By reaching back into the dawn of creation in this way, the paint box which colours the picture of the future suggests that it is nothing less than a new creation. God's care for his people, for every single one of them, is not bounded by time, but is itself as sure as creation (verse 16).

✻ *Deep calls to deep in the roar of your cataracts,*
and all your waves, all your breakers, sweep over me.
By day the LORD grants his unfailing love;
at night his praise is upon my lips,
a prayer to the God of my life.   *Psalm 42.7-8*

Tuesday September 4   *Habakkuk 2.1-3*
Watching for wisdom
An ancient city was defined as a 'city' by being enclosed with walls. And with the walls came watch-towers, elevated and defended structures that allowed the city's watchmen to see enemies or allies approaching from afar. The symbol of a watch-tower was a potent one in the last centuries of the kingdom of Judah, in the decades before Jerusalem succumbed to a Babylonian siege. People understood only too well what the prophet Habakkuk was meaning when he compared his ministry to a 'watch-tower'. It was essential always to keep on the look-out: there was, and is, a 'vision' (2.3) for each season, but only those who were prepared to continue looking, even when the night was dark, could expect to see what they were looking for, whether it was in hope or in dread.

To give up dreaming – looking for the vision – may sometimes feel the easiest, or most logical course. But, said another ancient prophet, 'Where there is no vision the people perish.' The vision depends on us, as much as it does on the one who gives it. We cannot hope to see a new world, unless we are prepared to keep open the eyes of our heart (Ephesians 1.18).

✻ *I will wait for the LORD with longing;*
I put my hope in his word.   *Psalm 130.5*

Wednesday September 5   *Isaiah 61.1-11*
Garments of glory
Those who were to return to Palestine and Jerusalem, after their captor Babylon was overthrown by the Persians in 538BC, were confronted by a ruined city and a devastated economy. In such circumstances – why dream of returning? But the dreams made a

return begin to feel possible. Isaiah 56-66 probably stems from this time, and the extravagant language seeks to dream dreams into reality. In these verses images and metaphors abound: the people will be like majestic and long-enduring trees (verse 3), like a bride or a bridegroom arrayed in glorious garments (verses 3, 10). Throughout the Bible the image of a change of garments stands again and again for a radical transformation. The world will become transformed into a place marked out by justice and compassion; it will be the location for God's Jubilee (verse 2).

Centuries later, Jesus began his ministry in Nazareth by quoting from this chapter (Luke 4.18-19). He caught up the dream and, in his ministry, gave it life. In situations of arid desolation we all need to revisit the dreams of our biblical forebears, and make them our own. Perhaps we shall discover to our surprise that the vision is the greater reality.

✳ *The day of Jubilation*
   Earth tell it out abroad!
   The Jubilee of justice,
   The Jubilee of God!
   From debt to equal living,
   From sickness unto health,
   Our Christ has purchased Jubilee
   Of earth's abundant wealth.   *Alison Norris*

Thursday September 6   *Isaiah 66.10-14*

A miracle of maternity

Sometimes the vision plants a seed that will only bear its fruit centuries – or millennia – later. Such is the case with the vision of God that is portrayed in these verses. In struggling to describe the compassion and tenderness of God, the prophet homes in on metaphors that picture maternity.

'As a mother comforts her son
so shall I myself comfort you' (verse 13).
Earlier God has actually described himself as the midwife of his people – again a female role (at least in biblical society). There are not many places in the Old Testament (or in the New) where such vividly female imagery is employed for God. Yet there are some. Deuteronomy 32.18 is a notable example, but these verses from Isaiah have a more evocative power.

In the last centuries of the Old Testament period, and in New Testament times, any feminine aspect of God was feared and frowned upon. Whether deliberately or not, there was a sort of censorship that presented God as safely masculine.

But the seed sown in such words as these from the book of Isaiah could not be permanently stifled. Here and there fresh metaphors for God sprang up. Among Syriac-speaking Christians the exquisite poetry of St Ephrem, or the haunting stanzas of the Odes of Solomon dared to excite us by crossing the limitations of masculine language. Centuries later the prayer of St Anselm, or the words of Julian of Norwich again drew from this 'Isaianic seed' to explore God in feminine terms.

Today we are both the heir and transmitter of the dream of Isaiah 66. It acts as a warranty and a defence for those who are challenged for exploring the feminine faces of God. For those who criticize them are not themselves being biblical.

✳ *Jesus, as a mother you gather your people to you:*
you are gentle with us as a mother with her children.

In your compassion bring grace and forgiveness:
for the beauty of heaven may your love prepare us.

Lord Jesus, in your mercy heal us:
in your love and tenderness remake us.
    From Michael Vasey's rendering of the prayer of St Anselm

Friday September 7   *Ezekiel 47.1-12*

Torrents from the Temple

One of the most vivid impressions that Jerusalem makes upon those who visit it, is the realization that the city is on the edge of the wilderness. You simply have to go and stand on the summit of the Mount of Olives to the east of the city. On one side you can look down on the great Muslim sanctuary of the Dome of the Rock (the former site of the Temple) and into the heart of the bustling city. On the other side the land immediately falls away, arid and barren, into the wastes of the Jordan Valley and the Dead Sea.

Jerusalem has always suffered the vulnerability that comes from being on this geographical frontier. It has clung to life, a life made possible only by the waters of the tiny Gihon spring at the base of one of its hills. In years of drought the desert can encroach and threaten to reclaim the city.

So the image that Ezekiel employs to express the wonder of God's return to his Temple after the Babylonian exile would have spoken powerfully to his audience. It told of a transformation that extended beyond people's hopes or dreamings. Instead of the insignificant Gihon spring, God's presence in the Temple would provide a source of life, a stream of water that would well up and transform the wilderness of Judah from death into life. It would even change the Dead Sea (so named because its waters are too salty for anything to live in it) into a Sea of Life teeming with living creatures.

In the Fourth Gospel John draws upon Ezekiel's vision to help him tell his story. In the Sea of Galilee too, one morning, the disciples discover empty nets suddenly teeming with fish, for the Lord of Life has come to them. Night is over and a new day has dawned (John 21.1-14).

✳ *There is a river whose streams bring joy*
    to the city of God...
The LORD *of Hosts is with us,*
the God of Jacob is our fortress.   *Psalm 46.4, 7*

Saturday September 8   *Revelation 22.1-5*
Faith to face
One of the riches of the Bible, and its gift to those who wrestle with it, is the way in which biblical texts and traditions are layered one on top of another, a later text interpreting an earlier one, in the light of a new experience to which it is now witnessing. So it is here. Revelation 22 draws deeply upon the vision of Ezekiel which we met in yesterday's reading. Once again we read of a river flowing in the city of Jerusalem. But this city of the future catches up and transforms the failures of the past, for now the riverbanks are lined with trees, including the tree of life: sought for during so many generations since the garden of Genesis.

But in this new city – not unlike the earthly Jerusalem – one thing is missing. Throughout history, from the time of Solomon, the rationale for Jerusalem was its Temple. It was why the city became a focus for pilgrimage. Jesus himself journeyed there. So it is perhaps strange that the writer of Revelation says, 'I saw no temple in the city' (21.22). Yet he provides the answer. The Temple, which had been built to be the place where human beings could encounter God, is now redundant – because through the life and death of Jesus, God is present with his people. The story of separation and alienation that began when a man and woman hid from God in a garden, finally now enjoys its healing in a city where the ancient desire for God's presence is granted 'faith to face'. The alienation that has separated human beings from God and from each other can be overcome. At last Jerusalem – the city called to be a vision of peace, yet so often a theatre of war – can finally honour its name.

✳ *O Lord, soften the stone hearts*
of those who preach and
practise intolerance and bigotry
– as the sun's setting glow
softens the stone walls of your
Holy City, Jerusalem.

Lord, the rocky hills, the valleys,
the deserts and the sea shores are filled with the echoes
of centuries of pain.
Lord, bring peace to house and village.

Comfort the mothers who fret
and those who mourn.

Lord, keep strong the twisted
old root of the olive tree,
and protect the young vine.

Lord of water and stone;
of bread and wine;
Lord of resurrection,
feed hope and bring peace
to the wracked and beautiful
Holy Land.
© *Gerald Butt*
Written in St George's Cathedral, Jerusalem

FOR REFLECTION – alone or with a group

What are the themes and images from the Bible which speak most powerfully to you of change and transformation?

INTERNATIONAL BIBLE READING ASSOCIATION

1020 Bristol Road, Selly Oak, Birmingham, Great Britain B29 6LB

ORDER FORM – For 2002 Books

Please send me the following books:

Name: _____

Address: _____

_____

_____ Postcode: _____

*To qualify for 2002 books at these special IBRA readers' prices, this order form must be used (photocopies not accepted). Your order will be dispatched when **all** books are available.*

Code	Title of Book	Quantity	Unit Price	Total
ZYW0991	Words for Today 2002		£5.00	
ZYL0992	Light for Our Path 2002		£5.00	
ZYL0993	Large Print Light for Our Path 2002		£9.00	
ZYF0897	Finding Our Way Together Book 1		£6.50	
ZYF0910	Finding Our Way Together Book 2		£6.50	
ZYF0938	Finding Our Way Together Book 3		£6.50	
ZYF0974	Finding Our Way Together Book 4		£6.50	
ZYF0897-SET	Finding Our Way Together series (4 BOOKS)		£20.00	
ZYS1000	Sharing God's Word 2002		£5.50	
ZYD0989	Discovering Christ *Advent & Christmas*		£6.50	
ZYD0994	Discovering Christ *Ascension & Pentecost*		£6.50	
ZYO0990	Online to God		£4.50	
ZYE0213	Everyday Prayers		£5.50	
ZYM0325	More Everyday Prayers		£5.50	
ZYF0495	Further Everyday Prayers		£5.50	
ZYL0781	Living Prayers For Today		£12.50	
ZYM0902	More Living Prayers For Today		£12.50	

I enclose cheque (Payable to IBRA)

Please charge my MASTERCARD / VISA / SWITCH

Card No:, Issue No (Switch): [ ]

[ ][ ][ ][ ][ ][ ][ ][ ][ ][ ][ ][ ][ ][ ][ ][ ]

Expiry Date: _____

Signature: _____

Total cost of books	
Post – UK free Overseas – add £3.00 airmail per book	
Donation to International Fund	
TOTAL DUE	

Payments in <u>Pounds Sterling</u>, please

The INTERNATIONAL BIBLE READING ASSOCIATION is a Registered Charity

International Bible Reading Association

Help us to continue our work of providing Bible study notes for use by Christians in the UK and throughout the world. The need is as great as it was when IBRA was founded in 1882 by Charles Waters as part of the work of the Sunday School Union.

Please leave a legacy to the International Bible Reading Association.

An easy-to-use leaflet has been prepared to help you provide a legacy. Please write to us at the address below and we will send you this leaflet – and answer any questions you might have about a legacy or other donations. Please help us to strengthen this and the next generation of Christians.

Thank you very much.

International Bible Reading Association
Dept 298, 1020 Bristol Road
Selly Oak
Birmingham B29 6LB
Great Britain
Tel. 0121 472 4242
Fax 0121 472 7575

Our solicitors are **Pothecary and Barratt**, Talbot House, Talbot Court, Gracechurch Street, London EC3V 0BS

Charity No. 211542

THE POWER OF DREAMING
5. Do dreams come true?

Notes based on the Revised English Bible by
Joy Mead

Joy Mead is a poet and writer who is involved in justice and peace work. She has recently edited Finding Our Way Together Book 4 (IBRA).

'You're a dreamer.' How many times have I heard that when I imagine a world where all life is valued, earth's good gifts shared and interdependence acknowledged and respected! Maybe this is dreaming, but what would the world be like without it? Imagination and creativity are not extras to life. They are, as this week's readings show, essentials. Neglect the imagination and we lose the ability to think of fullness of life for all people.

The Australian Aboriginal proverb says, 'Those who lose *dreaming* are lost.' It's the process of dreaming that matters.

Maybe dreams don't 'come true', but dreaming is truth.

Sunday September 9   *Genesis 45.1-15*
Sweet dreams!

Joseph is a good dreamer. He can imagine and see connections. He is sensitive and compassionate – a good person to have in government, but not always popular with those who feel threatened by the imagination's unlimited validity. Truths are to be found in the good dreaming – something beyond our little selves. When immediate events are unfavourable to him, Joseph passes no ultimate judgement but sees them as part of a bigger picture. Dreamers and poets know that responsibility begins in dreams – for telling dreams and writing poetry may destroy immunity to human emotions.

When Joseph recognizes the men asking for food as the brothers who had sold him into slavery, he doesn't condemn or pass judgement. He responds with love and wisdom, telling his brothers not to be distressed, for this is the way things are meant to be. All people will be fed, plenty will be shared – the ultimate dream.

✳ *God of multi-coloured dreaming,*
things that hurt us now will change when we are joyful.
Help us to understand the mystery of our suffering

211

so that we bear our hardships
and imagine life as it is meant to be for all.

Dreaming of Eden
Deuteronomy means 'second law'. It is meant to speak to future generations, so in many ways it is the book of dreaming. Our dreams are like trees, often planted for children and grandchildren – rooted in the earth with their heads in the heavens. Francis Mesah is a farmer in the Central Region of Ghana. His oil-palms are healthy and productive. Scattered throughout his fields are tall forest canopy trees in great demand by timber contractors, but Francis will not allow any of them to be cut. They give shade and help maintain the local water-table level. They are the future; they are the dream holders.

Today's passage is precise: choose life – 'life for you and length of days *on the soil*' – live in harmony with all creation – that's a cyclical not a linear law. If we lose the law of life in a relentless logic of 'progress' and destroy the dream of Eden, then we shall surely be cursed. But if we share in God's greening, we shall be blessed: life for you – life for all.

✳ *God of the dream-times,*
help us to root our dream of Eden firmly in the good earth.

Re-making our dreams
Jeremiah is a poet, prophet, dreamer: not an indifferent artist, but one who loves. His messages of apparent foreboding have the rootedness of one who remains deeply and creatively human, and pushes back the boundaries of the possible. He sees things as they are, and how they could be. He continually re-dreams the world.

We need to re-awaken our sensitivity to images of ancient dreams – what we once in our arrogance and ignorance called 'primitive objects'. The *Right to Hope* Exhibition – launched in South Africa to coincide with the 50th Anniversary of the United Nations – shows different ways of experiencing and responding to our world, different uses to which science and technology can be put to deal more effectively and creatively with poverty, illiteracy, unemployment and environmental degradation.

Jeremiah's lesson from the potter's shop is similar. Politics is the art of the possible; creativity the art of the impossible.

Creativity and imagination can change the shape of the future; there is always another way; it's not too late...

✳ *God, artist and re-shaper,*
help us to see as oppressive the lie that there is no other way
so that we may help to re-make humanity's dreams.

Wednesday September 12   *Matthew 11.2-6*

Ordinary miracles!

John, in prison but looking towards a day of liberation, asks, 'Are you my dream?' Jesus responds not by telling him who he is but what his dreams are made of: the human quest for justice and beauty, joy and peace; people showing the fruits of love, the work of the Spirit. This is the response that colours the night-time darkness of John's prison and it isn't about some sort of fantasy world. It's about the ordinary world where the miracles are of sharing, healing, transforming and the wonders are of love, courage and endurance. I think of little dreams of the Caribbean tucked away behind inner city railway tracks and busy roads. On traditional English allotments sunshine plants put down roots in British soil; people coax exotic plants to thrive even through dank and dark English winters so that they explode like fireworks on the grey city scene.

Wherever good things are happening, there we see the life-transforming, on-going strength of the dream – not an end but a singing, dancing, growing process.

✳ *God of good dreaming,*
help us to see that what we dream of
is the essence of who we are
and sustenance for our grey and empty moments.

Thursday September 13   *Acts 2.1-18*

Free to dream

The Pentecost story points us back to Joel's vision of unity in diversity: a world in which all sorts of people live together in a new way. It's a story about breaking down barriers and living fully and freely in community – a liberation story which uses the imagery of wind and fire to tell of the life-giving energy deeply embodied in the wonder of creation. If Pentecost signals the beginning of the Church, then it is a church that joins with all laughing, weeping, dancing, loving, living; a church that like a dream catcher holds the good dreams of ancestral spirits so that they may be dreamed afresh by the next generation; a church that celebrates the people's hopes and frees them from guilt and fear; a church that radiates energy and life; a church that we create and continually image and re-image.

Pentecost is about having power, confidence and energy to make the things we dream of happen.

✳ *God, make us a church that joins in with your loving,*
as you cherish and challenge, rein in and release,
a church that is winsome, impassioned, inspiring;
lioness of your justice and lamb of your peace.

> *Kate Compston – in Dare to Dream,*
> *ed. Geoffrey Duncan (HarperCollins)*

Friday September 14   *Romans 15.22-33*

Dreams find their release

Paul's hope is that he will visit the Christians in Rome 'in a happy frame of mind' on his way to Spain, but first of all he will visit a community in Jerusalem – poor but able, hopeful and imaginative. We can picture them – a loving, caring community working against great odds. We might hear of similar people today, maybe on one of our troubled housing estates. As small neighbourhood groups they seek to establish food co-operatives, credit unions, youth groups... keeping alive their dream of a loving, caring community free from crime and abuse.

We know that Paul doesn't make it to Spain. He ends up in prison in Rome (Acts 21.18 to 22.29). How many of us long for Spain... and end up imprisoned in Rome? It's a familiar story. We have to learn to live in a world where our highest hopes aren't realized and transform the disappointments into opportunities for loving and giving wherever we are – that's how dreams come true.

✳ *God of the upside-down dreams,*
help us to follow faithfully
the man who came to tip the balance with fishermen
and fools
and totally reverse what we think of as success.

Saturday September 15   *Philemon 1-21**

Getting personal

In this little letter Paul is getting personal, but his concern is also political. The more personal we are the more we need to confront

214

the needs of community and then the personal becomes political
– the two are inseparable. Paul's concern for Onesimus is also a
concern about the community to which he, Paul, is sending him
back. If he neglects one, he neglects the other also. Onesimus is
returning to be included and live out Paul's dream of a new
pattern of life where his voice will be heard.

In his book *Faith in the Poor* (Lion Publishing), Bob Holman
has collected some extraordinary stories by economically
excluded people – our brothers and sisters whose voices are not
usually heard. They tell their own stories – personal stories that
are also political stories. They haven't lost the dreaming – if our
society could understand that then they would have the same
faith in them as Paul has in Onesimus.

✳ *God of the one and the many,*
   give us faith in people and passion for justice;
   turn our misunderstandings into music
   and our prejudices into poetry.

FOR REFLECTION – alone or with a group

- What does resurrection faith mean? How much does it have to
  do with dreams, with not being resigned to hard facts?
- Why are we so unready to acknowledge that we all speak and
  act from our own experience? Is it because we become
  vulnerable and open to the personal experience of others?
- What are the responsibilities that begin in dreams?

FOR ACTION

Be still: wonder and dream good things for our earth. Give form to
your dreams – as poems, stories, paintings, pottery, sculpture...
and the way you live in community.

THE POWER OF DREAMING
6. God beyond the dreams

Notes based on the New Revised Standard Version by
Pauline Webb

Pauline Webb is a broadcaster, writer and Methodist local preacher. She regularly presents the Daily Service on Radio 4 and Pause for Thought on Radio 2, programmes which try to help people see beyond the immediate moment to the eternal significance of what God is saying to us through contemporary events. She has also recently co-edited a book, entitled 'Worship in Every Event' (Oxford University Press), which emphasizes the connection between the worship of God and the crises of everyday life.

Many people can recall moments of special illumination when the 'God light' streamed into their lives and faith became a natural response to the sense of God's presence. But beyond the vision of our dreaming lies the more demanding experience of learning to walk with God through daily routine. This week's readings show us how some of the great prophets managed to turn such fleeting moments of spiritual inspiration into a constant sense of companionship with God.

Sunday September 16   *Numbers 12.1-8*
Rivalry or recognition?
Even prophets can fall out with one another, especially if one seems to be given greater prominence than the others. Miriam and Aaron both had considerable prophetic gifts themselves. Miriam's songs had encouraged the Children of Israel through the long trek in the wilderness. Aaron's eloquence had enabled him to become his brother's spokesman. But now they see their brother Moses as their rival, and complain about his marrying one who is a foreigner to the family. Moses is humble enough not even to hear their complaint. But God does hear and rebukes them for their jealousy, bidding them recognize that Moses has a specially intimate relationship with God, which relies not just on particular moments of inspiration, dreams and visions, but on daily living in God's presence (verses 6-8).

It is always sad when those who are gifted themselves fail to recognize the different gifts God has given to others. Two world-renowned cellists were once asked if they considered themselves as rivals. 'No', they replied, 'because we are both only servants of the great masters of music. When we play Bach we are both humbled.' The gift of humility is itself a most important spiritual gift.

✳ *Lord, teach us to be grateful for the particular gifts*
you have given to each of us, but teach us also
the humility to recognize that you have given others
even deeper insights into your ways,
so that we might learn from them
how to live daily in your presence.

Monday September 17   *1 Kings 3.1-15*
A listening mind
This prayerful dialogue sounds like a vigil rather than a dream. Anyone who has ever had to take up a new responsibility from a renowned predecessor will sympathize with Solomon's sense of personal inadequacy and his need for a time of quiet preparation. He retreats to the tent of meeting which Moses had established in the wilderness.

I remember once myself, on the eve of taking up a new and daunting job, feeling the need to go for a weekend to a retreat centre. There I was able to spend a much longer time than usual in quiet prayer and preparation for the task ahead of me. Strengthened by that vigil of prayer, like Solomon I was able to return to the city to take up my task with a new-found confidence.

Solomon's prayer and God's response to it teach us the most important lesson for anyone placed in a position of leadership – whether we be parents or teachers, counsellors or politicians, church officers or secular employers. We all need to learn the importance of *listening*, first to God, and then to those over whom we have been given any kind of power.

✳ *Lord, give to all who are called to positions of leadership*
wisdom to seek your guidance,
willingness to listen with an understanding mind,
and ability to discern between right and wrong policies,
for the good of the people, and for your name's sake.

Tuesday September 18   *Ezekiel 1.22-28*
Above the Dome
Since the Millennium celebrations last year, London has been given a new symbol on its skyline – the great dome which housed

the 'Millennium experience'. When Sir Christopher Wren was commissioned to rebuild the fire-razed cathedral for the city of London, he insisted on constructing a dome rather than replicating the original tall spires. A dome signifies an over-arching splendour crowning all that is contained within it.

In Ezekiel's vision, even beyond the glory of the dome, glowed the grandeur of the architect of the universe itself, seated on a throne. He appears to have human form. It is as though the visionary sees, beyond the greatest of marvels, an extraordinary glimpse of the humility by which God himself will come to share our human experience. And around the throne he sees that other great symbol of the mercy of God, the rainbow reminder of God's covenant with the whole of humanity. At the sound of God's voice, even the angels let down their wings, and the prophet falls down in reverence. But this God beyond the dome has a message to be delivered to the people, and we, like Ezekiel, must get up on our feet and proclaim it to the nation.

✳ *Lord, help us to see beyond*
  our pride in human achievements, even beyond
  our wonder at the splendour of the universe,
  that our greatest glory is that you have shared
  our human predicament and in your mercy
  opened heaven to us, through Jesus Christ our Lord.

Wednesday September 19   *Isaiah 60.1-5,19-22**

The glory beyond the sun

To be deprived of sunlight can become a serious affliction. Appropriately, the acronym 'SAD' stands for 'seasonal affective disorder'. Just as people need light and sun for their physical well-being, so too they need vision and hope for their spiritual health. In this passage the prophet is speaking to a dispirited people who have been deprived of their land and separated from many of their loved ones. The exiles have been dispersed through many lands. He reminds them that not even the darkness of their present circumstances can blot out the light of God's love and purpose for their lives. They must try to penetrate beyond the present clouds to the glory that will shine upon them in the future, when all the exiles will return home and peace and justice will once more flourish in the land.

Once we learn to live with the kind of hope which faith can give, our joy no longer depends on the brightness of the sun nor on the comfort of our immediate circumstances. Our faith is a faith for all seasons, and the glory of God can brighten up all our days.

✳ **Lord, whose glory outshines the sun**
   and whose goodness outlives human evil,
   we pray particularly today for those who are sad,
   for whatever reason, that in some way
   they may hear a word of hope, bidding them look up
   to the everlasting light of your presence. Amen

Thursday September 20   *Luke 15.1-10**
Beyond the pale
It is important to notice the context in which Luke places this familiar picture of Jesus as the shepherd bringing home the lost sheep. It gives emphasis to the latter part of the parable – the shepherd calling all his friends and neighbours to come and share in his rejoicing over the successful search. He expects them to have shared his concern over the one who was lost. But the first two verses of the chapter make it clear that the Pharisees and scribes by no means shared Jesus' enthusiasm over reclaiming sinners and even treating them as friends. To make the point clear not only to the men in his audience but to the women as well, Jesus reminds the women how any woman would want her neighbours to rejoice with her if she had found a precious coin she had lost. Part of the joy of the find is sharing it with others.

Both parables emphasize how precious the lost are to Jesus, and how persistent is his search 'until he finds' them. If sinners are so precious to him, who are we to write off anyone as 'beyond the pale', and so be content to leave them there?

✳ **Lord, teach us to share your concern for all who have lost**
   their way in life; show us how we can join in your search for
   them; and give us the grace to welcome those who find their
   way back home.

Friday September 21   *Acts 26.4-23*
Not disobedient to the vision
Among the many letters of sympathy I received at the time when my father died was one which quoted these words from St Paul's speech to King Agrippa. The writer pointed out that my father, who was a greatly loved Methodist minister, had had a varied and

sometimes difficult ministry. It had spanned two world wars and survived many setbacks and sudden changes of stationing. 'But', said the writer, 'he was never disobedient to the heavenly vision.'

St Paul would have approved of such constancy. The proof of the reality of his own conversion experience was that it gave him a confidence that never deserted him. Long after the blinding light had dimmed and the heavenly voice had fallen silent, Paul continued steadfastly in the vocation to which God had called him. It had taken him on many long journeys and led him into dangerous situations, but never once did he regret that first response he had made to the Jesus who spoke to him personally by name. Damascus Road experiences are inevitably fleeting ones and may take many different forms. The true test of our discipleship is how steadily we keep right on to the end of the road!

✱ *Lord, I thank you for the way in which my own journey of faith began. I remember those moments when it seemed as though you were speaking to me by name. Keep me faithful to the vision you have given me, especially at times when I am in danger of losing it.*

Saturday September 22   1 Timothy 1.12-17*

Grace beyond limit

One of the best ways of defining the word 'grace' which St Paul uses here is to think of its opposite – 'disgrace'. To be in disgrace is to be made aware of how much we are to blame for some wrongdoing, deserving to be punished for it, and even to be shunned by those whom we have hurt by it. Grace, on the other hand, forgives the sin, saves us from the penalty and restores us to the fellowship of those whom we have wronged.

This was St Paul's experience from the moment of his conversion. There is no record of anyone in the Christian community treating him with suspicion or revenge because of his past cruelty against them. And Jesus himself had shown utmost patience with this man who was meant to be a prototype of true Christian discipleship. No wonder that these words of testimony to Timothy begin and end with words of thanksgiving to God.

Try reading the passage through again, applying it to your own experience, substituting your own failings for those which St Paul outlines in verse 13. Then, like St Paul, you too may feel like ending up on your knees reciting that closing doxology.

❋ *Amazing grace (how sweet the sound)*
That saved a wretch like me!
I once was lost, but now am found,
Was blind, but now I see.   John Newton (1725–1807)

FOR REFLECTION – alone or with a group

- Do you believe everyone needs to have some special moment of spiritual vision if they are to come to a full commitment of themselves to Christ? If not, what else can draw people into such discipleship?
- What is the most inspiring building, painting or work of sculpture you have ever seen? In what way did it draw you closer to the worship of God?
- For a fuller understanding of what grace means, read if you can Paul Tillich's sermon entitled 'You are Accepted', in *The Shaking of the Foundations* (Pelican Books).

CHALLENGES FOR CHANGE
1. Why Change?

Notes based on the Good News Bible by
the Grassroots Team

Grassroots is an ecumenical mission and development programme based in Luton and brings together mission partners from different parts of the world.

Pamela Parenzee *is a South African ordinand working on contextual Bible study.*

Jackie Gleeson *is a Loreto sister who has worked as a machinist in a factory and now works with Grassroots on Spirituality and Justice.*

David Cowling *works on links with other parts of Europe and community theology.*

Shanthi Hettiarachchi *is a Sri Lankan working with Interfaith dialogue and cross-cultural community work.*

Ann Hyde *is a social worker supporting a women's community project in Luton.*

There has been a tendency to emphasize personal sin as the reason why people need to change. In the readings for this week the focus is not so much on personal sin but on the injustices in wider society. Our personal relationship with God is important but it is suggested that it should result in changes which affect society. That could be depressing when we consider the degree of suffering and injustice today, but it is tempered with the assurance that the God of Israel is active in this world.

We are called to share in the mission of God which is to bring justice, healing and peace for all.

Sunday September 23   *Amos 2.6-16*
Fear of prophets
Thirty years ago, South Africa looked like the nation that is described in today's reading. People's land, homes and dignity were taken and sold to others who already had wealth. Those with little land and simple homes became poorer, and those who were rich became richer. Through a legalized system of corruption poor people were robbed of everything they had. The people responsible for this system believed they had been given

the land by God, and they used the Bible to justify it. Prophets were imprisoned and silenced.

Being 'black' was synonymous with being poor and if you somehow managed to retain a semblance of decent living you became suspect. A worse tragedy was that many black people thought it was the will of God that they remained poor, oppressed, abused, and beaten. They could not believe that God was on the side of the poor. When missionaries brought the good news of Jesus Christ to South Africa over 300 years ago, there also came a host of oppressive structures that had nothing to do with God nor his will for his people.

There are prophets today whose message is unpopular. They challenge us to change when we wish they would be quiet.

Pamela Parenzee

✳ **Heavenly Father, help us always to be mindful**
of the truth of your gospel. Amen

Monday September 24   *Amos 6.4-7**

A time for mourning

God's warning against injustice is severe and sure. We bring catastrophe upon ourselves when we lack hearts of compassion and refuse to share our riches with those in need. It was mind-boggling that rich South African whites were killing themselves (husbands and fathers) and very often took their families with them when their businesses folded. Many young teenagers committed suicide when pressures became too great.

We have to turn our compassion into grief and action. I will never forget the scene as I watched, on different occasions, both Beyers Naude (a great Afrikaans-speaking theologian) and David Bosch (author of *Transforming Mission)* break down and weep for South Africa – asking forgiveness for what their people had done to the people of the land. That grief and mourning was the beginning of change. Many of those who were not able to recognize the injustice of affluence existing side by side with poverty have found that their feasting has come to an end and some have chosen to go into exile.

Archbishop Desmond Tutu has said, 'Reconciliation can only come through forgiveness.' South Africa only began to change when people were willing to pay the price of that sort of reconciliation. We had to learn how to share... we are still learning. It is not easy, but it is possible. As South Africans we are living proof of that ongoing process and a model for the world to follow and learn.

Pamela Parenzee

Tuesday September 25   *Isaiah 9.8-17*

Trust the people

There is a big difference between punishing to bring out the best and punishing to destroy. Experience proves that if we are threatened or bullied we do not produce our best, but that, once it is recognized, generosity perpetuates itself.

In the workplace, excessive pressure for efficiency and quality has created an atmosphere of fear and threat; the worker feels under-valued and the product seems more important than people. This does not build confidence; it lowers morale and, in the long-run, is counter-productive.

In this passage God can see the destruction Israel is choosing, and does everything possible to bring the people to their senses. In this struggle, God recognizes that it is Israel's leaders who are to blame and so deals with them. Even after all this, the conflict is not solved; God remains angry but faithful.

If leaders in the workplace were able to trust the values revealed in this passage, their employees would be happier and profits would soar! Instead they are fighting a losing battle.

If we are trusted we become trustworthy – if we are valued we grow in self-worth and confidence.   *Jackie Gleeson*

✳ *We give thanks, Lord, for you are good,*
   your mercy and loving kindness endure forever.
   Israel now says, your mercy and loving kindness
   endure for ever.   *Based on Psalm 118.1-2*

Wednesday September 26   *Jeremiah 6.9-15*

Challenged by truth

It is often said that once you tell a lie, it becomes easier and easier to repeat other lies. I believe it is the same with truth. If you have avoided telling the truth a few times, you tend to do it more often than not, and the boundaries between the two become blurred. Eventually the lie becomes the truth in your own mind. That was certainly true when we, as young South Africans, were fighting for our freedom against Apartheid during the late seventies and early eighties. We were first indoctrinated by our families, school system and the Church that, although Apartheid was unjust, that was the way things were and it could not be changed. We were told to accept things as they were and so stay alive. We were pacified with many half-truths and untruths. We were blinded to the real truth, by those who said, 'Peace, Peace' where there was no peace. It was not until a young student died – and the country was shaken to its very roots – that similar young people realized that the worst vice was choosing to be victims. Change can only happen when we allow ourselves to see the truth for what it is. Then we are motivated to do something about it. *Pamela Parenzee*

✳ *Dear God, forgive us*
  when we have chosen not to believe in the truth.

Thursday September 27 *Jeremiah 23.1-4*

The end of fear

Kennet visited his mother in South Sudan. There was nothing unusual in that, you might think, but Kennet is one of two million people displaced as a result of conflict in Sudan. He has been living in Khartoum and after thirteen years travelled south to see his ageing mother. She had gone blind but was overjoyed that she was able to touch her son again. 20 million people have been forced to leave their homes and families, to live in an alien place.

Jeremiah recognizes the responsibility of those in leadership, but this does not 'let us off the hook'. The challenge is to all who are supposed to take care of people. Those in political leadership may have a greater influence but, in a democratic society, we all share responsibility for actions which may benefit us but harm others.

'My people will no longer be afraid or terrified', is the promise. Who are the people afraid and terrified in our community? What must we do to change that situation? In our society the result may not be physical flight or scattering but a loss of security and values: children in fear of those with whom they live; women locked in relationships that are dominated by violence; employees working in oppressive conditions... The promise is for all people, and we are called to change situations that create fear. *David Cowling*

✳ *Grant us the courage, merciful God,*
  to do away with harmful and abusive situations.

Friday September 28 *Luke 16.14-18*

Cloaked in righteousness

In the Gospels, the Pharisees have a reputation for looking down upon the ordinary masses. They are presented as self-righteous, and their religious pride and exclusive social behaviour has made people react negatively. Luke criticizes their attitude by alluding to the symbolism of marriage.

The relationship between God and Israel had been like a marriage, ratified irrevocably through the Covenant, and based on the just and caring behaviour laid down in the Law. The Pharisees thought they were holy because they observed the Law in intricate detail, but Jesus reminds them that marriage is also a matter of the heart. There has to be love, reciprocity, spontaneity, and the joy of caring for one another. He challenges their legalistic understanding of religion but warns them against 'throwing out the baby with the bath water'. The good news about the Kingdom of God does not replace the Covenant but rather gives it deeper meaning. God and his people are not to be separated or divorced.

Luke wants us to see that what separates us most from God is a self-proclaimed righteousness which alienates vulnerable people and leads to gross social exclusion. Luke is clear that only God is righteous: to claim what is God's is nothing less than idolatry. Righteousness is a virtue to be pursued by those who obey God's covenant. It is an invitation for the disciples of Christ to work in the world, cloaked in righteousness, in example and motive.   *Shanthi Hettiarachchi*

✴ *Reflect: Mother Theresa said that is not the privilege of the few to be holy but the right of all ordinary people.*

Saturday September 29   *Isaiah 1.11-20*
Reaching outwards
Just when we might be thinking that our salvation is secure, because we have always been regular 'church-goers', Isaiah challenges us with a God who, to our utter amazement, hates sabbaths, assemblies, festivals and solemnity.

We are told in no uncertain terms that we should learn to do good – help the oppressed, be just to the orphan, plead for the widow. If we don't happen to know any orphans and widows, or anyone who is oppressed, we still cannot breathe a sigh of relief. We have to search for justice. We had better think about doing some reaching outwards as well as upwards.

The good news is that God knows just what we are like in our narrow selfish ways and suggests that we can learn to do good and that we can talk it over with him. We need to be pro-active in finding ways of helping and supporting the defenceless and the marginalized – it is not a choice but a requirement of our God.

Recently my prayer and meditation time has been invaded by thoughts of how to carry forward work in the area of social care. Perhaps the frustration with my lack of a concentrated 'spiritual' experience is unjustified. Perhaps I am actually using my prayer time wisely after all!   *Ann Hyde*

✳ *Praise to you, Lord; you hear the cry of the poor.*

FOR REFLECTION – alone or with a group

● What would you do to make sure the truth is the truth – always?
● Are you in an abusive relationship? What are you doing about it?
● How can you act to be God's instruments of holiness?

FOR ACTION

What can you change in your own situation?

CHALLENGES FOR CHANGE
2. Hear the cries of the poor

Notes based on La Biblia Latinoamericana (Spanish) and The
New Revised Standard Version by

Marcella M Althaus-Reid

*Marcella Althaus-Reid, an Argentinian theologian, is a lecturer in
the Department of Christian Ethics and Practical Theology in New
College, the University of Edinburgh, Scotland. Marcella is a
Quaker and belongs to the Britain Yearly Meeting.*

This week we are challenged by the suffering of many of our
sisters and brothers. These are the poor who cry for justice and
for peace in a world afflicted by wars, natural disasters and
economic disorder, a world where many despair and feel that
'nobody cares'. The Bible, however, tells us that even if the
powerful of this world won't listen to their claims, there is
Someone who is listening, who cares a lot and exhorts us to put
our faith into action. We are talking about our God, the same God
who encouraged the Israelites to depart from a nation which
oppressed them; the same God who listens attentively to an
unimportant person, an impoverished widow pleading with a
judge for justice. This is our God, our Witness when in distress,
the One who listens to us. God sees and remembers our
sufferings, and encourages us to work in solidarity with each
other to overcome injustice and violence in order to fulfil God's
will of justice and peace for the world.

Sunday September 30   *Exodus 3.1-10*
The witness of the poor

When I first came to live in Britain, I was befriended by some
women refugees. The life of many refugees is one of poverty and
difficulties, but perhaps the saddest thing of all is a feeling of deep
loneliness which is difficult to compare with any other situation in
life. A refugee feels she has lost the people who knew her from
childhood, the witnesses of her life. That is the painful reality, not
only for refugees, but for many people in times of deep crisis
when everything seems lost. We do, however, have a witness to
our life: God. God knows about our pain and the injustices we
may have suffered even if apparently nobody else does. 'I have
observed the misery of my people,' and that means that God is

our witness. God has seen, God remembers and God delivers us by giving us courage and discernment. As with the Israelites in captivity, God promises to help us while encouraging us to depart from places of injustice. It may be a physical departure, or a departure on moral grounds, that we must take. And if today the time to depart has arrived for us, God, who observes our sufferings, promises to travel with us on the journey, just as in the Exodus.

✳ *Help us, God, to remember that you are the witness*
of the suffering of the poor among us,
and that you call us to act for peace and justice.

Monday October 1   *Amos 8.4-7**

Would you like to know my story?

Several years ago at an international Christian conference which was organized in Latin America, people from the poor communities were asked to contribute with an opening act of worship. They did so, but what happened was that the conference only took place in the 'spare moments' because the worship lasted during the entire three days of the event! Why? Because the people were giving testimonies. Testimonies are very important in the worship of the poor in Latin America. In this way people express the memory of what God has done for them, while proclaiming what we were reflecting on yesterday: the 'I'll never forget' of God in relation to the actions of oppression against the weakest in our society. The poor express not only their sufferings but also how God acts on their behalf, and the courage or inspiration they received. Such is the faith which sustains us, a stubborn faith which is based on belief in a God who remembers the injustices committed and reassures us that, in due time, God's justice will prevail.

✳ *Caring God, help us to remember with gratitude*
your action of deliverance in our lives.

Tuesday October 2   *Luke 16.19-31**

'Are you listening to me?'

I used to work in a poor community where people refused to speak to the authorities because they thought that they would not understand them. 'Perhaps there is something wrong with our accent,' they said, and instead asked someone to speak on their behalf. They presented carefully written petitions made by people who knew how to write with 'nice words', asking for clean water, decent houses, or a free school. The authorities understood them, but they did not listen and act on what was required.

'You never listen to what I say.' How many times have we heard these words meaning, in reality, 'you have not changed'? The text for today tells us of how difficult it is not just to listen but to change, to do that something different that God expects from us, for that is what happens when conversion takes place. This is the challenge of the gospel. In the story of the rich man and poor Lazarus, it seems that if words do not come with actions for justice, we close our ears to God's will. It is not only by hearing and saying 'yes' that we become Christians but by our deeds. In the Christian life, actions for justice are the test of understanding.

✳ *God, help us today to put into practice what we believe.*

Wednesday October 3   *James 5.1-6*

Today it is my turn

Tomorrow it is yours... A Brazilian theologian, Cardoso Pereyra, wrote that weeks after having had her first child, she saw a poor beggar washing a baby with dirty water from the streets. As Cardoso was coming from buying sterilized cotton wool for her own baby, she was shocked. Suddenly she remembered that in the Scriptures there was always an element of 'retribution'. She understood as if the poor woman was telling her, 'Today is my turn to suffer poverty with my daughter; tomorrow it is yours' *(Nancy Cardoso Pereyra, La Profecía y lo Cotidiano in RIBLA No 14, Chile, 1993).*

In the difficulties of the Brazilian economy this is easy to understand. Hyper-inflation sooner or later affects everybody. 'Now it is the turn of the rich,' says our text for today. What does this mean? Is it not that God is compassionate to all creatures, poor and rich alike? Of course God is! But the text may be telling us that we live in a world of connections. The poverty of the Third World affects the whole world, as the destruction of our environment threatens every form of life alike. It shows us that evil doing has consequences for everybody, not only the oppressed, because the whole creation is linked as God's family.

✳ *Pray that God will help us to see that we are all God's creation and must be concerned for each other.*

What does a humble person look like?

The late Dom Helder Camara, Archbishop of Olinda and Recife in Brazil, tells us how, during a Church Council, he carried a wooden cross in contrast with other bishops who carried decorated golden ones. When photographers arrived to take pictures of him, as they wanted to portray him as a humble bishop of the poor, Camara felt uneasy. He explained that it was the way he felt in his heart – not the fact that his was not a golden cross – which could make of him a faithful man of God. If he was going to be identified as humble and close to the poor simply because he refused to carry a golden cross, then, in his own words, 'It was a grave error' *(Helder Camara, 'Through the Gospel with Dom Helder Camara',* New York: Orbis, 1985).

In our text for today, we see Jesus as a servant of God, not attributing to himself priestly titles or external decorations because they were not needed: Jesus was known by his actions, and not by worldly forms of recognition. Real humility has little to do with external demonstrations of humility but, as we reflected in previous readings, in the courage required by God to stand for justice and for others who need us.

✳ *Pray that God will show us true humility of heart, manifested in actions of solidarity with others.*

Voce e muito importante, Ven!

A Portuguese hymn says: 'Come and join! Get in a circle with all the people; you are a very important person! Come!' Poor people do not feel important but, on the contrary, they feel as if they do not count. The first time I heard this hymn I was in a church worship service; we danced and sang these words to each other. Beside me, a woman wept with emotion as she told me that she had never heard anybody tell her these words before. At that time she needed courage to go through a divorce, because she was a battered wife. That worship gave her confidence.

It reminded me of the story for today. That poor widow probably never heard anyone say: you are important, valuable, and God (your Witness) is also your Lawyer. Come, with confidence, with your problems! But in spite of this she was persistent. Faith has this quality of persistence. She kept presenting her case and the judge recognized the importance of her claim.

The poor count for God. Everybody counts for God; we are all important in God's eyes and, when we claim justice for ourselves and our communities, God listens and asks us to persevere in faith. There lies the strength of the poor: in solidarity and perseverance in working together for justice.

✳ *Today, let us pray that God will help us to give courage to each other to persevere in our search for justice.*

Saturday October 6   *Isaiah 65.17-25*
A worship service is postponed

A Pentecostal minister from a poor church in Perú told me this story. She was ready to start worship one Sunday when she was told that a man from the congregation had died. After her initial shock, it occurred to her that the poor family had now been left destitute. What was she to do? She decided to start by asking the congregation if they would like to postpone the worship and go instead to visit the widow and offer help. The people, full of solidarity, were happy to do that and they went to support that family. Men offered to help build the half-finished house where the widow and children were living. Women helped with the housework and they also prayed. That was their Sunday worship!

When my friend told me this story, her church had been working for several years in a community project, working for solidarity after Sunday worship. The promises for today come from a text where God speaks about abundance: houses built, land, prosperity and health. Such promises are among us. When people, even if they are poor, come together to show love in action in God's name, the promises of the Kingdom become reality.

✳ *Pray that God will remind us that the Kingdom is among us, and that we are God's co-workers.*

FOR REFLECTION – alone or with a group

● In which ways can we hear today the cry of the poor?
● By remembering how many Christians took courage to break the chains of injustice, what other actions for transformation could happen in our societies? Can we use testimonials to praise God in community action, and to inspire us to act?

FOR ACTION

Read the newspaper with an open Bible beside it, in order to pray for discernment for action in our church communities.

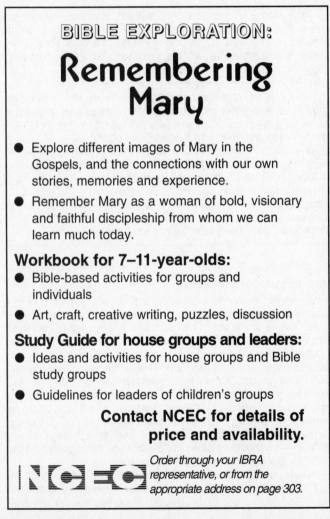

CHALLENGES FOR CHANGE
3. Change is possible

Notes based on the New International Version by
Norman Taggart

An Irish Methodist minister and author, Norman Taggart has served in Ireland, India, Britain and Sri Lanka. He has been the minister of churches in Ballymoney and Coleraine since 1994, and is due to retire in 2001. He was President of the Methodist Church in Ireland from 1997 to 1998.

Change can be regarded as either friend or foe. Within the Church, many are determined to oppose it, or at least to resist it, for as long as possible. They take refuge, for example, in the hymn, 'Abide with me', which associates change with decay and presents God as the one who does not change. Others, however, claim that the eternal 'always changes'; that Jesus Christ makes all things new; and that, as well as comforting us, the Holy Spirit disturbs and renews us. In society generally, resistance to change is common among those who feel they have most to lose. For Christians, change is to be welcomed when it is a response to God's Spirit and attempts to be true to gospel principles.

Sunday October 7   *1 Samuel 2.1-10*
Through prayer and action

In her prayer, Hannah is confident and joyful. The Lord is in a class of his own (verse 2). He understands human need (verse 3). He comes to the aid of the poor and needy, acting decisively to redress imbalances (verses 4-10).

Hannah's joy and assurance are based not on hearsay or on academic knowledge about God. They arise from what she has discovered to be true in her own experience. Being at first childless, she eventually bears a child after prayer, counselling and action (chapter 1). Though problems in life are often not resolved so clearly, faith still makes an enormous difference. Hannah's radical outlook – personal and social, religious and political – is echoed by other people of faith, notably Mary (Luke 1.46-55). Such faith is always transforming.

People of faith are remarkable for their capacity to hold the past, the present and the future together. They recall occasions when God turned situations around. Believing that he still does this, they are fully engaged in the present. They look for saving possibilities even in the most adverse circumstances and uphold in prayer those who are distressed. They anticipate the successful consummation of all things in Christ.

✴ *God to enfold you,*
Christ to uphold you,
Spirit to keep you in heaven's sight;
so may God grace you,
heal and embrace you,
lead you through darkness into the light.

From 'Love and Anger', Iona Community

Monday October 8   Lamentations 3.19-26*

Change in God's time and ways

Lamentations is a sad book, a funeral lament for the sins of the people, the fall of Jerusalem and exile in Babylon. These are real rather than anticipated or imagined tragedies, with countless numbers of people suffering.

For dramatic effect in part of chapter 3, the writer imagines the people's calamities falling on one person. 'I am the man who has seen affliction' (verse 1). 'My skin and my flesh grow old', due to severe hunger and hardship (verse 4). 'I have been deprived of peace; I have forgotten what prosperity is' (verse 17). Most difficult of all to bear, he becomes the laughing-stock of all his own people (verse 14). There are echoes here of the sense of utter lostness and devastation experienced by many people in the world today in disasters and tragedies.

Incredibly the prophet finds comfort and hope, first because of the Lord's own nature and character. The Lord's love is steadfast. He is good in all his dealings with us, a covenant God who can be trusted. Second, the Lord is our portion, always resourceful. Interestingly in Hebrew, the word for 'good' comes first in verses 25, 26 and 27. Huge difficulties remain, but we look for his deliverance in hope.

✴ *Yet, in the maddening maze of things,*
And tossed by storm and flood,
To one fixed stake my spirit clings;
I know that God is good!

John Greenleaf Whittier (1807-92)

When we get our priorities right

If you can, read the incident also in Matthew 19.16-30 and Mark 10.17-31. The differences and similarities are illuminating.

Things are moving fast in Jesus' ministry. There is talk of his approaching death, yet he makes time and space for this young man. Jesus accepts him on the basis of his approach, but makes clear what he expects of him. He sets standards which prove to be unacceptable (verses 22 and 23).

Jesus' respect for the young man is remarkable. The encounter between the two is not about trifling issues but about the most vital, such as eternal life (verse 18), entering the Kingdom of God (verse 24), following Jesus (verse 22) and being saved (verse 26). Jesus fully respects the young man's right to hold a different set of values and to go his own way. Jesus looks at the young man, loves him and, incredibly, lets him go! He leaves the matter in the hands of God, and keeps the door open. There are important lessons here for parents, pastors and others.

✷ *Give us, we pray, gentle God,*
  a mind forgetful of past injury,
  a will to seek the good of others
  and a heart of love,
  that we may learn to live
  in the way of your Son, Jesus Christ,
  through whom we pray. Amen

© *The Anglican Church in Aotearoa, New Zealand & Polynesia*

Perhaps sooner than we think!

To all appearances Zacchaeus was a winner. As the chief tax collector in a major town, he had security, status, power and wealth, all considered essential for a fulfilled life. But in reality Zacchaeus was a loser. True, he had made it to the top of his profession, yet life for him had turned sour and become empty. He was a 'sinner' (verse 7), 'one of the lost' (verse 10).

Loneliness was a major element in the emptiness he felt. How many people had he hurt as he elbowed them aside in his pursuit of power? By working for the Roman authorities he came to be regarded as a traitor. He had lost touch with his own people, with God and with himself. In an increasingly secular and selfish society do we too run the risk of losing touch with our roots?

Zacchaeus undergoes a personal and spiritual transformation when he encounters Jesus. He becomes a whole person again. There are too far-reaching social consequences. 'No one who meets Jesus ever stays the same' (Philip Yancey).

✴ *God of the nations,*
to whose table we are all invited
and in whose kingdom no one is a stranger:
hear the cries of the hungry
and mercifully extend to all the peoples on earth
the joy of your salvation;
through Jesus Christ our Lord. Amen

Thursday October 11   Luke 19.45-48

Through action and teaching

The incident is one in a series in which teaching and action clearly belong together, each calling attention to, and reinforcing, the other. For integrity in the Christian life, words and actions are both needed.

Unfair, exploitative trade should be resisted wherever it takes place, whatever the consequences. Jesus is particularly angered by the fact that here it is practised within the Temple area, which in the eyes of some people might appear to give it legitimacy. In driving out the traders, he engages in high profile behaviour which is bound to lead to trouble. Not surprisingly, prominent people feel threatened and share a common desire to kill him. Under what circumstances would we be prepared to challenge traditional practices which we felt to be unjust and contrary to the spirit of the gospel? What risks would we be prepared to take?

In Luke's Gospel the cleansing of the Temple takes place towards the end of Jesus' life. John places it very early in Jesus' ministry (John 2). It fits well in either place, reminding us that the Church is in constant need of renewal. The Church denies its nature if it fails to be a house of prayer for all people (Mark 11.17).

✴ *Holy God,*
you liberate the oppressed
and make a way of salvation.
Unite us with all who cry for justice,

237

and lead us together into freedom;
through our Lord and Liberator, Jesus Christ. Amen
The Methodist Worship Book (Methodist Publishing House)

Friday October 12   Luke 20.1-8
When backed by integrity
The question of authority is crucial. Change is more acceptable if the credentials and integrity of those suggesting it are good. Yet Jesus did not immediately respond to the question regarding his own authority. Was this because he could see into the hearts of his questioners, and recognize that their motivation was not pure? Disclosing the nature of, and authority for, his mission too early would have frustrated it. In putting a question back to his critics, was Jesus also inviting them to re-examine their motives, and appealing to them to reconsider their position?

The parable of the tenants (verses 9-19) is Jesus' reply to the question in verse 2. In it he claims, first, to possess the full authority of God himself. Second, those who oppose him resist the purposes of God and ensure their own downfall. His critics take the point, and become even more determined to silence him.

✳ *Tell out, my soul, the greatness of his might!*
   Powers and dominions lay their glory by;
   Proud hearts and stubborn wills are put to flight,
   The hungry fed, the humble lifted high.
          Verse 3 from 'Tell out my soul' © Timothy Dudley-Smith

Saturday October 13   James 1.9-18
When we are open to others and to God
A poor person becomes rich when he realizes he is a child of God (verse 9). A rich person is humbled when he recognizes that the sole source of his worth lies not in his riches, but in God (verses 10-11). The poor and the rich are brothers and sisters together in the family of the Father (verses 9, 10 and 17).

Those who persevere in the love of God in times of trial, receive the crown of life (verse 12). Those who fall from grace have only themselves to blame (verses 13-15). God provides for us in abundance, so that we can be the first fruits of a new creation, a new order of things (verses 16-18).

Verse 17 does not say that God does not change, but that he who is 'the Father of the heavenly lights... does not change like shifting shadows'. He is the dependable one. His love, goodness and purposes stand.

✳ *Lord, may nothing perturb us and nothing make us frightened;*
for all things are passing and you alone are changeless.
Those who possess you lack nothing
and you alone meet all our needs. Amen

Teresa of Avila (1515-1582)

FOR REFLECTION – alone or with a group

- The Church is in constant need of renewal. What changes would you like to see to enable it to be truer to its nature and to fulfil its mission better?
- It has been claimed that Christians, perhaps more than others, should be 'can-do' people. Do you agree, or is this much too glib? Do we have special resources to make a difference in difficult situations?

FOR ACTION

Take some practical steps to affirm an undervalued group or individual in your area.

CHALLENGES FOR CHANGE
4. Pray for change

Notes based on the New International Version by
Marian Strachan

Marian Strachan has taught in Papua New Guinea, Western Samoa, and Britain. She is a part-time lecturer and freelance writer. Marian is the wife of a minister of the United Reformed Church, and in her spare time works with international students, children and young people in the Church.

Our world is changing at an awesome rate. We are all aware that some of the changes are beneficial and many are not. During this Week of Prayer for World Peace, we are invited afresh to open windows, through prayer and God's Word, so we can look out, and glimpse some of the ways in which God seeks to change people and situations, and to see where we can be involved.

Sunday October 14   *Daniel 6.10-22*
Changing the unchangeable
The story of Daniel was written to encourage the people of God to be faithful, at a time when foreign ruling powers were setting up idols and persuading the people to break their religious laws.

In the face of overwhelming problems and pressures many situations seem unchangeable. As Christians, we believe that change is possible, even though it may take a long time. When we seek change in environmental, economic and political systems which appear immovable, we need to be faithful in prayer and action: to pray, to go on praying, and not to give up!

Last year on television, millions of people watched the first country to greet the new millennium. As the sun rose, the islanders of Kiribati in the South Pacific sang and danced on the beaches. It was beautiful! The news presenter then announced that, if global warming and rising sea levels continue at the present rate, in thirty to forty years' time, Kiribati will disappear into the ocean. Gas emissions, mostly from wealthy countries, are affecting global climate. Some small islets in the Pacific have already been swamped. In Kiribati, the islet of Tebua Tarawa, once a landmark for fishermen, has gone. Similarly, Tuvalu and other islands are threatened.

✻ *Creator God,*
The oceans you formed will soon cover our
island homes and land.
What shall we do? To have no land brings shame on us.
Who will hear? When will human destruction cease?

Monday October 15   *Luke 11.1-4*

The power of forgiveness to bring about change

Some of the most spine-chilling and painful words I hear, thankfully only occasionally, are, 'I will never forgive him/her/ them.' To be unwilling or unable to forgive, is to inhibit the circulation of love, freedom and growth in our lives.

Jesus used the word 'forgive' twice in the prayer he taught his disciples and it was one of his last words from the cross. As Christians, we experience every day the power of God's forgiveness to bring healing, change and freedom in our lives and relationships. And we know that learning to forgive others often requires us to grow in understanding, to love and to change.

Forgiveness, reconciliation and understanding, between individuals, divided communities, and nations, are challenges that we are called to take up again and again. We are seeing, in the beginnings of the remission of the debts of poorer countries, and in reconciliation between some peoples in previously war-torn areas, something of the power of forgiveness to effect change.

✻ *Loving and forgiving God,*
be with us and all who are struggling
to forgive people and to change situations
which are causing pain and injustice.

World Food Day, Tuesday October 16   *Luke 11.5-13*

Praying for change – food for the world

In Malawi twenty months ago we visited a friend and his family. An elder from the local church called to see us and told us how, on the previous night, his crop of corn had been stolen. He was sad but not angry. There had been too much rain just before the harvest was ready to be gathered and much of the food had been destroyed. As a result, people were stealing to feed their hungry children and to stay alive.

In his teaching, Jesus taught his disciples to ask God, not only for spiritual gifts but also for the daily necessities of life. 'Father...

241

give us each day our daily bread.' Jesus taught the disciples to ask, to be direct, and to go on asking.

We don't have to travel to see hunger. People with disabilities and street children beg for food and money in our major cities and some of our towns around the world. Often they are desperate, hungry and frightened. Then there are those who are too proud or ashamed to beg. Are we tempted sometimes to think that food for everyone is an impossibility?

In times of crisis, we are bombarded by the media with pictures of hunger and suffering. But many areas of the world never hit the headlines, even though they are in desperate need of food, and of programmes to help them become self-supporting. Do we need to take more time and trouble to be informed about our world and its peoples' needs?

Praying for change will include a willingness to stand alongside people in their suffering, empathizing with their pain, and entering into God's anguish over what we are doing to each other and to his world.

✴ *Yes, Lord, it's all a bit too much sometimes,*
this constant reminder of a hungry world.
Thank you for our own daily food.
Help us never to grow weary or indifferent
about praying and working to eradicate hunger.

Wednesday October 17   *Luke 18.9-14**
Open to change

The confident Pharisee talked a lot! He wanted to be sure that God knew he was better than others, and that in his religious duties he even went beyond what was required. Do you think that sometimes 'church folk' seem – to those who don't belong – a bit like the Pharisee? What can we do to change this? The second man, hated and despised by most of the people around him, asked for God's forgiveness.

The tax-collector is commended for his openness to God and his willingness to admit his part in exploiting the poor. The changes for which we long and pray must begin in ourselves. The tax-collector becomes a different person. God can work through people like him.

This Week of Prayer for World Peace provides an opportunity for us to share, in private prayer, or with others. It is a time to come in humility and to be open to what God is wanting to say and do in and through us, and in our world.

✳ *Our dear God,*
I pray for peace in our countries around the world.
Without your help, Lord, we can't find peace.

Pililan Chukambiri (age 10), Malawi

Thursday October 18   1 Kings 8.22-23, 33-40

A chance for us all to start again

At the Autumn festival, Solomon gathers the leaders and people of Israel for the dedication of the Temple and speaks of the covenant of love which God makes with those who are open to him.

In his prayer, he asks God for forgiveness for the times when they sin and turn away from him. Solomon's prayer reminds his people that when things go wrong for individuals or communities, they can turn to God and make a new start. If they genuinely want change, he will heal and work with them.

The dire situations in many parts of our world today are rarely the simple result of the wrongs of those most affected. People far away may bear the guilt and responsibility. In the Pacific, for example, there is continuing concern about the unknown long-term effects of former nuclear testing in the seas. The dumping of toxic waste in the Pacific should now have ceased but is difficult to monitor. Recently, there have been protests against shipments of plutonium and other radioactive wastes through the Pacific.

✳ *Lord God, you said, 'Let the water teem with living creatures.'*
Thank you for providing us with food from the sea.
Help us to protect our children's food cupboard
and playground.

Friday October 19   1 Kings 8.41-43, 54-61

For all the peoples of the earth

Israel's prosperity in the reign of Solomon would have suggested to surrounding nations that their God was great and powerful. We may not identify prosperity with God's blessing in such a simplistic way, but we are still called to demonstrate the reality of God in our lives.

Solomon is aware that foreigners would come and pray to Israel's God and he asks God to listen and respond to their prayers. Do you believe that God is bigger than the Christian community? That he is available and listens to all people of faith? The increasingly rich and diverse communities in our countries give us an opportunity to share our cultures and beliefs and to learn from each other. It is in such sharing, and in coming together, that we will come to see the truth that God has revealed to us all.

✲ *May the Lord our God be with us...*
May he never leave us nor forsake us...
May he turn our hearts to him, to walk in all his ways...
so that the peoples of the earth may know
that the Lord is God. 1 Kings 8.57-60

Saturday October 20 1 Timothy 2.1-8

Praying for decision makers and leaders

The early Christians here were being challenged to a broader view of the scope of prayer. Their intercessions and thanksgiving were to go out to embrace all people, including the Roman Emperor and government officials. They were to pray, not out of fear of the authorities, but out of recognition of God's love for every person. The authorities provided the external conditions in which the gospel was being spread.

In our time, leaders and politicians have terrifying responsibilities, with power to influence or change world situations and events. We cannot fully understand the pressures on politicians, especially in the different countries and cultures where, for example, the expectations of extended families may add to the difficulty of maintaining integrity and honesty.

Would you agree that whilst being critical of leaders of nations, governments, public or private institutions, or the Church, we also need to be supportive, where appropriate, and give thanks for all who work hard and sacrificially for others? Certainly we need to surround the decision makers daily with our prayers.

✲ *Dear God,*
In this hurting world,
Help the world's leaders
to speak and work for peace. Emily Kiddle (age 10)
Prayers for Wednesday and Friday are from 'Online to God',
Marian Strachan and Jane Taylor (IBRA – see page 245)

FOR REFLECTION – alone or with a group

● Make a list of five things you would like to see changed in our world. In what ways can you become involved? Make these issues part of your prayers.

- Do you believe that praying for peace makes a difference? If so, how?

FOR ACTION

Do you have an atlas or world map? Look at the map of the Pacific Ocean. The islands vary in size, but millions of people live in or around the Pacific. Try to think of ways in which you can increase your own and other people's awareness of life there, its joys and problems. Encourage a group, or your church, to pray and perhaps find out more about this region.

CHALLENGES FOR CHANGE
5. A new respect
(the book of Ruth)

Notes based upon the Book of Ruth in the *Five Scrolls* (CAAR Press, New York 1984) – translation and introductions by Albert H Friedlander and Herbert Bronstein. The text from Jeremiah uses the translation of the Jewish Publication Society of America.

Albert H Friedlander

Albert H Friedlander is Dean of the Leo Baeck College in London and Rabbi Emeritus of the Westminster Synagogue. He was a Fellow of the Wissenschaftskolleg in Berlin and has served as visiting professor at many universities. His books on theology and history have appeared in various languages. He is the Associate President of the Conference of Christians and Jews, President of the London Society for the Study of Religion and Philosophy, an Honorary President of the World Conference of Religions for Peace, and co-editor of 'European Judaism'.

The first reading comes from the book of Jeremiah, who comforts those taken away from Jerusalem into the first captivity. He teaches them to adjust to change, now that they have been transplanted in a new land. Hope for the future is the golden thread running through all the books of the Bible.

The other readings come from the book of Ruth – a nightingale song of love and trust – as Ruth follows Naomi into a new world and finds new faith.

'Perhaps the self-same song that found a path
Through the sad heart of Ruth, when, sick for home,
She stood in tears amid the alien corn...'

Keats in 'Ode to a Nightingale'

Ruth lived in the time of the Judges, when war and poverty raged. The book of Leviticus, with its injunctions to leave part of the harvest for the needy and a legal system which protected widows, is part of that new world. Yet it is her courage in not deserting Naomi, and her faith in God which enable her to meet the new challenges in her life which inspire us.

A pastoral letter

Jeremiah writes to people taken captive to Babylon: 'Build ye houses, and dwell in them; and plant gardens, and eat the fruit of them. Take ye wives, and beget sons and daughters... And seek peace for the city where I have caused you to be carried away captives, and pray unto the LORD for it; for in the peace thereof ye shall have peace.' His teachings are clear. One must not carry hatred into the new situation. God is everywhere, not only in the Holy Land. Let them accept their fate, and maintain self-respect. Prayers link these captives to their neighbours, and are said for all of society. Create a better world where you are, and encourage the next generation of children and your children's children. They must not dream of what once was, and reject what is. In all houses of worship, we pray for the government of our land, and hope for peace and justice for all.

✳ *O God, let me encounter you on my way*
   when it leads through darkness.
   Let me feel your presence in others,
   and give me hope for every new tomorrow.
   Give me vision to live in the future,
   even when I honour the past. Amen

Initiative: Find an organization which works for refugees. Can you help them?

Responding to adversity

When there was famine in her land, Naomi became a refugee and moved to Moab. Her sons married fine Moabite girls; and she adjusted to the change. Then her husband died, and so did her sons. Again facing poverty, she decided to return home, and her daughters-in-law came with her. Naomi respected this, but gently told them to stay in their land, with their families – why should they also become refugees? The girls wept, kissed her, and wanted to share her fate. Naomi knew how harsh life was for widows. She pleaded with them to return, prayed for them, and insisted they leave and not share her future: 'Oh, no, my daughters, I would be all the more bitter on your behalf; for the hand of the Lord has gone out against me.'

Often we only see the misfortunes of those who suffer. Here, we come to see the dignity and courage within those families who give love and comfort to each other. Let us recognize the greatness of human beings even in their adversity.

✴ *God, preserve me from darkness.*
Give me understanding for those who suffer,
and let me reach out to them and share with them;
for we are all your children. Amen

Initiative: How are your churches helping those in need?
Can you help?

Tuesday October 23   *Ruth 1.15-22*
Choosing life

There are times when an irrevocable decision has to be made. Orpah decided to return to her people. Ruth was totally loyal to Naomi. And she made another choice:

'Entreat me not to leave you... For wherever you go, I will go. Wherever you lodge, I will lodge. Your people shall be my people, and your God my God.'

In times of suffering, sometimes on a journey, we confront a vision which changes our life. Revelation does not only come to great leaders and prophets. It can happen to anyone at any time. Ruth realized that she loved Naomi; but she now also knew that the God of Israel was her God. Naomi said no more, even though her own life had become dark. When they arrived in Bethlehem, people remembered Naomi as 'the sweet one'; but she told them to call her Mara now: 'the bitter one'. This happens to us, and then we learn that help comes from unexpected quarters. The book of Ruth stresses family loyalties, but it also teaches that when we choose God, we choose life.

✴ *There are times when I grow bitter and feel very old.*
Teach me, O God, that help is always near,
and that it can come through my family. Amen

Initiative: Study the stories of people who found faith in time of need; and think of all those who are willing to help, both in Kosovo and in your own street.

United Nations Day, October 24   *Ruth 2.1-23*
Global ethics in the global village

We cannot live without others: they are part of our identity. This we can learn at home. And we learn it in the world, knowing that nations who go to war destroy themselves. We need each other. Naomi discovered that she had a support network in her birthplace, Bethlehem. Boaz was her kinsman, and she could send Ruth into his fields so that they would not starve. Just as the poor nations of our world are entitled to help from their neighbours, so Naomi and Ruth had ancient rights to work and to food. Boaz immediately felt affection for Ruth, and became her protector. He gave her extra opportunity to glean at harvest, and saw to it that she was protected from unwelcome advances from others. When she pointed out that she was 'only an alien' he assured her that the kindness and loyalty she had shown Naomi had been noted, together with her courage to come to a people whom she had not known before.

Today, when we also live in a world of mass migration, we recognize that universal ethics unite us with others, and the stranger in our midst 'should be as the home-born to us'. The book of Ruth is a pastoral tale, but it contains universal dimensions. The cries of the poor must be heard, and we must learn to 'love our neighbour as ourselves'.

✷ *Lord, let me not fall into want, but give me courage*
 to encounter all the changes and chances of life,
 and the hope that your love will always sustain me. Amen

Initiative: On this United Nations Day, make a special attempt to support an endeavour which is vital for the peace of the world.

Thursday October 25   Ruth 3.1-18

A new respect

The story of Ruth reaches a new, delicate aspect. Naomi tells her that, according to tradition, Boaz should marry her. She advises Ruth to go to him at night, lie next to his bed, and to trust him fully. She accepts the advice, and Boaz shows himself a man of integrity. In a position of total authority, he shows respect for a person without power. He does not take advantage of her, but explains the legal position: there is another kinsman with greater rights. He must consult the court, but will marry her if the other person will not do so. 'If he does not want to redeem you, then – as the Lord lives – I shall redeem you.'

The weak within society need the particular respect which Boaz gives Ruth. She leaves him early in the morning, before gossip can destroy her, carrying presents to Naomi to give additional assurance to these wanderers in search for security. As the story reaches its climax, we learn that there must be legal safeguards in the structure of our society to ensure that the weak are treated with respect and honour.

* *O Lord, teach me to respect others*
  so that I can respect myself.
  Let me not abuse my authority,
  and let me always remember that we encounter you
  in our neighbours in all actions of life. Amen

Initiative: *This story deals with family obligations. Have you examined your relationship to those you love? Have you shown respect for the old and young whose rights need to be respected?*

Friday October 26   Ruth 4.1-12

Due process of law

If you enter Old Jerusalem through the Damascus Gate, it almost looks like a tunnel. In biblical times, the gates were built that way, so that a court could take place there – as it did in the days of Ruth. We read that Boaz sat in the city gate, asked the next-of-kin to sit down with him, and called ten city elders to join them. The court was in session. He asked the man whether he wanted to buy the land of Ruth's father-in-law, and the man agreed. 'Ah,' said Boaz, 'then you must also marry Ruth the Moabitess to perpetuate the family name...' The man refused and took off his shoe (an ancient form of oath). Now, Boaz could proclaim: 'I will purchase the land and marry Ruth!' The court and the onlookers confirmed and cheered his decision, and the elders blessed the marriage. Much happened here.

The rights of women still suffer in patriarchal societies, but they are implicit in the law if it is rightly applied. Enmity between nations – Moab and Israel were bitter foes – was pushed aside when these two came together in love and respect, and history was changed.

* *O Lord, I am filled with prejudice, and afraid of the stranger.*
  Teach me that there cannot be peace
  until we learn to trust others;
  and may others come to trust me. Amen

Initiative: Visit a court and see how difficult it is to let justice be done – and how necessary it is as well.

Saturday October 27   Ruth 4.13-22

History is hope

We sometimes think that genealogies – those boring lists of names in the Bible – can be omitted. Here, we discover that the genealogy is the climax and triumph of this story of love and devotion. Boaz and Ruth marry, and have a child. Now Naomi, the 'bitter one' is sweet again. The baby is placed into the arms of the grandmother, and her friends rejoice: 'There is a son born to Naomi'. Yet Ruth, no longer a refugee but honoured and happy, is still the proud mother, alongside Boaz the father.

Look at the last name: David. David, king of Israel. Ruth, the foreigner from Moab, becomes a founder of the royal house of Israel, which tradition links with the future coming of the messianic Kingdom, the time of universal love and peace. In the book of Ruth, this 'nightingale song of love and trust' has embraced the vision for all humanity and teaches the importance of love which links all of us together.

✳ *God, help me to judge others for what they are,*
  and not for what they may appear to me.
  And let me look at my child – at all children –
  and discover in them Your divine plan
  which gives meaning to my days and nights. Amen

Initiative: Look at the first lines of the New Testament (Matthew 1) and read the genealogy which is a continuation of the text of Ruth. What can you learn from it?

FOR REFLECTION – alone or with a group
Reflect again on the initiatives given for each day, and decide how you will respond to them.

LETTERS TO THE THESSALONIANS

Notes based on the Revised English Bible by
Edmund Banyard

Edmund Banyard is a minister and former Moderator of the General Assembly of the United Reformed Church. He is a committed ecumenist and currently edits 'All Year Round' for Churches Together in Britain and Ireland.

These letters, written from Corinth around AD50, are almost certainly the earliest of our New Testament documents and they are extremely important for what they tell us of the life and faith of churches being established at that time. Paul and Silas (Silvanus), possibly accompanied by Timothy, came to Thessalonica after being forced to leave Philippi. The account of this visit is to be found in Acts 17.1-10a, though they must have stayed in Thessalonica for a considerably longer period than this brief record suggests. In the letter to the Philippians written at a later date, Paul refers with gratitude to the Philippian church, on more than one occasion, sending him aid in Thessalonica (Philippians 4.15-16). Eventually, however, Paul and his companions are forced once again to leave a city following rioting. Church planting in the teeth of opposition and helping new converts to grow in the faith forms the background to Paul's letters to the Thessalonians.

Sunday October 28   *1 Thessalonians 1.1-10*
Faith, love and hope
Paul couples Silas and Timothy in the warm greetings with which this letter opens and the intercessory prayers which were a vital part of his life. Remembering before God the many and varied needs of the converts he has made and the churches he has planted is clearly for him a top priority.

The Thessalonian church, only established a short time before these letters were written, had turned from idols (1.9). This means that most, if not all, of its members came from a Gentile, pagan background, for Paul would not have written that of Jewish converts. He had been extremely anxious to know how they stood up to pressure after he was forced to leave them and was delighted with the news Timothy had just brought (3.6).

They have, he writes, put faith into action, expressed love through hard work and, despite difficult times and much hostility, their hope remains firm. Faith, love, hope – this theme will recur in later letters, especially 1 Corinthians 13. But the way in which Paul uses it for the first time here shows a church in which the gospel is really alive!

✳ *Thank you, Lord, for all with whom I share my faith,*
both for the friends I know
and the vast multitude I do not know.
Be with me and all who seek you this day,
that in joyful hope we may reflect in our living
something of the great love you have
for the whole of humanity.

Monday October 29   *1 Thessalonians 2.1-12*

Living what you preach

The old faiths were dying and there was a lively market in religion. A wide variety of people were proclaiming new faiths and many were making a good living out of it. In marked contrast, Paul reminds the Thessalonian church that he and his companions had not been promoting themselves or seeking to make any personal profit. On the contrary, they had worked hard to earn their own keep so that they should not be a charge on their new converts. It is clear from the way Paul writes that this had only been achieved through long hours of hard labour, often when they were already dead tired. In verse 12 Paul reminds the Thessalonians how he and Silas had appealed, encouraged and urged them to live lives worthy of the God who calls them into his Kingdom; but I think we may be sure that, earnest as their preaching had been, what carried most conviction and made the biggest impact was the striking way in which Paul and Silas were seen to live the faith they professed.

✳ *Forgive me, Lord, I pray,*
the many times when my living has fallen short
of the faith I profess, and help me this day
to live closer to the example you have set before me.

Tuesday October 30   *1 Thessalonians 2.13-20*

Out of sight, but never out of mind

The first missionary visit to Thessalonica ended abruptly when Paul and Silas had to be smuggled out of the city under cover of darkness. But the church they planted, in the short time they had been there, was strong enough to survive, despite continued and often violent opposition. Paul reminds them that such persecution has been a common experience of the Church from the very beginning, indeed hadn't Jesus himself been crucified? But what particularly comes through, and especially from the second half of this passage (verses 17-20), is Paul's deep ongoing concern for this young church. He desperately wanted to visit them again but it had not been possible. Most likely the situation in Thessalonica itself was such that his reappearance would only bring more trouble. We saw at the beginning of the letter how important intercessory prayer was to Paul, and here again he shows that, though he cannot visit them, this congregation – together we may be sure with many others – was never ever really out of his mind.

✳ *We lift up to you our relatives and friends,*
especially those we do not often see. Though out of sight,
we hold them lovingly in our thoughts before you
and pray for their well-being.

Wednesday October 31   *1 Thessalonians 3.1-6*

Keeping contact at all costs

When they had been forced to leave Thessalonica, Paul and his companions had made their way to Beroea where they were well received. However, news of the success of their work was received back in Thessalonica and some hostile members of the Jewish community made it their business to go to Beroea to stir up trouble. This hostility centred in particular on Paul, so he had gone on ahead of his companions to Athens. It was evidently after Silas and Timothy had joined him there that his impatience to have direct contact again with Thessalonica caused him to send Timothy back. Timothy stayed a while and eventually rejoined Paul (who by this time was in Corinth), bringing him a good account of the life of the Thessalonian church.

The peace and stability of the Roman Empire had made such widespread travel easier than ever before. Even so it was far more difficult and demanding than it is today. Yet keeping in touch – not only by prayer, but by whatever human contact was possible – was to Paul a top priority.

✳ *Lord, thinking of Paul's efforts*
to keep in touch with people
for whom he was deeply concerned, reminds me,
should I – with all the means of communication

available today – need reminding
of those to whom I should be reaching out
with messages of love.

Thursday November 1   *1 Thessalonians 3.7-13*

Thanksgiving and blessings

Paul had only a few months to establish the little church in Thessalonica, his stay being cut short by intense opposition from within the Jewish community. That hostility had continued after he left, and there would also have been other pressures on these new converts to resume their former way of life. Understandably Paul was deeply concerned as to how their faith would stand up to continual harassment. This was why, since he couldn't go back himself, he had sent Timothy to them. Now that Timothy has returned with the news that the church is in good heart, Paul is overjoyed. We see again how prayer is central for Paul; he had been lifting them up before God day and night and now he offers thanksgiving to God that these prayers have been answered. He still longs to be with them to lead them deeper into the faith and he prays that the way may be opened for him to return. Meanwhile, may their love overflow and their hearts be held firm. As words come tumbling out we find thanksgiving, petition, blessing, but above all joy that the gospel has been effectively planted and is being lived.

✻ *Lord, may I know you so close to me*
   that my love may grow and increase.
   Lead me, I pray, in paths you have chosen for me,
   and so strengthen and guide me
   that I may give glory to you
   in every part of my daily living.

Friday November 2   *1 Thessalonians 4.1-12*

A gentle holiness

For Gentile converts Christianity required a whole new set of moral values, which meant that they needed not only to change old habits, but also to break with many of the customs and practices of the society in which they had grown up. All sorts of pressures from family and daily companions could make their lives extremely difficult. We see the problems very clearly from some of Paul's other letters, but it does seem that the Thessalonian Christians have so far met these temptations very well indeed. Nevertheless Paul reminds them of the need for holiness, which in this context is equated with high moral standards, and again he speaks of the rule of love.

The amazing thing is that this very new church is already being commended for practising the rule of love towards fellow Christians 'throughout Macedonia'. Does this suggest that they were almost too good to be true? No, though Timothy's report has evidently suggested at least a little cause for concern. Were some men going a bit 'over the top' with their new-found faith? For one reason or another we find Paul gently reminding them that their first aim should be to live quietly and attend to their own business in a way that provides for their needs and commands the respect of those outside the Christian community.

✳ *Teach us the art of witnessing*
through simply living our everyday lives:
doing whatever comes to hand,
be it significant or insignificant, to the best of our ability;
and doing it all quietly and to your glory.

Saturday November 3   *1 Thessalonians 4.13-18*

The resurrection of the dead

There is no doubt that the first Christians expected the early return of Jesus, the Christ, in glory and power and the dramatic end of the present age. But what would happen about those who had died before that day came? And so Paul now turns his attention to the hope of the resurrection of the dead. At this time he shares the general expectation of an early coming again and what he writes is coloured by this expectation. He answers the immediate question by saying that when that day comes the living will have no advantage over those who have died; indeed the dead will rise first. The imagery which Paul uses will not be so meaningful for us as it was for them, but the heart of the message echoes the teaching of Jesus himself, for example: 'As for the resurrection of the dead, have you never read what God himself said to you: "I am the God of Abraham, the God of Isaac, the God of Jacob?" God is not God of the dead but of the living' (Matthew 22.31).

God is the God of all, past and present alike, and God holds us all in life. This is a message for Christians of every age.

✳ *We remember before you those we love who have died,*
rejoicing that you have broken the power of death
and hold us all in life, now and forever.

FOR REFLECTION – alone or with a group

● The Thessalonian Christians held to their faith despite the pressure put on them by persecution to abandon it. Is your Christian faith subjected to any pressures ? What form do they take? How do you stand up to them?

● Intercessory prayer and keeping in touch are both of great importance to Paul. Do you see them linked in this way? How far, in your experience, does intercessory prayer become a matter of 'Over to you, Lord – over and out!' ?

Sunday November 4   *1 Thessalonians 5.1-11*

At all times be on your toes

2000 years have passed, but there are still those who are obsessed with dates and times, predicting or arguing about the end of the age. The message here, which is repeated in other parts of the New Testament, is that this is a fruitless exercise. It distracts us from the more important duty of living each day as fully as we may so that at our life's end we may not be ashamed. Among the writings Dietrich Bonhoeffer smuggled out of the concentration camp where he was executed are the words: 'There remains for us only the very narrow way, often extremely difficult to find, of living every day as if it were our last, and yet living in faith and responsibility as though there were to be a great future' (*Letters and Papers from Prison – SCM*).

Paul concludes this section of the letter with a reference to the Christian's armour, another theme which he will develop more fully later, but here the armour is seen to be made up of the faith, love and hope we noticed earlier.

✻ *Lord God, teach me, I pray, to follow the way of Christ*
by living each day lovingly to the full
and strengthen within me faith and hope
in the great future you have prepared for all your people.

Monday November 5   *1 Thessalonians 5.12-28*

Work at maintaining the Christian community

Paul's letters tend to end somewhat reluctantly with a lot of last-minute thoughts. In these closing sentences he calls for a proper consideration for those who lead and guide the little community, and he goes on to remind the church that they all need to have a proper care for one another. 'Live at peace among yourselves' (verse 13b). Most of the other closing exhortations are developments of the same theme.

We should always beware of taking other human beings for granted in family, church, or indeed wherever else we may be. Christian love requires us to work at keeping all our relationships in good order. What Paul is saying here of the church applies right across the board: respect and esteem where they are due, working for peace and understanding, taking care not to repay wrong with wrong – these should be our goals at all times. Note the call to be joyful and to 'give thanks whatever happens' (verse 18a). This can be extremely testing at times, but the underlying thought is to look for and value the happiness we already have, to recall the things for which we have cause to be grateful and, above all else, never to forget that God holds us at all times.

✷ *May the God of peace make me holy through and through,*
keep me sound in spirit, soul and body,
and enable me each day, until my life shall end,
to find cause for thanksgiving.

Tuesday November 6　　　　　　　　　　　　*2 Thessalonians 1.1-12**

Faith put to the test

This second letter to the Thessalonians was almost certainly written within a few months of the first. Paul is again able to write warmly of their increasing faith and growing love, but he is deeply concerned about the troubles they are facing and wants to assure them that God rewards faithfulness. He then uses some vivid images of judgement (verses 5-10). That God is just, and will deal justly with his people, is a constant theme of the Scriptures, but any attempt to describe the form that judgement will take is inevitably coloured by the times in which the writer lives. The punishments experienced under Roman justice were extremely harsh and cruel by our standards today, but this was the only justice they knew and it would colour all images of justice. It is reasonable to suppose that just as the 'day of the Lord' is likely to take us by surprise so is the nature of the judgement when it comes. The really important thing for us all is that we should not get bogged down by what will happen to the wicked, but aim so to live that we may be found worthy of our calling whenever and however the judgement comes.

✷ *Lord, let me not live in an unholy fear of your judgement,*
nor let me be complacent because you come as Saviour;
help me so to respond to the warmth of your love

that I may make the most of the life I have been given
and have something to offer back to you
when the 'day of the Lord' comes.

Wednesday November 7   *2 Thessalonians 2.1-12**

Keep your feet on the ground

This passage may be the main reason why Paul wrote a second letter so soon after the first. There were those in the Thessalonian church who were so anticipating the 'day of the Lord' – the end of the age – expecting it to come at almost any minute, that it was adversely affecting their living. If you are expecting to have to move out because your house is to be demolished you are unlikely to start doing any repairs. If you expect the world to end next week you are unlikely to be planning anything very far ahead. So here we see some people getting extremely unsettled by various predictions and expectations and finding it difficult to cope with, or just opting out of the normal duties of everyday life.

What Paul has to say about secret evil, which has yet to be brought to light, is really only secondary to the earlier and very important word, 'don't lose your heads'; your first duty is to keep on with the business of living fully, putting as much as you can into life in the world as it is.

✳ *Lord, preserve me from vain speculation.*
When you come for me, may I be found
busy at the work you have given me to do.

Thursday November 8   *2 Thessalonians 2.13-17**

Stand firm

In the few sentences covered by these five verses we find Paul once again expressing his joy in the life of this young church and repeating how he thanks God for them. Firmly believing that all that happens is within the will of God, he goes on to tell them that it is no accident that they have been gathered into the fellowship of believers. Yet Paul knows that God is not a puppet master and so he reminds them that they still have to play their part in a difficult and challenging situation. They must stand firm and hold fast to the faith they have received. This means living it to the best of their ability, whatever the difficulties they may have to face. He rounds it all off with a prayer that the love and grace which they have already experienced may continue to encourage and strengthen them. So while the central message is 'stand firm', it is accompanied by great encouragement and a reminder that if they look to him, God through Christ will supply the strength they will surely need.

✳ *Lord, I have been blessed,*
for I have experienced in my life your love
and encouragement. Continue with me, I pray,
and so guide and strengthen me that I may find
many opportunities to serve you by word or deed.

Friday November 9   *2 Thessalonians 3.1-5*
Pray for others as others pray for you

It couldn't have been an easy task to write down Paul's letters as he dictated them; ideas came tumbling out. For a moment Paul's thoughts turn to the ongoing wider mission, 'Pray for us', he says, and particularly that he and his fellow evangelists 'may be rescued from wrong-headed and wicked people' (verse 2). Paul certainly needed the prayers of all who loved him for he was constantly facing bitter opposition, but even as he dictates this sentence his thoughts go back to the Thessalonian Christians. Following the sense of what has gone before we might have expected 'the Lord keeps faith' (verse 3) to be followed by 'he will strengthen us', but no, his thoughts have gone back to those he is writing to and so it becomes, 'he will strengthen you.' Once again we see that 'the care of all the churches' is uppermost in his thoughts and his love for those he is now addressing shines out through the prayer which rounds off this short passage.

✳ *Lord, I pray that you will ever lead me*
into a greater understanding of the love of God
and grant me more of the steadfastness of Christ.

Saturday November 10   *2 Thessalonians 3.6-18**
Never tire of doing right

In Acts 2.42-47 we find that for a while a close-knit Christian community was formed where they held all things in common and the better-off supported the neediest. Something of this sort probably happened for a while in Thessalonica and the little church could well have attracted some who were merely looking for an easy life and a free meal ticket. So Paul, while he had been with them, had given the ruling: no work, no food. The general warmth of this correspondence shows that these could only have been a small minority, but a very irritating one, playing on the generosity of the others.

The final exhortation is: friends, never tire of doing right. 'Doing' is of course the operative word. It is not a matter of 'being right', but of positive activity, deeds of love. Notice that with the final greeting and prayer, Paul adds a word in his own hand and the letter is rounded off with a grace.

✳ *May the Lord of peace grant me*
and those for whom I pray
his peace which passes human understanding
and which can hold us fast at all times
and in all circumstances.

FOR REFLECTION – alone or with others

● How difficult is it to live in expectant hope of God's great future and at the same time to keep our feet firmly on the ground?
● In the light of Paul's deep concern for maintaining the unity of the Christian community, how important do you think the ecumenical movement is today? How much time and energy would you say should be put into the efforts to bring the various branches of the Church closer together?

FOR ACTION

Consider whether there are any relationships in church, family or among neighbours which you ought to be working to repair.

DAVID – THE POET KING

Notes based on the Revised English Bible by
Bernard Thorogood

Bernard Thorogood began his ministry in Polynesia, serving with the London Missionary Society, mainly in the Cook Islands and concentrating on the training of ministers. He became General Secretary of that society, which developed into the Council for World Mission, and then served the United Reformed Church as its General Secretary. Since 1992 he has lived in retirement in Sydney, Australia.

During these three weeks we read the key passages in the story of David, from the time of his calling to serve Saul through to his death. It is a remarkable life. His gift of leadership was outstanding, for he carried his people from defeat to strength in a hostile world. He dealt successfully with greater powers: the Philistines along the sea coast and the Egyptian kingdom, still a mighty force, to the south. He was also a musician, a poet and a singer. He was a man who could rise to great heights and fall into grievous sins. David is worth studying, especially as we approach Advent: from him the family line is traced to Jesus of Nazareth.

We remember that we are reading about a wild period of history, 1000 years before Christ, when many tribes were clashing in the struggle for fertile land, many gods were worshipped, and savage fighting was the common way of dealing with disputes. Perhaps, as we read the daily news, we may hear echoes even today.

Sunday November 11   *1 Samuel 16.1-13*
God's choice

How splendid it would be if we could hear God's choice of people as Samuel did. All those committees which have to decide on candidates for the ministry, working so patiently through interviews and reports, would long to hear the word, 'Rise and anoint him: this is the man.' When we cast a vote in an election, responding to the manifestos of all the candidates, we would be on sure ground if we could hear that voice. But it is not so, or very rarely so. We are usually having to make up our minds on the variety of evidence.

In this part of the Bible we meet conversations with God reported with simplicity. That is the story-teller's art. It brings the scene alive. But perhaps the reality was more like our own experience, with Samuel taking time, looking, listening, praying until the conviction was strong in him that the right person stood before him. That is a firm basis for all choosing of people for God's service. An archbishop once said, 'If you get seven out of ten appointments right, you are doing well; and the test of your ministry is how you live with the other three.'

✳ *When you call, Lord, may I respond;*
when you command, may I obey;
when you choose, may I affirm your will
in the way I live and serve.
And today, as we remember
the ending of the first World War, we pray for peace.

Monday November 12   *1 Samuel 16.14-23*
A troubled King
We are introduced here to Saul, the first of the kings, who had made his capital at Gibeah and was fighting a guerrilla war against the Philistines in order to establish his territory. He was a deeply troubled man, and the writer of this history sees him as invaded by an evil spirit. He was subject to fits of violence. We may see this as a recurrent illness, perhaps like epilepsy or schizophrenia. And it was this troubled state that led to his need for a companion who would soothe him with music. So David, the shepherd lad, entered the royal household. It was a great change and a test of character.

Thanks for all those who minister to the troubled spirits among us. Music may well be one of the calming influences that help to heal, and there are many others. For some it is the quietness and beauty of a garden, or the voice of a loved and trusted friend, or the atmosphere of a church, and these are just as true healers as the medicines that modern science provides. We are learning that body, mind and spirit all need the peace of God.

✳ *We pray for all who suffer from deep disturbance*
of heart and mind, that they may know
the touch of God's hand today.
'My peace I give to you.'

Tuesday November 13   *1 Samuel 18.6-16*
The fever called Jealousy
What excitement in the camp that night, how splendid the songs, how bright the firelight and how eloquent the toasts to the victory!

And as all that celebration went on, so the name of David was lifted high and the name of Saul was given a secondary place. We can almost see that very tall, regal figure glaring suspiciously through the smoke of the cooking fires as the fever grew in him. 'So it's David now, is it? David's the conqueror! And all my fighting and suffering goes for nothing and this youngster takes my seat.' So fear and jealousy grew until it almost drove the older man mad.

We may not be consumed in that way, but the seed of jealousy often begins to send out its shoots and roots in our hearts. I have seen it happen in ministers of the church when a colleague, with energy, skill or imagination, has made a great success of some project, and at once grounds for criticism emerge: 'It's bad theology', or 'He's getting involved in politics'. But it is often jealousy. We can become jealous of personal friendships in which we don't share, and jealous of gifts we don't possess. And then we cease to thank God for all that we ourselves have and are.

✳ *Save me, dear God, from resenting*
   the success of friends and colleagues,
   but let me rejoice with those who rejoice
   even if they leave me behind.

Wednesday November 14   *1 Samuel 19.1-18*

Drama in the palace

The story is told with directness. We are introduced to Jonathan, who, as Saul's son, might well have been jealous of David but who was his great friend. Here Saul is so maddened by his anger that he tries to kill David, and this passion within him remained like a poison through his later years. He had this fixed image of David as the usurper who would snatch the crown. So Jonathan was torn between support for his father and love for his friend.

Then we meet Michal, Saul's daughter and David's wife. We shall meet her again in 2 Samuel 6 where she seems a rather superior and pompous wife. Here she is loyal to the limit, but suggests in verse 17 that she had acted under threat. We note in verse 13 the presence of a household god, a statue of some sort, that could be disguised on the bed to look like a sleeping man. This suggests that in the king's household there was a variety of worship, including Canaanite influences, and idols were not yet abolished in spite of the constant instruction from the time of Moses.

What complex human relationships are suggested here. Are we honest as we cope with divided loyalties?

✳ *In this place we need your Spirit,*
so that we may be true to one another,
as friends of Jesus Christ.

Thursday November 15   *1 Samuel 24.1-22*

Keeping the peace

Saul, with his troops, had been chasing David because he still saw him as an ambitious rebel. This incident in the rocky wilderness shows us how wisdom prevented a bloody feud. Saul was at David's mercy. By a quick stroke of the sword Saul's life could have been ended and David could have claimed the spoils of victory. But his sense of duty prevailed and he spared Saul. In verses 16-21 we see that Saul, in a moment of great insight, could be wise and could recognize the quality of David's character. Because of this he looked on David as his successor.

Across the whole family of humanity we need such wisdom to prevent feuds which are handed down through the generations. That is the promise Saul asked for (verse 21). It is our burden that such feuds embitter life for many people today as they remember the wrongs done centuries ago. We know the sorrows of the Balkans, with a thousand years of strife. And I cannot see the marches of the Orange Order in Ireland without praying for wisdom that will allow the past to rest in the past. You will think of your own context and the ancient enmities that still divide people. So we pray:

✳ *Help us to act generously,*
to think without prejudice,
and to hold out a hand of friendship
wherever we sense that an old pain
keeps us apart.

Friday November 16   *2 Samuel 1.1-16*

Defeat and death

The end of the first book of Samuel tells of the defeat of Saul by the Philistines. It was a complete rout. The three sons of Saul were killed in the fighting and Saul himself, in utter despair, ended his own life. In this passage the story is told a little differently, with the Amalekite messenger claiming to have given Saul the final blow, at Saul's agonized plea. And for doing that he too lost his life. Even in the heat of battle, and even at the urging of Saul himself, it was still inexcusable for anyone to execute 'the Lord's anointed'.

This was a day of sorrow for all the people of Israel. Many would have thought that God had deserted them. Others would have said that it was a punishment from God for their lack of faith. We might say that numbers, or equipment, or tactics were all in the Philistines' favour and that Saul had lost his way as a general. We need to be careful about blaming God for our losses when often we should blame ourselves.

'The fault, dear Brutus, is not in our stars,
But in ourselves, that we are underlings.'

From Julius Caesar, William Shakespeare

Do you think Shakespeare got it right?

✳ *There are moments of defeat in all our lives,*
and so we pray, Lord Christ, for your light,
for the courage to continue,
and for wisdom to learn from our failures.

Saturday November 17   *2 Samuel 1.17-27*

Song of sorrow

Here the poet turns tears into eloquence, for it is a song that spans the centuries and speaks today for many who have seen their own people defeated. We can only try, in fellowship, to share with those who suffer, to weep with those who weep, and to keep clearly in our hearts the renewing power of the Holy Spirit. It is good to note how David mourns for Saul despite all the pain that Saul had caused him; the respect was still there.

There is a point that has caused a good deal of debate. From verse 26 it has been suggested that the love between David and Jonathan was homosexual in character, and that David was here mourning the loss of his lover. I do not think this can be so. First, it was not part of the Hebrew culture to approve homosexuality, as it was approved in Egypt and later on in Greece. Yet David was never accused of it. Second, David's personal life was strongly heterosexual, and that was where he fell into strife. So I believe that here in this song we have an expression of deep, youthful friendship.

✳ *Man of Sorrows, you are near us when we weep;*
you know our sense of loss;
you entered into the darkness;

now, today, receive our prayer
for all who tread that road.

FOR REFLECTION – alone or with a group

● In these readings we have met the savagery of life among warring tribes. What has the world learned about resolving conflicts in better ways? Have we made progress?

● Saul had fits of violence. Can you relate this to examples in the Gospels of Jesus bringing peace of heart and mind? And is there such healing today for people with mental illness?

Sunday November 18   *2 Samuel 2.1-11*

Royal succession

Royal families are often in turmoil about the succession. Marriages that were intended to make an alliance break up, a son expected to succeed dies early, a likely princess flies to another country – and then, when the king dies, there is a power struggle that threatens to tear the nation apart. That was the risk for Israel on the death of Saul.

Our readings describe two movements. The first is David's move to Hebron, in the south of Palestine, in the area of Judah. He takes his two wives, which indicates a permanent move to a new capital. In 1 Samuel 25.44 Saul gave Michal, David's first wife, to another man. So here are wives numbers two and three, an indication of the marriages that were acceptable at the time. It was at Hebron that David was anointed king – but over what nation? At first it was only over Judah, one tribe only.

A soldier had other ideas. Abner used his position as a general to take Ishbosheth, a son of Saul, and proclaim him king at Manahaim, which was on the east of Jordan. From there he was to rule the northern tribes. This was clearly an opposition party setting up camp and so dividing the nation. The later story of this attempt is more blood and sorrow, for Ishbosheth was murdered in his bed by two of his own guards (2 Samuel 4.5-8).

A divided nation – that is not a distant story but very much with us still. Race, colour, language, religion, local loyalty, oppression – all may cause such deep fractures in our human society that we wonder if they can be healed. The gospel is about the breaking down of the walls of division, and the Church is called to that ministry. Are we obedient?

✳ *'Spare no effort to make fast with bonds of peace*
the unity which the Spirit gives.'   *Ephesians 4.3 (NEB)*

So grant us the will and the patience
to follow the Spirit's lead.

Monday November 19   *2 Samuel 5.1-12*

The City of David

When Ishbosheth was killed, his party no longer had a candidate for the throne. In verses 1-3 the meeting at Hebron brought all the groups together with acceptance of David as the one man who could unite the people. So, after a very eventful life, at the age of thirty, he assumed full responsibility for the security of his nation. It was a dangerous task.

A primary project was to find a suitable site for his capital. He needed a neutral place, not already claimed as a tribal centre, and it had to be in a good defensive position. He found such a site in Jerusalem, occupied by Jebusites, descendants of the tribe that lived through the patriarchal days. David captured the site, and verse 8 tells of the water shaft as the hidden way through to the citadel. The reality of this came to light in 1867 when a Captain Warren climbed through a hole above the spring called Gihon – 'bubbler' – along a shaft and found himself in the middle of the city. Archaeology confirms this ancient text.

So a long story began, the story of a place where the heights and depths of human nature were to be revealed, a city still built with passion and fought over with faith. It has become, through the centuries, a focus for three great religious traditions, and it is a test for all three whether they can live in peace.

✷ *'Unless the Lord builds the house,*
its builders labour in vain.
Unless the Lord keeps watch over the city,
the watchman stands guard in vain' (Psalm 127.1).
So may we build
with trust in the greatness of God.

Tuesday November 20   *2 Samuel 6.1-23*

The Ark comes home

The Ark was the most precious heritage of the people of Israel, their talisman. It was said to have been the very focus of Moses' faith, carried through the desert, across the Jordan and into the Promised Land. It stood for the authority of God, holy and eternal. At the beginning of the book of Samuel it rested at Shiloh. Now, in the newly united kingdom, with its new capital city, there was a secure home for the Ark, and David realized the importance of its journey. It was a great national celebration. There was music and feasting, and great care for this precious symbol.

It was the music and dancing that raised eyebrows, particularly those of Michal! She thought such conduct was unfitting for a king. David knew better. His outpouring of joy that day was an expression of his faith, not to be silenced. There is a fuller account in 1 Chronicles 15, where the names of the musicians and choir leaders are listed, and the day's events set out. It is good to know that celebration has its place in worship. We all need quietness and dignity and reverence, but there are also times when dancing for joy and singing with delight are the right way – and in some cultures the only way – to express our thanks to God.

✳ *Praise the LORD...*
Praise him with fanfares on the trumpet,
praise him on harp and lyre;
praise him with tambourines and dancing,
praise him with flute and strings...
Let everything that has breath praise the LORD!　　*Psalm 150*

Wednesday November 21　　　　　　　　　　*2 Samuel 7.1-17*

A House for God

This passage tells us of the major social transition when the people of Israel adopted an urban way of life after their long history as a nomadic, pastoral people. Their tradition told them that God had indeed met them as a journeying people in the wilderness. Their worship had been in transportable tents. Their unity as a people and their morality were all geared to that nomadic life. So settlement in Canaan was at first in small tribal camps scattered over the country, and only later did the concept of a city become a reality. Then the question was whether God can dwell in the city.

So there is hesitation about the Temple. Can the simple worship of the past be translated into a much more formal and regular liturgy with an established priesthood? What might be lost and what could be gained? The answer here is that David should not attempt the change but leave it to his successor.

All great social changes raise similar issues. To move from an absolute monarchy to a democracy is a big shift for public life. Should the Church become a democracy too? Or do we stay with clerical authority? From static rural life to modern human mobility is a major change. Is it the end of the parish?

✳ In farm and field or city street
each day eternity we meet;
in crowded buses and on trains
we meet an unknown neighbour's pains;
so may the Spirit touch us here
and help us live our daily prayer.

Thursday November 22   *2 Samuel 7.18-29*

David accepted as king

David had the future of his people in his heart and mind. So his prayer looked back and forward: back to the foundation of the nation, which was always seen as the exodus from Egypt, and forward to the need for stability amid the power blocs of the area. The prayer is a confirmation of the covenant between God and the people. As it was, now let it be so.

We also see in this prayer that David was now wholly convinced that all the idols of Canaanite worship were to be banished for ever (verse 22). Israel's God reigns, is to be obeyed, and is the people's security. This sense of God and nation bound together gave strength in all the crises ahead. But it was also a danger, for it made faith and nationalism one package. That was to be at the heart of the Jewish story for the next five hundred years. It was only with the *Diaspora*, the scattering of Jews, and then the Pentecost experience for Christians that the slow disentangling began. In modern Israel how do you think Jews might understand verses 24 to 26? And how do Christians and Arabs understand them? We all need to recall that these words belong to their historical context.

✳ Bind us together, Lord, with love,
that we might be your people;
Bind us all together, Lord, with love,
that the human family may be at one with you.

Friday November 23   *2 Samuel 8.15 to 9.13*

Welcome for a cripple

In verses 15-18 we read of the leadership group which ruled, rather like a modern cabinet, under David. The position of Jehoshaphat is interesting, for he was called the *Sopher*, or the Writer of Chronicles, the Recorder. The ability to write laws and records was highly valued; there was a sense of history at the seat of power.

Chapter 9 brings us a moving story of David's personal grace. He wanted to honour the family of Saul, not bury them, and this one descendant was known, a son of Jonathan. But he was a cripple, and so would be considered by many to be an outcast from society.

David had him brought into the palace, made him at home there, found people to care for him, and welcomed him to the royal table.

For most of history disabled people have had a rough deal from society. We pretended they were not there. Our buildings were designed in ways that always put them at great disadvantage, and employers often rejected them. It has taken a long time for that attitude to be reversed, and it has not yet changed everywhere. We do now consider access for people with disabilities to all new public buildings, and that is a start. Perhaps more important still is for the majority to appreciate the gifts they bring into the common life. I cannot see the Paralympic Games without astonishment at the strength, skill and courage of physically handicapped people. We need them.

✳ *Lord of all, we all have our handicaps*
but some have major life-long problems.
Help us all to understand, to respect and to hear
those who find every day a struggle.

Saturday November 24   *2 Samuel 11.1-27*

The corruption of power

The story is familiar and splendidly told; it is very human. David's position of power gave him the opportunity not only to take for himself the beautiful Bathsheba, but also to dispose of her husband in a way that would not implicate himself. No doubt he thought that Uriah would disappear conveniently to be heard no more – a classic cover up.

So David, who could rise to the heights of faith, devotion and graciousness, fell into conduct that was 'wrong in the eyes of the LORD' (verse 27).

This is the temptation of power. It is insidious and universal. 'Power tends to corrupt and absolute power corrupts absolutely' *(Lord Acton)*. We know this very well in politics. The greater the power held by one ruler, the more the likely it will be misused. This is why the 'separation of powers' has been a strength for democratic societies, so that no one person, and no single party, can control all the life of the nation. But there is power in churches too, and it is just as dangerous. The power of popes to pronounce anathemas or cursings was often used in earlier centuries for political purposes. Still today if the power to promote, to appoint, to decide who teaches is all in one person's hand, then we run a risk. So David stands for us all as a warning, that power is to be handled with humility and with safeguards.

✲ *'Do not remember the sins and offences of my youth,*
but remember me in your unfailing love' (Psalm 25.7a).
Yes, Lord, for we all fall into sin
and need your cleansing grace.

FOR REFLECTION – alone or with a group

● This week we have read of the establishment of a nation, a united people under one ruler. Do we see nationalism as a blessing or a curse? Or is it both?

● As we read about David we may say, 'Human nature doesn't change.' Is that so? In what ways are we the same sort of people as they were 3000 years ago?

Sunday November 25   *2 Samuel 12.1-14*

You are the man!

The prophet: Here the man of God had to take a personal risk. He felt compelled to challenge the king for his wickedness, and knew that in doing so he might lose his own life. We admire his sensitive method of attack, for his story led the king to convict himself, and that is a very powerful form of self-discovery. What a hard calling it is to be a prophet! To be aware of God's call, to perceive how it applies, to challenge the status quo, to expose the powerful when they lead people astray, to put up with all the accusations of the guilty, and still to remain humble and open to the word of God – such prophets are precious people in every age. Too often the Church of God has failed to be such a prophet, preferring to share the seats of power, but we thank God for the insight and courage of the few, whose faith shines for ever.

   The king: Once the accusation had come home to David, there was no attempt at self-excuse. 'I have sinned against the LORD' (verse 13). He did not try to bluster his way out with a speech of self-justification as so many people do, for he was a man of quick, direct feelings, moved by a sense of the holiness of God. When we can confess, both to God and to any whom we have hurt, then we are on the way to spiritual health.

✳ God, be gracious to me in your faithful love;
in the fullness of your mercy blot out my misdeeds.
Wash away all my iniquity
and cleanse me from my sin.
Lord, open my lips,
that my mouth may proclaim your praise.   *Psalm 51.1,2,15*

Monday November 26   *2 Samuel 12.15-25*

Dealing with grief and guilt

At this moment David was full of guilt; he knew that in some way it was his own sin that had brought the tragic illness on the small child. We might be much more cautious about linking a father's sin with a son's sickness, for we know a lot more about the origins of disease, but for David, Nathan and Bathsheba the link was obvious. So David pleaded with God for the life of the child by his fasting and prayer. Then the boy died, and it is as though the whole episode is over, the tragedy has cleared the air, the tears are wiped away, and life can be normal again.

We often meet guilt within our grieving. Why did I not care more? Why didn't I tell her how much I loved her? Why did I fail to take him to the best hospital? Why did we allow them to use the car that night? Why did I ignore that pain she complained about?

So we recognize our human solidarity, that we touch each other deeply and cannot escape from our own influence and responsibility. Yet to carry guilt for ever is the most unproductive thing; it prevents a creative and hopeful life. Dealing with guilt is a gospel gift. In Jesus Christ we find that God is offering forgiveness and a new beginning to all who bring their burdens with humility and trust. We cannot escape from the sorrow when a loved person dies, for that is our humanity, but in faith we can move on.

✳ 'God, my sacrifice is a broken spirit;
you, God, will not despise a chastened heart' (Psalm 51.17).
With all my past, my doubtful record,
I trust and hope in the burden-bearing Christ.

Tuesday November 27   *2 Samuel 18.1-18*

Intrigue and consequences

Chapters 13-17 tell a powerful story of struggles within the royal family. It is a drama of passion, we might say a melodrama. In David's extended family there was great ill-feeling among the next generation; in particular between two sons, Amnon and Absalom. Amnon was murdered and Absalom went into hiding for three years, and then was invited back to Jerusalem. But he was proudly independent and set himself up as a competitor to David, and this became civil war. Yet even when things were at their worst David could not altogether condemn his son. So in this passage we find David seeking to protect Absalom during the fighting.

It was of no avail. In the heat of the battle Absalom was caught up in the branches of a tree and there was killed by the spears of the king's men. It was the sorry end to a sorry life. A man who was 'admired for his beauty' (2 Samuel 14.25), who had courage and ability well above average, wasted his life in trying to compete with his father for the loyalty of the people. It seems to happen in powerful families – in the past, for example, in the family of Caesar Augustus and his successors – that children may lose all sense of respect for parents. So we thank God for genuine family faithfulness wherever it is found.

✳ *Thank you, ever-faithful God, for our families.*
May we reflect your care,
in good times and bad,
and honour those whose name we bear.

Wednesday November 28   *2 Samuel 18.19-33*

Waiting for news

Waiting for the telephone call.
Waiting for the doctor's verdict.
Waiting for the school report.
Waiting for the election result.
Waiting for the judge to pass sentence...
A time of worry or fear, of sleeplessness or bravado, a weary time.

So as we read of David watching and waiting for news of the battle, and then receiving the worst of news, that his son has been killed, we think of those who today wait with anxiety.

✳ *Lord our God, you wait for us*
to learn your way of life.
Jesus Christ, you waited at Nazareth
until your moment came.
And the world waits still for the peace
which the Spirit brings to our hearts.
Be with those who now wait anxiously for news;

that both hope and realism may live in them;
and that courage and grace may be your gift.

Thursday November 29   *2 Samuel 19.1-15*

Healing the feud

Once again David was faced with a divided people, for all the followers of Absalom had deserted the king. Now, in verses 1-8, his own close friends wondered if he could be trusted, for David was mourning for Absalom, the enemy, and ignoring the soldiers who had won the battle. But to David Absalom was a son. The death of his son was more crucial than anything else. Personal relationships before politics. Is that the right way round? Should family loyalties shape political conduct? It is not easy to give a single answer, for there has to be a very personal decision.

In verses 9-15 the rebellious element realized that without Absalom they had no credible leader and so returned to their old allegiance to David. Again we see the skill of David as he addressed them, 'You are my brothers, my own flesh and blood' (verse 12). The defeated enemies were at once lifted up again, restored to fellowship, not ground down with penalties. And the rebel general, Amasa, became David's commander. It is a pointer on how to end a feud, a remarkable sign of grace.

✳ *May we learn how to make peace, Lord,*
instead of learning how to make war.
Teach us through Christ the road of forgiveness,
as we all need to be forgiven.

Friday November 30   *2 Samuel 22.1-7, 17-31*

David's psalms

The Book of Psalms is a great collection of Hebrew devotion, and much of it (particularly the early part) is attributed to David. It is plain that he inspired the poets and singers of Israel. We can think of the songs that rose out of the shepherd experience and out of the family struggles. Some developed from the experience of kingship, others from personal sorrows and joys. All the psalms show us a faith in God who is directly involved in the life of his people.

At the end of the books of Samuel we have the long psalm in chapter 22 which thanks God for his strength and aid during the tough times of war. It is a song of victory, full of images of the power of the Lord assisting his righteous servant. Can we sing such a song in modern military victories? I think the answer is No. Not because we are in any way superior to David's Israel, but because we know that war is always a great tragedy and that the people on the other side are also the children of the one God. As we look at the Christ of the cross we cannot sing,

'You grant me vengeance, God,
laying nations prostrate at my feet' (verse 48).
This song belongs to David's era.

✳ *Yes, Lord God, you are with us*
in all the events of life and all the years,
teaching us the way of holiness.
Be patient with us; have mercy,
for we are slow learners.

Saturday December 1   *2 Samuel 23.1-7*

Last words

Although there is further material before the end of the book, this passage is given to us as the last words of David, 'the singer of Israel's psalms.' Verses 2-5 are a splendid summary of all that David prayed that he might be. It is a text to be preached for any government. Justice for the people and faithfulness to God go hand in hand.

David had been an exceptional leader, always aware of human frailty and battered by family conflict; a man of passion and poetry; consistent in his desire to keep the people united; skilful in mending quarrels; a man of song; the founder of Jerusalem; the sinner who was penitent before God and before the prophet; above all a leader who knew that he stood under the mighty hand of God.

✳ *'One thing I ask of the LORD,*
it is the one thing I seek:
that I may dwell in the house of the LORD
all the days of my life' (Psalm 27.4a).
So may we all be members of God's household
in faith, confidence and solidarity.

FOR REFLECTION – alone or with a group

● The readings this week have shown us the highs and the lows of David's spiritual life. Do we sense the presence of God in both these experiences?

- Chapter 19 is a remarkable witness to generosity towards enemies. Are there examples of this in modern history for which we should thank God?

To take this further

Psalms 1-41 are specially linked to David, either as the author or as the inspirer. Which of these psalms can we all sing with Christian conviction? Which are difficult for us? And what makes the difference? Then try to write your own psalm about a key event in your life.

ADVENT – GOD WITH US
1. David's descendant

Notes based on The Revised English Bible by
Alec Gilmore

Alec Gilmore is a Baptist minister with 20 years' experience in pastorates in Northampton and West Worthing followed by a literature ministry for the benefit of the Third World and Eastern Europe as Director of Feed the Minds. He lives in Sussex and is a freelance writer and lecturer, mostly on biblical topics. His recent books include A Dictionary of the English Bible and its Origins (Sheffield Academic Press), Aid Matters, Preaching as Theatre (SCM Press), and Agenda for Development (SPCK).

David was almost the only king to keep his reputation intact. Any others who managed it were thought to be following in his footsteps. They were his 'sons'.

Anyone therefore who might be thought the 'hope of the future' must measure up to him and, though Jesus himself seems not to have made much of it, there is little doubt that the early Church needed to see 'their man' in that succession.

With the passing of time the David-link has become more important and when you think of the Coming of Jesus it is an obvious place to begin.

1st Sunday of Advent, December 2   *Jeremiah 33.14-16*
Thankfulness and hope

Jeremiah is writing to a people at rock bottom. Their land, which they had always thought of as a gift from God, had been conquered by Babylon whom they regarded as pagan. Jerusalem, their holy city, had been sacked. The Temple, centre of their worship, was in ruins. Their natural leaders and many of their personal friends had been carried off into exile. Even the Sabbath was rapidly becoming history. For at least fifty years things had been getting worse!

But just now there is a light at the end of the tunnel. Persia has conquered Babylon and rumour has it that they can hope for better things. A restoration! Jeremiah latches on to it.

First, the great and glorious days of David are not over for ever. Second, what the future holds will have a direct connection with what has gone before. Of David's line! But third, they are painting on a broad canvas and will need patience. David is 400 years behind. Jesus, we now know, was 600 years in front. But then God is like that! Always with us.

✳ *Lord, when the day is dark, help me to look back*
with thankfulness, and forward with hope.
Help me to bridge the gap between the two
and give me patience to wait your time.

Monday December 3   *Matthew 1.1,17-25*

A foot in the present

Verses 2-16 need not be taken literally. What matters is that Jesus fits into the plan, and the plan covers a very long time. Verses 17-25 suffer from sheer familiarity, but the point not to be missed is that God is with us.

Events may happen once, and once only, but the presence of God in those events is the timeless bit which provides the link over those 42 generations (verse 17) and at the time bridges the gap between all that and what has happened over a similar period of time until now.

The God of Abraham, through David to Jesus, is the same one as is 'with *us*' in Jesus through Luther to Mandela (or whomever), and the one who was 'with us' in the exodus, the exile and the incarnation is the same as the one in the abolition of slavery, the civil rights movement or the emancipation of women.

Every foot in the present bears the footprint of a timeless God, and nowhere more than in familiar, everyday experiences such as surprise and puzzlement, fear and anxiety, joy, pain, and even embarrassment, which manifest themselves in so many ways, but right here and now in the birth of a baby.

✳ *Lord, keep me aware that you are 'with us', now as then,*
just as you have always been 'with them',
and teach me how to bridge the gap
between the present and the eternal.

Tuesday December 4   *Matthew 22.41-45*

A new dimension

Just as playful kittens may grow up to be cantankerous cats, and cuddly babies become independent-minded adolescents – and it is not always easy to see the connection between the two – so in the case of Jesus, thirty years down the line, his contemporaries were still trying to work it out. Is he, or is he not, a true Son of David?

In this somewhat difficult encounter (which harks back to Psalm 110) Jesus tries to put the discussion on a different level.

The Jews knew that the Messiah (i.e. the anointed one) was 'bigger' than David but had always thought of him either as the child (son) of David or the fulfilment of David. Some suggested he was *the inspiration* of David and Jesus seems to suggest that this is where we should look. Not in events nor at individuals, however worthy! Seek rather to discover the Spirit who moves and inspires them. Who makes them tick? For it is there that we shall find God.

✳ *Father, help me today to look beyond, beneath and above*
 the events I see and the people I encounter
 that I may see your Spirit who moved in prophets,
 priests and kings as well as in ordinary people,
 and whose fullest expression came in Jesus Christ.

Wednesday December 5   *John 3.1-17*

Beginning in a different place

Steinbeck, in a short story called 'Differences', relates how he once met the Indians of the Gulf on a short trip to Guaymas. What they did for him and his companions was 'without hope or plan of profit', or if it was profit it was 'not the kind we are used to, not of material things changing hands'. Yet always something was exchanged, 'some unnameable of great value'. These Indians were living on a different plane.

So it was with Jesus and Nicodemus: two people of quite different background and experience with enough in common to want to meet but, when they did, they quickly became aware that they were living in totally different worlds, with different mindsets.

True faith is not acquiring knowledge or information. Nicodemus had both, but he was a materialist. He could not see what human life means – what is 'beyond and above'. If he really wanted to meet Jesus he needed to begin in a different place. That is what is meant by 'new birth'. How Nicodemus responded is left an open question.

✳ *Father, no one can decide to be born again.*
 But can you touch my life in this season of Advent
 so that I can begin in a different place and come closer to you?

Widening circles

This is probably an adaptation of a hymn with two verses, one linking Christ with creation (verses 15-18a), the other with redemption and renewal (verses 18b-20). Both broaden our understanding of Christ. The Colossians had a reputation for honouring *all* the cosmic powers. Paul wants them to know that Christ is supreme. All other powers are dependent on him. He was there, in creation, before they were, and the reference to his 'blood on the cross' (verse 20) clearly refers to his role in redemption.

This is a hymn 'to sing' when we find ourselves limiting the gospel to humanity. It takes us out into the world of animals and nature, ecology and the environment, and the heavenly bodies. All are part of God's agenda.

It is a hymn 'to sing' when faced with personal catastrophe, human or natural disaster, what the insurance companies call 'acts of God' and many others describe as 'bad luck'. Evil forces of many kinds, beyond our comprehension, may be at work everywhere but their power and time span are limited. Christ is in control.

It is a hymn 'to sing' when clearly self-seeking and evil-minded people are 'successfully' pursuing their wicked ways and many 'innocents' are suffering as a result. Christ still reigns.

✳ *Lord, I believe. Help my unbelief.*

A re-discovery

Christians in Rome were obviously having difficulty getting on with one another – mainly Jews accepting Gentiles. But not only that. It was also strong people relating to weak people, and hence the problems we are familiar with: majorities and minorities, traditionalists and modernizers, what we were brought up on and what we are now asked to believe and do, and so on. In short, relating to anybody who is 'different' or any *thing* that is unfamiliar.

But the coming of Christ has set up a new order which overcomes antipathies, dissolves divisions, breaks down barriers and embraces all. God did, when he came in Jesus. Why can't we?

When we do, we often re-discover the Christ we thought we were losing, often to our surprise: in places and people where we never thought he existed or expected to find him. Like a Mother

Teresa among the poor of Calcutta. Or parents coping with a handicapped child, and finding reserves and resources of love they never knew they had. Or a white racist missionary with all the gospel at her fingertips finding Christ in a totally different culture.

✳ *Lord Jesus Christ, as a mother loves her child,*
  help me to learn to accept and love others
  and to find you present in them.

Saturday December 8   *Isaiah 2.1-5**
Capturing the vision
The vision of what might be, if only we could learn to accept one another, is not confined to today, nor indeed to Christianity, and didn't even begin with Jesus. Isaiah had it. So apparently did Micah (4.1-4), and perhaps many others too.

What matters for Isaiah is that the vision is linked with Jerusalem, the holy city, city of David, capital of the kingdom of David, home of the Temple and centre of worship.

What matters for the early Christians is that Jesus is linked with that Davidic line to satisfy those who saw Jerusalem as the city of David, the forerunner of the Messiah.

What matters to us is that he finds a place today with all those who are working to fulfil the vision: sound teaching, instruction and obedience (verse 3), faithful justice (verse 4a), and food before arms (verse 4b). This is seeing the light, engaging with the light and walking in the light towards its fulfilment.

✳ *O God of all truth, all justice and all peoples,*
  open our eyes to the vision you have set before us
  and enable us to join with all those who are seeking fulfilment.

FOR REFLECTION – alone or with a group
● Identify a situation which five, ten, twenty-five or fifty years ago seemed hopeless. Reflect on it for five minutes to see how it looks different today. What brought about the change and what does this say to us about the future? In group discussion share your stories.

● Choose an everyday story, personal, in the press or in a 'soap', which is charged with human emotion (e.g. fear, anxiety, joy) and try to work out who (or what) is coming to new birth as a result? Can you find the 'baby' and so see the hand of God?

- Think of three people, personal acquaintances or people in the public eye, about whom you know a great deal: one whom you like, one you don't like and one of whom you are profoundly suspicious. Think about what makes them tick and then see if all three can in some way be related to the God of the New Testament.
- How do you think God might touch a life so as to bring about a new birth?
- What difference does it make to your faith to think of God as concerned with ecology and the universe?

FOR ACTION

Find three stories in the press this week, one motivated by a vision for sound teaching and instruction ('right living'), one by a concern for justice, and one by a desire to see a peace-loving community. Choose one and write 200-300 words (for your eyes only!) setting out how that person, idea or incident is related to the gospel of Jesus Christ.

ADVENT – GOD WITH US
2. Advent prophets – then and now

Notes based on the Jerusalem Bible by
John Medcalf

John Medcalf, a Roman Catholic priest, was ordained in England in 1963. After five years in a parish in Brighton, he volunteered to work in Latin America. He founded the Rural Library Network in Peru and set up a chain of Rural Arts Centres in the war-zone in Nicaragua. From 1992-98 he worked in a shanty town in San Salvador where he founded the theatrical group ELSINORE. Publications include 'That's my Boy' – an illustrated life of Christ (Collins Liturgical) and 'Letters from Nicaragua' (Catholic Institute of International Relations, London).

The growing gap between North and South, haves and have-nots, is our generation's biggest challenge. Unless health, education and employment can be improved in Asia, Africa and Latin America there is little or no chance of a lasting world peace.

The Advent prophets warn us sternly in words that are as significant today as when they were originally written. There can be no good news at Christmas unless we are prepared to recognize the bad news that is mostly the work of human hands.

2nd of Advent, Bible Sunday, December 9   *Isaiah 52.1-12 ***
How beautiful are your feet!

It's not so much the feet that are beautiful as the eager, hurried footsteps that carry the gospel of Isaiah to an anxious world.

In China the Barefoot Doctors' Network is still good news for millions of peasant families. This new concept in health care enables the largest ethnic population on our planet to extend primary health facilities to the remotest of its people.

In Peru several hundred librarians carry books over the Andes mountains to isolated families. They are sometimes carried on horses or mules, but more often by the bare feet of men and women volunteers. The books are often read aloud by a child who has learned to read and write in a village school. The women (mostly illiterate) are stimulated to learn to read, through Church or government programmes, by books on health, farming, nutrition, and local history.

The good news of peace, salvation and the reign of God is proclaimed in a special way in the Bible. On this Bible Sunday we should ask ourselves whether our footsteps are heading outwards in eagerness and joy towards those in need of God's Word.

Are our feet beautiful in God's sight?

✴ *Lord, may your Word be always*
a lamp for our feet.

Human Rights Day, Monday December 10   *1 Kings 18.17-39**
Baaled over!
The new turn-of-the-millennium gods are just damp squibs, like the *baalim* of Mount Carmel:

GLOBALIZATION means Dallas and Dynasty lifestyles for a few north-westerners and malnutrition for the south of the planet;

FREE MARKET ECONOMY means an average lifespan of nearly 80 years for Western Europe and barely 45 for Bolivians and Haitians;

WESTERN-STYLE DEMOCRACY works tolerably well in a handful of countries in the northern hemisphere, but cannot be imposed successfully in Africa or Asia without radical adaptation.

Elijah, in one of the greatest of God's manifestations in the Old Testament, invites the Jews to choose (verse 21) between the true God of history who brought them out of Egyptian slavery, and the false baals of their neighbours. Jesus will later echo this passage to his own generation: 'No one can be the slave of two masters... God and money' (Matthew 6.24).

Human Rights Day is a reminder that ALL human beings have sacred rights – from womb to tomb, as the saying goes. A social order that penalizes the poor to favour the rich cannot have the true God as its author.

✴ *Help us, Lord, to unmask, recognize and denounce*
the false gods of our time.

Tuesday December 11   *Amos 5.4-15*
Amos who roared!
Amos is the prophet of social justice. In a period of prosperity and class inequality this sheep-breeder from Tekoa (five miles south of Bethlehem) condemns injustice, especially when directed against the poor.

During Advent, we remember that the gospel of Jesus Christ is not just speaking to us as individuals. Matthew 25.31-46 reminds us that there will also be a judgement of the nations. Society and the world family of nations are also 'groaning in one great act of giving birth' (Romans 8.22) for the coming or advent of Christ into our present history.

Amos would have roared against present-day bankers and the International Monetary Fund. The unpayable debts owed by Third World countries would have infuriated him. They should infuriate us too.

✱ *You who pull down the mighty from their thrones*
lift up, we beg you, the weak and downtrodden of our world.

Wednesday December 12   Jeremiah 7.1-15

Wanted – a new Jeremiah!

Which is the world's most significant building? Possible candidates are: the Great Wall of China, The Taj Mahal, the Kremlin, Chartres Cathedral, the Sydney Opera House...

For Jews in Old Testament times the Temple in Jerusalem was not just beautiful and significant. It was a sign of God's special approval and blessing. Psalms were composed and sung in its honour. It was thought to be indestructible.

But for the prophet Jeremiah the Temple provided a false sense of security. The house of the Lord had become a den of thieves. The Jews were failing to care for their neighbours – especially widows, orphans, and foreigners – and putting their trust in a mere building.

Buildings come and go. Fires, earthquakes and wars can destroy your parish church, your ancient monastery, your proud cathedral. The real Church is not made of bricks and mortar, and the only cornerstone is Jesus Christ.

Great buildings of the past, like the Egyptian pyramids, were often built by slave labour. Today the marble-fronted banks of Zurich, Wall Street and the City of London are sustained by vast interest payments on capital loans made to the impoverished countries of the South, or rather to their despotic and irresponsible leaders.

We need a new Jeremiah.

✱ *O come, thou Rod of Jesse, free*
thine own from Satan's tyranny.   18th century Latin

286

Power corrupts!

During my visit to Paraguay in 1978, I heard the following announcement on the national TV station: 'This morning President-General Alfredo Stroessner inaugurated the new Alfredo Stroessner Airport, twelve kilometres to the south of Alfredo Stroessner City...'

Dictators and corrupt politicians have had a field day in the final century before the millennium. General Stroessner was a murderous fascist who clung to power for 35 years. In the nightmare republic of Haiti, the Duvalier dynasty was even worse. Stalin, Hitler, Mussolini... Political corruption is not just a fact of Third World politics, nor of our own times: Oliver Cromwell acted in Ireland like a bloodthirsty thug.

The Advent prophet Ezekiel denounces false shepherds of Israel. These shepherds are not the priests and prophets, but the political leaders, as is made clear by the text.

Political corruption depresses us. But we should remember with joy those who resisted corruption, those good shepherds who refused to trade in their conscience. Favourites of mine are: King Stephen of Hungary, Sir Thomas More, Abraham Lincoln, Nelson Mandela... Add your favourites...

✴ *O God of earth and altar,*
Bow down and hear our cry;
Our earthly rulers falter,
Our people drift and die;
The walls of gold entomb us,
The swords of scorn divide,
Take not thy thunder from us,
But take away our pride.   *GK Chesterton (1874-1936)*

Comfort ye my people!

As a returned mission partner from Latin America, I am frequently disturbed by the premature deaths of those I have known and loved in Peru, Nicaragua and El Salvador. Most have died from what could have been cured in any First World hospital. I get angry. I argue with God. I stop saying my prayers.

The anonymous 'second Isaiah' faced a similar problem. His response was (depending on your translation) to console, comfort or strengthen the people. They too had known exile, humiliation and premature death. The deliverance of Israel, especially of Jerusalem, was for them a new liberation.

When will deliverance come for the peoples of Asia, Africa and Latin America? When will the nations be united? When will the countries of the planet act as a functional family? When will South and North, East and West acknowledge their need for each other?

We Christians are called to be leaven, salt and light: quality rather than quantity; to permeate rather than to dominate; to inspire and perspire rather than to pull and push.

✴ *Out of the depths I cry to you, O Lord,*
Lord, hear my cry.   *Psalm 130.1-2a (NIV)*

Saturday December 15   *Matthew 3.1-12**

Prophets, martyrs, alive-alive-O!

A prophet speaks the truth, come what may. He or she applauds what is good, denounces what is evil.

I once had the privilege of knowing a Basque Jesuit in El Salvador. Father Amando had given his life to evangelize the poor. He could have had a comfortable teaching position in Europe, but he chose to go to a country where comfort was scarce.

El Salvador is a feisty Central American republic. Its people are renowned as hard-working. When they emigrate to the USA they are snapped up for illegal and underpaid jobs. Sweatshops for cheap clothes allow them to send back dollars to their families at home.

Sadly, successive administrations in Washington DC have propped up a series of corrupt, pliant military governments in El Salvador. In November 1989, Fr Amando was one of six Jesuit priests murdered by a government death squad. Like John the Baptist before them the Jesuits had prophesied in favour of the poor and against the rich and corrupt. Prophets are frequently martyred.

Are we the stuff that martyrs are made of?

✴ *Hark! A herald voice is calling:*
'Christ is nigh' it seems to say;
'Cast away the dreams of darkness,
O ye children of the day!'
                                          6th Century, tr. E Caswall (1814-78), alt.

FOR REFLECTION – alone or with a group

What is your commitment to party politics? How can you justify not joining the party you consider most likely to put God's will into action?

FOR ACTION

Join an Amnesty International group in your area. If there isn't one, help to set one up, making sure that it's not totally taken over by Christians.

ADVENT – GOD WITH US
3. A voice in the wilderness

Notes based on the Revised Standard Version by
Andrew Wingate

Andrew Wingate is an Anglican priest who has been involved in theological education for the last 25 years, in South India, at Queen's College, Birmingham, and as Principal of the United College of the Ascension at Selly Oak. He has now moved to Leicester, where he is Director of Ministry and Training in the Diocese. He has written articles and books in the areas of mission, interfaith dialogue and theological education.

The last century of the old millennium was a time of unprecedented progress in science, technology and communications. But socially, politically, environmentally and culturally, there was a sense often of having been in an unparalleled wilderness. This was perhaps even more so spiritually. As we move to the third millennium, which are the voices crying in the wilderness to bring hope of transformation? Perhaps we should go back and hear again voices at the dawn of the first millennium, and learn from them anew.

3rd Sunday of Advent, December 16   *Luke 1.57-66*
A voice of hope

Naming a child has deep significance in most cultures. It may be because of meaning as, for example, within the Muslim or Hindu religions, where it is felt that a child may take on the characteristics symbolized in the name. In other contexts, a family name will be handed on. Hence the shock when Elizabeth and Zechariah indicated that their son should be called John. It was a new name for a new situation, for one who was to be the last great prophet of the pre-messianic period, and whom the Messiah was to call 'the greatest of the prophets'.

His voice was to have universal significance. But first, like his cousin Jesus, he was to become fully a Jew, by going through the rite of circumcision. God acts, not through the universal, but through the particular, as that is the only way that history can work. Both Judaism and Christianity are historical faiths.

Each human birth is a miracle. Let us never lose our sense of wonder at the birth of any child, and ask the question expressed by the crowds here, 'What then will this child be?'

* *Down in a slum a new-born babe stirs in her sleep.*
  She wakes, she looks, she looks into my eyes.
  She looks into my eyes and I know we have hope.
                    Procession of Prayers, ed. John Carden (Cassell)

Monday December 17   *Luke 1.67-79*

Where is wisdom?

After a long absence, when there was no more prophecy in the land, Luke records the Spirit as returning to a series of people: to Elizabeth (1.41), to Mary (1.35), to Zechariah (1.67) and to Simeon (2.27). Such people have been described as the *anawim,* 'the holy poor', or the 'poor of Yahweh', those who live lives of simple piety and know their daily and ultimate dependence upon God. They know they owe all to God as do the poor in Isaiah 41.17-20. They are the 'poor in spirit' who are blessed in Matthew's version of the Beatitudes. The majority are old. In Western culture, the wisdom of the old is often not valued. In *The Book of Life,* by Andrew Jackson (Gollancz 1999) is the story of a young Englishman's journey round the world meeting the oldest men and women he could find in each culture. He found them also the wisest. Do we recognize the wisdom of the elderly around us? Zechariah's wisdom is revealed in his song.

The songs in Luke 1-2 point to a radical transformation taking place in history at that time, though at that moment it could only be seen by a few. At the beginning of Luke's other book, the Acts, he describes how at Pentecost the transformation becomes public with a great outpouring of the Holy Spirit on old and young of every language and culture.

* *Ageless God, let me not just grow old.*
  Let me grow.   *Prayer from the USA*
                    Procession of Prayers, ed. John Carden (Cassell)

Tuesday December 18   *John 1.19-28**

A voice of challenge

I recently saw an exhibition of paintings by Gordon Bennett, an Australian artist whose work expresses the anguish he felt when, as a teenager, he discovered that his mother was half Aborigine. The paintings are a deeply disturbing expression of a man bleeding for his people who have lost their language, culture and dignity. Through his paintbrush he tries to bring them hope within the wilderness. John did this for his Jewish people, not through a brush but through his voice. He pointed them, not to himself, but to the one who would bring them hope in the wilderness of their political and spiritual disarray.

A 'John the Baptist of our time' was Archbishop Oscar Romero of El Salvador. He was killed as he celebrated Mass in March 1980, because the oligarchy who dominated his country could not bear his voice crying out in the wilderness of the poverty, exploitation and death suffered by his people. Two weeks before his death he expressed his readiness to die for the poor: 'Martyrdom is a grace from God that I do not believe I have earned. But if God accepts the sacrifice of my life, then may my blood be the seed of liberty, and a sign of the hope that will soon become a reality.' Let us have the courage to be a voice for someone who is voiceless, and to challenge our church to be a voice for the poor.

✳ *Unless the grain of wheat falls to the earth and dies, it remains only a grain. But if it dies, it bears much fruit.*
John 12.23-26 (from the reading at Romero's last Mass)

Wednesday December 19 Luke 3.10-14,18-20

The voice of repentance

John does not impose ethical requirements on those to be baptized. Instead, he responds to their question, 'What shall we do?' It comes from three groups, the multitudes, tax collectors and soldiers. Later the same question is asked of Jesus by a lawyer (Luke 10.25) and a rich ruler (18.18). The three groups approaching John for baptism are despised: those whom the respectable call 'common', and those whose profession involved co-operation with the Roman colonial power over its Jewish puppets. John anticipates 'the one who is to come' by his appeal to these groups who were not normally in the synagogue or Temple. Their question, 'What shall we do?' indicated a desire to change. Each group was given an ethically demanding challenge. 'The good news' John preached demanded repentance as well as baptism, action as well as faith.

What would John demand this Advent? Of you personally, and of your community? He might also ask, 'Where are the unexpected or "common" people?' Are they part of your church community? If not, why not?

✳ *Lord, thank you for revealing the mystery of your truth and love to the poor.* Procession of Prayers

292

Who was John?

Who was John the Baptist? The Gospels vary in their answers to this question. In the Fourth Gospel, as we have seen, John is quite explicit, 'I am not Elijah, the prophet or the Messiah.' John is a voice of witness, no more and no less. In Luke, he comes 'in the spirit and power of Elijah' to make ready for the Lord a people prepared (Luke 1.17). In Mark and Matthew, he is unambiguously Elijah returned. On the Mount of Transfiguration in Mark, Jesus declares 'Elijah has come' (Mark 9.13), and here again Jesus testifies, 'He is Elijah who is to come' (verse 14). These two Gospels are eager to show the fulfilment of the prophecy of Malachi (4.5) of the return of Elijah. But they make a clear change, nevertheless. For Malachi, Elijah's return will be to herald 'the great and terrible day of the LORD'. For all four Gospels, John's coming is to herald the coming of salvation for all, Gentile and Jew alike, with the coming of a Messiah for the whole world.

With six questions here (verses 7-10), Jesus emphasizes that who John was became clear only to those who 'have ears to hear'. Most were not willing to accept, particularly the powerful who killed the messenger. In previous verses (2-7) John had asked just one question from prison, 'Are you the one who is to come?' Are we asking the right questions this Advent? A characteristic of children is to ask questions. Such may become tedious. But, unless we become as children, we will not become even the least in the Kingdom of heaven.

✴ *Lord Jesus, light of the world, John told the people to prepare, for you were very near. As Christmas grows closer... help us to be ready to welcome you now.*

The Promise of his Glory

The choice

John's way of austerity led to his being mocked as demonic, while Jesus' way of identifying with ordinary life in terms of eating and drinking only led to accusations about the company he and his disciples kept. The small parable of the children vividly indicates this (verses 16-17). But the choice before those who met John and Jesus was not a choice about whether to join a game or to sulk at the side of the market place. It was whether to respond to the gospel, whether to enter the Kingdom of God by the door open before them. By questioning the lifestyle of Jesus and John, they missed the heart of their message – the call to repentance and new life – even though it had been put clearly to them. Today, people make excuses to avoid going to church – this church is too noisy, this one too austere... Such will always be. But within all the attempts to be modern and satisfy, the central message is still clear, that God was with us in John the greatest of the prophets, and is still with us in Jesus born in poverty in Bethlehem, the One who was a friend of tax gatherers and sinners. And that means all of us.

✳ *Almighty God... give us the sensitivity*
to hear prophetic voices today,
that we may turn from unjust deeds
to wait in happiness... for Christ our Liberator.
Anesia Nascimento, Brazil – More Living Prayers for Today (IBRA)

Saturday December 22   *Luke 1.46-55**

A voice of liberation

Mary's song, the *Magnificat*, has become one of the most loved of Christian hymns, but its familiarity can blind us to its radicalness. It is the voice of a young peasant girl who became the most honoured woman in history, because of the child she bore. She speaks here with the voice of radical prophecy, ranking with that of her cousin's son, John.

Verses 46-49 record her overwhelming sense of the grace of God in making her what she is to become; as St Paul was to say, God chooses what is weak in the world to shame the strong (1 Corinthians 1.27). In verses 50-55, Mary sings of the transformation that is to come upon power relationships in the world through her Son. As that Son says later, 'Blessed are you poor, for yours is the kingdom of God.' In the Christmas story itself, it is the poor – Mary, Joseph, the shepherds, older people like Simeon and Anna – who are to touch the reality of the beginning of the Kingdom, not the powerful Herod. It is no wonder that Liberation theologians and activists of Latin America, South Africa and other places have found in the *Magnificat* a key text for their social gospel.

What is also clear is that in Europe Mary has largely been a symbol of submissive obedience, and the import of this passage has rarely been heard. Let us hear it anew, and reflect on its implications for us wherever we are.

✳ *Jesus our brother, born of the woman Mary,*
You confronted the proud and the powerful,

And welcomed as your friends those of no account...
Help us to commit ourselves to struggle against evil
And to choose life.   Iona Community Worship Book
                                          (Wild Goose Publications)

FOR REFLECTION – alone or with a group

- Examine the way you are hearing and responding to the questions of the young in your place, and how far you are giving space to learn from the wisdom of the old.
- What are the main features of the wilderness lying around your context? What voices are crying out to bring hope there?

FOR ACTION

Are there individuals or groups who are voiceless in your situation? How can you become their voice or, better, enable them to speak for themselves?

CHRISTMAS – GOD WITH US
4. Born of God

Notes based on the New Revised Standard Version by

Helen Richmond

Helen Richmond, a minister of the Uniting Church of Australia, has spent the last four and a half years working as Tutor in Mission Studies at the United College of the Ascension, a jointly sponsored Methodist and Anglican (United Society for the Propagation of the Gospel) College at Selly Oak, Birmingham. She has lived in Indonesia and has a keen interest in mission, women's theology, and Indigenous Peoples' theology. Helen is married to Ben Suherman and they have two boys.

In so many ways our world is the same as the world into which Jesus was born. Then people were waiting in hope, in a country occupied by foreigners. Now, in many parts of the world, people are also longing for freedom from oppression, for light in the darkness, for things to be different. Ours is a world still groaning as in childbirth, waiting for new life to be born.

Can a baby born in Bethlehem so long ago
really make a difference to our lives, our families, our world?
Is there something here, Lord?
Something that can kindle again the flickering flame of faith?
That can bring energy and vigour to our jaded lives
and renew your world?

The promise of Christmas is that God creates life even when human expectation has dried up and hope has been eclipsed. Let us keep alive this fragile hope. God still chooses to enter our life so that we will affirm the possibility of God being reborn in us and our world.

4th Sunday of Advent, December 23   *Isaiah 7.10-16**

God's sign of commitment

If there was ever need for conflict resolution the Kings of Judah, Israel and Aram needed it. Political alliances meant Judah was to be on the receiving end of some nasty treatment. Surrounded by enemies, Ahaz King of Judah and his people expect the worst (Isaiah 7.2). In the midst of political turmoil Isaiah conveys the message of God's protection and care. God promises Ahaz and the people of Judah that those plotting their destruction will be dealt with (7.7). Ultimately Ahaz learnt that it is not political manoeuvring or military might that determines the outcome but God who intervenes to liberate and rescue. In response to God's promise Ahaz trusts God, despite appearances to the contrary. Ahaz took God at his word and needed no additional assurance but nevertheless God gives a sign of commitment to Ahaz: a child will be born whose name is *Immanuel*, 'God with us'.

✳ *O God, the mighty ones are still plotting*
and we await a sign that you have not abandoned
your children, and that the poor will not for ever be
at the mercy of the rich and powerful.
Immanuel, come to us, and to our world,
overthrowing the mighty ones, lifting up the lowly. Amen

Christmas Eve, December 24   *Luke 1.26-45*

How can this be?

Mary's initial question when confronted by the strange message-bearer was, 'How can this be?'. But in the end Mary says, 'May it be to me as you have said.' Mary, after some reassurance, was able to relinquish her fears, doubts and disbelief, and grasp the significance of what was happening to her. Nothing was impossible for God to accomplish. God could use her to nurture the life of the One who would bring life to the world.

If you and I have sensed God's blessing in our life – we had better start feeling troubled! God has an uncanny way of asking us to do things we would never have imagined were possible. Mary and Elizabeth were the first to hear and embrace this good news. With them can we be open to the crazy dreams of God, trusting in the creative power of the life-giving Spirit?

✳ *Mary and Elizabeth,*
our sisters and mothers in the faith,
you believed, accepted and welcomed God's irruption
into human history. We are inspired by your 'yes'.
O God, help us, like them, to cooperate with,
rather than resist, the plans you dream up.
Be born, O God, in us. Amen

Christmas Day, December 25   *Luke 2.1-20**

Listen to the angels sing

Shepherds were at the lowest rung in the ancient social scale and yet it is they who hear the song of the angels. Why is it that these folk, rough and ready, simple and humble, were visited by angels who sent them to Bethlehem to get a first look at the Christ child? It wasn't to some learned rabbi or well-to-do town folk. Perhaps the shepherds, who knew what being despised and rejected meant, had eyes of faith to see and believe that God could come to them in the form of a small and helpless baby, born in poverty in a smelly stable.

They gaze in wonder and then go home rejoicing. God has sent as Saviour One who is truly born among us, one of us. This God enters our experience, identifies with our longings and brings the poor and the humble into the centre of his saving concern.

✳ *Open our hearts, Lord, that we will not be distracted*
or too busy to hear the angels sing.
Help us this day to travel to Bethlehem
to receive the vulnerable Christ child
and welcome him as Saviour. Then, like the shepherds,
we will return to our ordinary lives with hope kindled,
joy in our hearts, changed by the good news of his birth.

Wednesday December 26   *Titus 2.11-14**

Awaiting his coming

Christmas time, often characterized by festivities and excessive consumption, can also be a time when family breakdown and violence is on the increase. We find it difficult to transfer the message of Christmas in a lasting way to the rest of our lives. Today's reading invites us to move our attention away from the manger to its implications for our living. This pastoral epistle, written to Titus and his community in Crete, reminds believers that through God's grace they are called to live a lifestyle that reflects holiness and goodness. It is not enough to give verbal assent to our faith at one time of the year. We need to let Christ remake us from the inside to the outside, transforming our self-centredness and redirecting our worldly passions towards a passion for what is right. Believers then and now are challenged to keep alive the hope of Jesus' final return and to live out their lives in the light of this point of reference.

✳ *If we outwardly confess Christ but our words*
and actions betray him, Lord, have mercy.
If we welcome the birth of Jesus but fail
to follow him, Lord, have mercy.
If our faith is sentimentalized
and our hope quickly extinguished, Lord, have mercy.

The Word became flesh and dwelt among us

Excluded from the synagogue and condemned as heretics, the Johannine community around 90AD experienced first-hand the reality of following the rejected one. The opening prologue of John's Gospel reaches into the depths of a mystery. Jesus, the One from God, the Word of God, the life for the world, is rejected by the world. Here key themes are introduced that will echo throughout the Gospel. Light has come into the world but humankind prefers darkness. God's grace and truth are disclosed but humanity fails to recognize God when he comes to us. Yet there will always be witnesses who point us towards the truth. John the Baptist, the desert prophet, was the first. Downplaying his own importance he announced the coming of Christ. The Johannine community too were witnesses: experiencing persecution and ridicule they were to remain faithful to Christ.

And what of us? We are invited to join this crowd of witnesses. It is a costly path but 'to all who received him... he gave the right to become children of God'. Remember those who are persecuted for their beliefs, or for standing up for truth and justice.

✳ *Pray – thanking God for the faithful witness of those who have gone before us.*
Pray that we too may continue their testimony.

Every tribe and nation

One way the persecuted early Christian communities sustained their faith was by holding on to a sense of the bigger picture. Whilst all around them chaos reigned, the bigger picture – represented in the Apostle John's vision – shows that God is still in control. The crucified Jesus is the One enthroned in glory and majesty. Peoples from every tribe and nation and all creation, including the heavenly host, celebrate the victory he has won. As at his birth the angelic voices heralded his coming, so now, with his mission accomplished, myriads of angels sing, 'Worthy is the Lamb who was slain...' The vision of John puts the redeeming work of Christ at the heart of what God is doing within human history. God's purposes may be delayed but nevertheless the future is being unrolled. John's great statement of faith, wrapped up in richly symbolic and apocalyptic language, involved a way of seeing that went far beyond what was visible to the naked eye.

Outwardly it would have seemed a joke to claim that the beleaguered Christian communities with a crucified leader amounted to anything much, and yet John was able to see with different eyes. What appears worthless and weak is often, in God's scale of things, truly worthy.

✳ *O God, give us a new way of 'seeing'*
that we may not be tricked into thinking that the loudest,
the biggest and the flashiest are the best
but recognize the significance of the One born in poverty
who becomes the Lamb enthroned in your Kingdom.

Saturday December 29   *Revelation 22.6-21**

I am coming soon!

Maybe it is only those who know the terror of persecution, those who have been defenceless in the face of authorized and deadly state brutality, those who have seen a loved one dragged away or 'disappeared', who know what relief and overwhelming joy is felt upon hearing the words, 'I am coming soon!'

Throughout the world, many people over the last year have cried out to God, wondering when their pain will end; wondering when they will be able to return home; wondering when they will not have to see their loved ones die before their time. The community with which John shared his vision was one that lived in hope that their suffering wasn't all in vain. Jesus, who is Lord and Judge, is coming. For many Christians today it is difficult to feel over-excited at the promise of Jesus – I am coming soon. But for those who thirst for righteousness, the vision of John is received with ecstatic jubilation. God has not abandoned his people. No cry has gone unheard. Evil will not prevail over good. Justice will come and each will be rewarded according to what s/he has done (verse 12).

Light a candle for the places in the world where people are standing firm in the face of suffering or persecution. Pray that they may have a share in the fruit from the tree of life.

✳ *God of the bruised ones, who inspires the prophets,*
we thank you for those who, in the face of evil,
defiantly proclaim that Jesus is coming
and that victory is his. Help us to grasp their vision
and to share their thirst so that together
we may live out our days and face the future
with courage and hope. Amen

Show me what love is

Calls for debt relief for the poorest nations have not fallen on deaf ears, but the challenge is that we find ways to pattern the life of our world so that exploitation of the poor and destruction of the environment are not accepted as inevitable.

John is writing to a community that is experiencing schism and division. He calls them back to their essential calling and he doesn't mince his words when he spells out what it means. Those who are rich must open their lives to the poor. John didn't think this was impossible even though he knew the community was riddled with conflict and inequality. We too mustn't lose sight of a vision of a world guided by love for one another. The authentic mark of the followers of Christ is love, and the Spirit enables us to keep alive Christ's vision for a redeemed world. Talk, talk, more talk – it's just not enough, writes John, to believe the right things and say the right things unless we also do the right things. Being united to Christ means sharing his passion for the world into which he came.

✳ *God, show us where our speaking and our living*
fail to match. Reveal to us our blind spots.
Help us to take the actions that are needed,
that demonstrate justice and sharing of resources
so that none go without. Amen

God is love

Many of us have been loved by others into the Kingdom of God. I recall my mother, my aunts, and those who nurtured me and challenged me in the Christian life. Through them I began to understand God's love for me and realize that God wanted me to share life and love with others. So what is it that you and I are passing on to those around us? There are many things we value and can share with others, but the greatest of them is love. As we greet the new year may it be an opportunity to realign ourselves with what is really important in life.

A number of years ago I sat with a man who knew he was dying of cancer. He was in his mid-forties. What surprised and impressed me was that, instead of railing against God for robbing him of years of his life, he said that cancer had enabled him to see things more clearly. He had been given time with his family and friends instead of the 'workaholic' life he had led up till then.

He was grateful to discover what is most important – relationships – and to realize what a precious gift love is.

John says that the source of love is God. In the relationship between the Father and the Son we glimpse this love that always reaches out to us before we ever respond. *Agape* (the quality of divine love) is John's resounding theme. We have been made friends and lovers with God.

✳ *God, lover of Creation, you call us friends.*
We thank you for your astounding love.
Help your Church to live out this love in action.
And may we be those who build bridges of reconciliation
and loving friendship wherever we are.

FOR REFLECTION – alone or with a group

● What has it meant for you to ask God to be born in your heart?
● As you look back over the year what is it that you want to thank God for?
● As you prepare to begin a New Year what is the deepest desire of your heart? To what do you believe God is calling you? Are there things you need to let go?

FOR ACTION

There are those you know who are finding it difficult to welcome a new year: who are experiencing loss or grief, taking up a new challenge or move and are feeling unsure of themselves, those who feel alone or lost... Take time to reach out to someone you know needs assuring of God's love.

INTERNATIONAL BIBLE READING ASSOCIATION

– a worldwide service of the National Christian Education Council
at work in five continents.

HEADQUARTERS

1020 Bristol Road
Selly Oak
Birmingham
Great Britain
B29 6LB
and the following agencies

http://www.ncec.org.uk
ibra@ncec.org.uk

AUSTRALIA

Uniting Education (previously The Joint Board of Christian Education)
PO Box 1245 (65 Oxford Street)
Collingwood
Victoria 3066

GHANA

IBRA Secretary
PO Box 919
Accra

INDIA

All India Sunday School Association
PO Box 2099
Secunderabad – 500 003
Andhra Pradesh

NEW ZEALAND

Epworth Bookshop
PO Box 6133, Te Aro
75 Taranaki Street
Wellington 6035

NIGERIA

IBRA Representative
PMB 5298
Ibadan

SOUTH AND CENTRAL AFRICA

IBRA Representative
Box 1176
Sedgefield 6573

IBRA READINGS FOR 2002

1. **BECOMING DISCIPLES: Matthew's Gospel**
   God with us - Strangers - Child of Abraham - Testing -
   New teaching - Integrity - Clear choice

2. **LENTEN ENCOUNTER**
   In sin and in forgiveness - In danger and in safety -
   In doubt and in faith - In darkness and in light -
   In death and in life - In rejection and in recognition

3. **EASTER PEOPLE, EASTER PLACES**

4. **BREAKING THE MOULD**
   Breaking Traditions - Breaking Expectations -
   Breaking and Shaping - Breaking Bread

5. **ROUGH PASSAGE TO THE PROMISED LAND**
   Numbers 20-36

6. **DIFFERENT WAYS OF LEARNING**
   Learning from each other - From the past - Through stories
   Through precepts - By doing - Through worship

7. **UNCOMFORTABLE WORDS**
   Difficult texts - Difficult sayings

8. **FROM GLORY TO GLORY**

9. **PHILIPPIANS**
   The mind of Christ - The life of Christ

10. **LIFE TOGETHER**

11. **AMOS** - The challenge of justice

12. **MISSION**
    Gathering in - Going out - Proclaiming the good news -
    Hearing the good news

13. **ADVENT: THE COMING KINGDOM**
    Readings in Mark's Gospel

The themes and books studied each year are linked with the Revised Common Lectionary.

Order your copy now through your local bookseller, your church IBRA secretary, or direct from IBRA using the booking form on page 209.